BROWNING

VOLUMES IN THIS SERIES

PUBLISHED AND IN PREPARATION

EDITED BY WILL D. HOWE

Arnold,	Stuart P. Sherman
Browning,	William Lyon Phelps
Burns,	W. A. Neilson
Carlyle,	Bliss Perry
Dante,	Alfred M. Brooks
Defoe,	William P. Trent
Dickens,	Richard Burton
Emerson,	Samuel M. Crothers
Hawthorne,	George E. Woodberry
Lamb,	Will D. Howe
Lowell,	John H. Finley
Stevenson,	Richard A. Rice
Tennyson,	Raymond M. Alden
Whitman,	Brand Whitlock
Wordsworth,	C. T. Winchester

Etc., Etc.

Robert Browning

ROBERT BROWNING

HOW TO KNOW HIM

By
WILLIAM LYON PHELPS
Lampson Professor of English Literature at Yale

WITH PORTRAIT

INDIANAPOLIS
THE BOBBS-MERRILL COMPANY
PUBLISHERS

TO
JAMES WHITCOMB RILEY
WITH SINCERE AFFECTION AND
RESPECT

PREFACE

In this volume I have attempted to give an account of Browning's life and an estimation of his character: to set forth, with sufficient illustration from his poems, his theory of poetry, his aim and method: to make clear some of the leading ideas in his work: to show his fondness for paradox: to exhibit the nature and basis of his optimism. I have given in complete form over fifty of his poems, each one preceded by my interpretation of its meaning and significance.   W. L. P.

Seven Gables, Lake Huron

CONTENTS

CHAPTER   PAGE

    I THE MAN   1

   II BROWNING'S THEORY OF POETRY . . .   34

 III LYRICS   71

 IV DRAMATIC LYRICS   96

  V DRAMATIC MONOLOGUES   169

 VI POEMS OF PARADOX   245

VII BROWNING'S OPTIMISM   294

     INDEX   377

LIST OF POEMS

	PAGE
ABT VOGLER	353
ANDREA DEL SARTO	208
APPARENT FAILURE	361
BAD DREAMS	168
BISHOP ORDERS HIS TOMB, THE	195
CALIBAN UPON SETEBOS	331
CAVALIER TUNES	111
"CHILDE ROLAND TO THE DARK TOWER CAME"	237
CONFESSIONS	164
COUNT GISMOND	179
CRISTINA	125
EPILOGUE TO ASOLANDO	373
EPILOGUE TO FIFINE AT THE FAIR	89
EPISTLE (AN) CONTAINING THE STRANGE MEDICAL EXPERIENCE OF KARSHISH	222
EVELYN HOPE	130
EYES CALM BESIDE THEE	75
FACE, A	87
GLOVE, THE	250
GRAMMARIAN'S FUNERAL, A	262
GUARDIAN-ANGEL, THE	324
HOME-THOUGHTS, FROM ABROAD	85
HOME-THOUGHTS, FROM THE SEA	85
HOW IT STRIKES A CONTEMPORARY	54
"HOW THEY BROUGHT THE GOOD NEWS FROM GHENT TO AIX"	191
JAMES LEE'S WIFE (two stanzas from)	86
JOHANNES AGRICOLA IN MEDITATION	108
LABORATORY, THE	201
LAST RIDE TOGETHER, THE	150
LOST LEADER, THE	114
LOST MISTRESS, THE	149
LOVE AMONG THE RUINS	158
MEETING AT NIGHT	140
MY LAST DUCHESS	175

LIST OF POEMS—*Continued*

	PAGE
My Star	167
Never the Time and the Place	94
One Way of Love	149
One Word More	15
Over the Sea Our Galleys Went	128
Parting at Morning	140
Porphyria's Lover	104
Prologue to Asolando	370
Prologue to Jocoseria	94
Prologue to La Saisiaz	93
Prologue to Pacchiarotto	92
Prologue to The Two Poets of Croisic	91
Prospice	359
Rabbi Ben Ezra	344
Rephan	365
Respectability	162
Saul	303
Sibrandus Schafnaburgensis	259
Soliloquy of the Spanish Cloister	187
Song from A Blot in the 'Scutcheon	83
Songs from Paracelsus	76
Songs from Pippa Passes	81
Statue (The) and the Bust	277
Summum Bonum	168
"Transcendentalism"	52
Up at a Villa—Down in the City	269
Which?	293

BROWNING

BROWNING

I

THE MAN

IF we enter this world from some other state of existence, it seems certain that in the obscure pre-natal country, the power of free choice—so stormily debated by philosophers and theologians here—does not exist. Millions of earth's infants are handicapped at the start by having parents who lack health, money, brains, and character; and in many cases the environment is no better than the ancestry. "God plants us where we grow," said Pompilia, and we can not save the rose by placing it on the tree-top. Robert Browning, who was perhaps the happiest man in the nineteenth century, was particularly fortunate in his advent. Of the entire population of the planet in the year of grace 1812, he could hardly have selected a better father and mother than were chosen for him; and the place of his birth was just what it should have been, the biggest town on earth. All his life long he was emphatically a city man, dwelling in London, Florence, Paris, and Venice, never remaining long in rural surroundings.

Browning was born on May 7, 1812, in Southampton Street, Camberwell, London, a suburb on the southern side of the river. One hundred years later, as I traversed the length of this street, it looked squalid in the rain, and is indeed sufficiently unlovely. But in 1812 it was a good residential locality, and not far away were fresh woods and pastures. . . . The good health of Browning's father may be inferred from the fact that he lived to be eighty-four, "without a day's illness;" he was a practical, successful business man, an official in the Bank of England. His love of literature and the arts is proved by the fact that he practised them constantly for the pure joy of the working; he wrote reams and reams of verse, without publishing a line. He had extraordinary facility in composition, being able to write poetry even faster than his son. Rossetti said that he had "a real genius for drawing." He owned a large and valuable library, filled with curiosities of literature. Robert was brought up among books, even in earliest youth turning over many a quaint and curious volume of forgotten lore.

His latest biographers have shown the powerful and permanent effects on his poetry of this early reading.

Browning's father—while not a rich man—had sufficient income to give his son every possible advantage in physical and intellectual training, and to enable him to live without earning a cent; after Robert grew up, he was absolutely free to devote his entire time and energy to writing poetry, which, even to the day of his death, did not yield a livelihood. The young poet was free from care, free from responsibility, and able from childhood to old age to bring out the best that was in him. A curious and exact parallel is found in the case of the great pessimist, Schopenhauer, who never ceased to be grateful to his father for making his whole life-work possible. In his later years, Browning wrote: "It would have been quite unpardonable in any case not to have done my best. My dear father put me in a condition most favourable for the best work I was capable of. When I think of the many authors who had to fight their way through all sorts of difficulties I have no reason to be proud of my achievements."

Browning's mother, whom he loved with passionate adoration, was a healthy and sensible woman; better than all these gifts, she was deeply

religious, with sincere and unaffected piety. She
was a Dissenter, a Congregationalist, and brought
up Robert in the nurture and admonition of the
Lord, herself a noble example of her teachings.
This evangelical training had an incalculably strong
influence on the spirit of Browning's poetry. She
loved music ardently, and when Robert was a boy,
used to play the piano to him in the twilight. He
always said that he got his devotion to music from
her.

In these days, when there is such a strong re-
action everywhere against the elective system in
education, it is interesting to remember that Browning's education was simply the elective system
pushed to its last possibility. It is perhaps safe to
say that no learned man in modern times ever had
so little of school and college. His education de-
pended absolutely and exclusively on his inclina-
tions; he was encouraged to study anything he
wished. His father granted him perfect liberty,
never sent him to any "institution of learning," and
allowed him to do exactly as he chose, simply pro-
viding competent private instruction in whatever subject the youth expressed any interest. Thus he learned
Greek, Latin, the modern languages, music (harmony and counterpoint, as well as piano and organ),

chemistry (a private laboratory was fitted up in the house), history and art. Now every one knows that so far as definite acquisition of knowledge is concerned, our schools and colleges—at least in America —leave much to be desired; our boys and girls study the classics for years without being able to read a page at sight; and the modern languages show a similarly meagre harvest. If one wishes positive and practical results one must employ a private tutor, or work alone in secret. The great advantages of our schools and colleges—except in so far as they inspire intellectual curiosity—are not primarily of a scholarly nature; their strength lies in other directions. The result of Browning's education was that at the age of twenty he knew more than most college graduates ever know; and his knowledge was at his full command. His favorite reading on the train, for example, was a Greek play; one of the reasons why his poetry sometimes seems so pedantic is simply because he never realised how ignorant most of us really are. I suppose he did not believe that men could pass years in school and university training and know so little. Yet the truth is, that most boys, brought up as Browning was, would be utterly unfitted for the active duties and struggles of life, and indeed for the amenities of social intercourse. With ninety-nine out of a hundred, such an education, so far as it made for either happiness or efficiency, would be a failure. But Browning was the hundredth man. He was profoundly learned without pedantry and without conceit; and he was primarily a social being.

His physical training was not neglected. The boy had expert private instruction in fencing, boxing, and riding. He was at ease on the back of a spirited horse. He was particularly fond of dancing, which later aroused the wonder of Elizabeth Barrett, who found it difficult to imagine the author of *Paracelsus* dancing the polka.

In 1833 appeared Browning's first poem, *Pauline,* which had been completed before he was twenty-one years old. His aunt, Mrs. Silverthorne, gave him one hundred and fifty dollars, which paid the expenses of publication. Not a single copy was sold, and the unbound sheets came home to roost. The commercial worth of *Pauline* was exactly zero; to-day it is said that only five copies exist. One was sold recently for two thousand four hundred dollars.

In 1834 Browning visited Russia, going by steamer to Rotterdam, and then driving fifteen hundred miles with horses. Although he was in Russia about three months, and at the most sensitive time of life, the country made surprisingly little impression upon him, or at least upon his poetry. The dramatic idyl, *Ivàn Ivànovitch,* is practically the only literary result of this journey. It was the south, and not the north, that was to be the inspiration of Browning.

He published his second poem, *Paracelsus,* in 1835. Although this attracted no general attention, and had no sale, it was enthusiastically reviewed by John Forster, who declared that its author was a man of genius. The most fortunate result of its appearance was that it brought Browning within the pale of literary society, and gave him the friendship of some of the leading men in London. The great actor Macready was charmed with the poem, and young Browning haunted Macready's dressing-room at the theatre for years; but their friendship ceased in 1843 when *A Blot in the 'Scutcheon* was acted. Browning wrote four plays for Macready, two of which were accepted.

Although Browning late in life remarked in a casual conversation that he had visited Italy in 1834, he must have been mistaken, for it is impossible to find any record of such a journey. To the best of our knowledge, he first saw the land of his inspiration in 1838, sailing from London on April

13th, passing through the Straits of Gibraltar on the twenty-ninth, and reaching Trieste on May 30th. On the first of June he entered Venice. It was on a walking-trip that he first saw the village of Asolo, about thirty miles to the northeast of Venice. Little did he then realise how closely his name would be forever associated with this tiny town. The scenes of *Pippa Passes* he located there: the last summer of his life, in 1889, was spent in Asolo, his last volume he named in memory of the village; and on the one hundredth anniversary of his birth, the street where he lived and wrote in 1889 was formally named Via Roberto Browning. His son, Robert Barrett Browning, lived to see this event, and died at Asolo on July 8, 1912.

The long and obscure poem *Sordello* was published in 1840; and then for thirty years Browning produced poetry of the highest order: poetry that shows scarcely any obscurity, and that in lyric and dramatic power has given its author a fixed place among the greatest names in English literature.

The story of the marriage and married life of Elizabeth Barrett and Robert Browning is one of the greatest love stories in the world's history; their love-letters reveal a drama of noble passion that excels in beauty and intensity the universally

popular examples of Heloise and Abelard, Aucassin
and Nicolette, Paul and Virginia. There was a
mysterious bond between them long before the personal acquaintance: each admired the other's poetry.
Miss Barrett had a picture of Browning in her sick-
room, and declared that the adverse criticism constantly directed against his verse hurt her like a
lash across her own back. In a new volume of
poems, she made a complimentary reference to his
work, and in January, 1845, he wrote her a letter
properly beginning with the two words, "I love."
It was her verses that he loved, and said so. In
May he saw her and illustrated his own doctrine by
falling in love with her at first sight. She was in
her fortieth year, and an invalid; but if any one is
surprised at the passion she aroused in the handsome young poet, six years her junior, one has only
to read her letters. She was a charming woman,
feminine from her soul to her finger-tips, the incarnation of *das Ewigweibliche*. Her intimate friends
were mostly what were then known as strong-
minded women—I suppose to-day they would seem
like timid, shy violets. She was modest, gentle,
winsome, irresistible: profoundly learned, with the
eager heart of a child.

Wimpole Street in London, "the long, unlovely

street," as Tennyson calls it, is holy ground to the lover of literature: for at Number 67 lived Arthur Henry Hallam, and diagonally opposite, at Number 50, lived Elizabeth Barrett. This street—utterly commonplace in appearance—is forever associated with the names of our two great Victorian poets: and the association with Tennyson is Death: with Browning, Love.

Not only was Elizabeth believed to be a hopeless invalid, but her father had forbidden any of his children to marry. He was a religious man, whose motto in his own household was apparently "Thou shalt have no other gods before me." He had the particular kind of piety that is most offensive to ordinary humanity. He gave his children, for whom he had a stern and savage passion, everything except what they wanted. He had an insane jealousy of any possible lover, and there is no doubt that he would have preferred to attend the funeral of any one of his children rather than a marriage. But Browning's triumphant love knew no obstacles, and he persuaded Elizabeth Barrett to run away with him. They were married in September, 1846, and shortly after left for Italy. Her father refused to see either of them in subsequent years, and returned his daughter's letters unopened. Is there any cause in nature for these hard hearts?

Browning's faith wrought a miracle. Instead of dying on the journey to Italy, Mrs. Browning got well, and the two lived together in unclouded happiness for fifteen years, until 1861, when she died in his arms. Not a scrap of writing passed between them from the day of her marriage to the day of her death: for they were never separated. She said that all a woman needed to be perfectly happy was three things—Life, Love, Italy—and she had all three.

The relations between Elizabeth Barrett and Robert Browning had all the wonder and beauty of a mediæval romance, with the notable addition of being historically true. The familiar story of a damosel imprisoned in a gloomy dungeon, guarded by a cruel dragon—and then, when all her hope had vanished, rescued by the sudden appearance of the brilliant knight, who carried her away from her dull prison to a land of sunshine and happiness— this became the literal experience of Elizabeth Barrett. Her love for her husband was the passionate love of a woman for a man, glorified by adoration for the champion who had miraculously transformed her life from the depths of despair to the topmost heights of joy. He came, "pouring heaven into this shut house of life." She expressed the

daily surprise of her happiness in her Sonnets, which
one day she put shyly into his hands:

> I thought once how Theocritus had sung
> Of the sweet years, the dear and wished-for years,
> Who each one in a gracious hand appears
> To bear a gift for mortals, old or young:
> And, as I mused it in his antique tongue,
> I saw, in gradual vision through my tears,
> The sweet, sad years, the melancholy years,
> Those of my own life, who by turns had flung
> A shadow across me. Straightway I was 'ware,
> So weeping, how a mystic Shape did move
> Behind me, and drew me backward by the hair;
> And a voice said in mastery while I strove, . . .
> "Guess now who holds thee?"—"Death!" I said. But,
>   there,
> The silver answer rang . . . "Not Death, but Love."

> My own Beloved, who hast lifted me
> From this drear flat of earth where I was thrown,
> And in betwixt the languid ringlets, blown
> A life-breath, till the forehead hopefully
> Shines out again, as all the angels see,
> Before thy saving kiss! My own, my own,
> Who camest to me when the world was gone,
> And I who looked for only God, found *thee!*
> I find thee: I am safe, and strong, and glad.
> As one who stands in dewless asphodel
> Looks backward on the tedious time he had
> In the upper life . . . so I, with bosom-swell,
> Make witness here between the good and bad,
> That Love, as strong as Death, retrieves as well.

Browning replied to this wonderful tribute by appending to the fifty poems published in 1855 his *One Word More*. He wrote this in a metre different from any he had ever used, for he meant the poem to be unique in his works, a personal expression of his love. He remarked that Rafael wrote sonnets, that Dante painted a picture, each man going outside the sphere of his genius to please the woman he loved, to give her something entirely apart from his gifts to the world. He wished that he could do something other than poetry for his wife, and in the next life he believed that it would be possible. But here God had given him only one gift—verse: he must therefore present her with a specimen of the only art he could command; but it should be utterly unlike all his other poems, for they were dramatic; here just once, and for one woman only, he would step out from behind the scenes, and address her directly in his own person.

Of course Browning could have modelled a statue, or written a piece of music for Elizabeth, for in both of these arts he had attained moderate proficiency: but he wished not only to make a gift just for her, but to give it to her in public, with the whole world regarding; therefore it must be of his best.

He calls her his *moon* of poets. He reminds her
how a few days ago, they had seen the crescent
moon in Florence, how they had seen it nightly
waxing until it lamped the façade of San Miniato,
while the nightingales, in ecstasy among the cypress
trees, gave full-throated applause. Then they had
travelled together to London, and now saw the same
dispirited moon, saving up her silver parsimoniously,
sink in gibbous meanness behind the chimney-tops.

The notable thing about the moon is that whereas
the earth, during one revolution about the sun, turns
on its own axis three hundred and sixty-five times,
the shy moon takes exactly the same length of time
to turn around as she takes to circle once around the
earth. For this reason, earth's inhabitants have
never seen but one side of the moon, and never will.
Elizabeth Browning is *his* moon, because she shows
the other side to him alone. The radiant splendor
of her poetry fills the whole earth with light; but to
her husband she shows the other side, the loving, domestic woman, the unspeakably precious and
intimate associate of his daily life. The world
thinks it knows her; but it has seen only one side;
it knows nothing of the marvellous depth and purity
of her real nature.

ONE WORD MORE

TO E. B. B.

1855

I

There they are, my fifty men and women
Naming me the fifty poems finished!
Take them, Love, the book and me together:
Where the heart lies, let the brain lie also.

II

Rafael made a century of sonnets,
Made and wrote them in a certain volume
Dinted with the silver-pointed pencil
Else he only used to draw Madonnas:
These, the world might view—but one, the volume.
Who that one, you ask? Your heart instructs you.
Did she live and love it all her life-time?
Did she drop, his lady of the sonnets,
Die, and let it drop beside her pillow
Where it lay in place of Rafael's glory,
Rafael's cheek so duteous and so loving—
Cheek, the world was wont to hail a painter's,
Rafael's cheek, her love had turned a poet's?

III

You and I would rather read that volume,
(Taken to his beating bosom by it)
Lean and list the bosom-beats of Rafael,
Would we not? than wonder at Madonnas—
Her, San Sisto names, and Her, Foligno,
Her, that visits Florence in a vision,
Her, that's left with lilies in the Louvre—
Seen by us and all the world in circle.

IV

You and I will never read that volume.
Guido Reni, like his own eye's apple
Guarded long the treasure-book and loved it.
Guido Reni dying, all Bologna
Cried, and the world cried too, "Ours, the treasure!"
Suddenly, as rare things will, it vanished.

V

Dante once prepared to paint an angel:
Whom to please? You whisper "Beatrice."
While he mused and traced it and retraced it,
(Peradventure with a pen corroded
Still by drops of that hot ink he dipped for,
When, his left-hand i' the hair o' the wicked,
Back he held the brow and pricked its stigma,
Bit into the live man's flesh for parchment,
Loosed him, laughed to see the writing rankle,
Let the wretch go festering through Florence)—
Dante, who loved well because he hated,
Hated wickedness that hinders loving,
Dante standing, studying his angel,—
In there broke the folk of his Inferno.
Says he—"Certain people of importance"
(Such he gave his daily dreadful line to)
"Entered and would seize, forsooth, the poet."
Says the poet—"Then I stopped my painting."

VI

You and I would rather see that angel,
Painted by the tenderness of Dante,
Would we not?—than read a fresh Inferno.

VII

You and I will never see that picture.
While he mused on love and Beatrice,
While he softened o'er his outlined angel,
In they broke, those "people of importance":
We and Bice bear the loss for ever.

VIII

What of Rafael's sonnets, Dante's picture?
This: no artist lives and loves, that longs not
Once, and only once, and for one only,
(Ah, the prize!) to find his love a language
Fit and fair and simple and sufficient—
Using nature that's an art to others,
Not, this one time, art that's turned his nature.
Ay, of all the artists living, loving,
None but would forego his proper dowry,—
Does he paint? he fain would write a poem,—
Does he write? he fain would paint a picture,
Put to proof art alien to the artist's,
Once, and only once, and for one only,
So to be the man and leave the artist,
Gain the man's joy, miss the artist's sorrow.

IX

Wherefore? Heaven's gift takes earth's abatement!
He who smites the rock and spreads the water,
Bidding drink and live a crowd beneath him,
Even he, the minute makes immortal,
Proves, perchance, but mortal in the minute,
Desecrates, belike, the deed in doing.
While he smites, how can he but remember,
So he smote before, in such a peril,
When they stood and mocked—"Shall smiting help us?"

When they drank and sneered—"A stroke is easy!"
When they wiped their mouths and went their journey,
Throwing him for thanks—"But drought was pleasant."
Thus old memories mar the actual triumph;
Thus the doing savours of disrelish;
Thus achievement lacks a gracious somewhat;
O'er-importuned brows becloud the mandate,
Carelessness or consciousness—the gesture.
For he bears an ancient wrong about him,
Sees and knows again those phalanxed faces,
Hears, yet one time more, the 'customed prelude—
"How shouldst thou, of all men, smite, and save us?"
Guesses what is like to prove the sequel—
"Egypt's flesh-pots—nay, the drought was better."

X

Oh, the crowd must have emphatic warrant!
Theirs, the Sinai-forehead's cloven brilliance,
Right-arm's rod-sweep, tongue's imperial fiat.
Never dares the man put off the prophet.

XI

Did he love one face from out the thousands,
(Were she Jethro's daughter, white and wifely,
Were she but the Æthiopian bondslave,)
He would envy yon dumb patient camel,
Keeping a reserve of scanty water
Meant to save his own life in the desert;
Ready in the desert to deliver
(Kneeling down to let his breast be opened)
Hoard and life together for his mistress.

XII

I shall never, in the years remaining,
Paint you pictures, no, nor carve you statues,

Make you music that should all-express me;
So it seems: I stand on my attainment.
This of verse alone, one life allows me;
Verse and nothing else have I to give you.
Other heights in other lives, God willing:
All the gifts from all the heights, your own, Love

XIII

Yet a semblance of resource avails us—
Shade so finely touched, love's sense must seize it.
Take these lines, look lovingly and nearly,
Lines I write the first time and the last time.
He who works in fresco, steals a hair-brush,
Curbs the liberal hand, subservient proudly,
Cramps his spirit, crowds its all in little,
Makes a strange art of an art familiar,
Fills his lady's missal-marge with flowerets.
He who blows thro' bronze, may breathe thro' silver,
Fitly serenade a slumbrous princess.
He who writes, may write for once as I do.

XIV

Love, you saw me gather men and women,
Live or dead or fashioned by my fancy,
Enter each and all, and use their service,
Speak from every mouth,—the speech, a poem.
Hardly shall I tell my joys and sorrows,
Hopes and fears, belief and disbelieving:
I am mine and yours—the rest be all men's,
Karshish, Cleon, Norbert and the fifty.
Let me speak this once in my true person,
Not as Lippo, Roland or Andrea,
Though the fruit of speech be just this sentence:
Pray you, look on these my men and women,
Take and keep my fifty poems finished;

Where my heart lies, let my brain lie also!
Poor the speech; be how I speak, for all things.

XV

Not but that you know me! Lo, the moon's self!
Here in London, yonder late in Florence,
Still we find her face, the thrice-transfigured.
Curving on a sky imbrued with colour,
Drifted over Fiesole by twilight,
Came she, our new crescent of a hair's-breadth.
Full she flared it, lamping Samminiato,
Rounder 'twixt the cypresses and rounder,
Perfect till the nightingales applauded.
Now, a piece of her old self, impoverished,
Hard to greet, she traverses the houseroofs,
Hurries with unhandsome thrift of silver,
Goes dispiritedly, glad to finish.

XVI

What, there's nothing in the moon noteworthy?
Nay: for if that moon could love a mortal,
Use, to charm him (so to fit a fancy),
All her magic ('tis the old sweet mythos)
She would turn a new side to her mortal,
Side unseen of herdsman, huntsman, steersman—
Blank to Zoroaster on his terrace,
Blind to Galileo on his turret,
Dumb to Homer, dumb to Keats—him, even!
Think, the wonder of the moonstruck mortal—
When she turns round, comes again in heaven,
Opens out anew for worse or better!
Proves she like some portent of an iceberg
Swimming full upon the ship it founders,
Hungry with huge teeth of splintered crystals?
Proves she as the paved work of a sapphire

Seen by Moses when he climbed the mountain?
Moses, Aaron, Nadab and Abihu
Climbed and saw the very God, the Highest,
Stand upon the paved work of a sapphire.
Like the bodied heaven in his clearness
Shone the stone, the sapphire of that paved work,
When they ate and drank and saw God also!

XVII

What were seen? None knows, none ever shall know.
Only this is sure—the sight were other,
Not the moon's same side, born late in Florence,
Dying now impoverished here in London.
God be thanked, the meanest of his creatures
Boasts two soul-sides, one to face the world with,
One to show a woman when he loves her!

XVIII

This I say of me, but think of you, Love!
This to you—yourself my moon of poets!
Ah, but that's the world's side, there's the wonder,
Thus they see you, praise you, think they know you!
There, in turn I stand with them and praise you—
Out of my own self, I dare to phrase it.
But the best is when I glide from out them,
Cross a step or two of dubious twilight,
Come out on the other side, the novel
Silent silver lights and darks undreamed of,
Where I hush and bless myself with silence.

XIX

Oh, their Rafael of the dear Madonnas,
Oh, their Dante of the dread Inferno,
Wrote one song—and in my brain I sing it,
Drew one angel—borne, see, on my bosom!

R. B.

The Brownings travelled a good deal: they visited many places in Italy, Venice, Ancona, Fano,
Siena, and spent several winters in Rome. The
winter of 1851-52 was passed at Paris, where on
the third of January Browning wrote one of his
most notable poems, *Childe Roland to the Dark
Tower Came*. One memorable evening at London
in 1855 there were gathered together in an upper
room Mr. and Mrs. Browning, Mr. and Mrs. Tennyson, Dante and William Rossetti. Tennyson had
just published *Maud* and Browning the two volumes
called *Men and Women*. Each poet was invited to
read from his new work. Tennyson, with one leg
curled under him on the sofa, chanted *Maud,* the
tears running down his cheeks; and then Browning
read in a conversational manner his characteristic
poem, *Fra Lippo Lippi*. Rossetti made a pen-and-
ink sketch of the Laureate while he was intoning.
On one of the journeys made by the Brownings
from London to Paris they were accompanied by
Thomas Carlyle, who wrote a vivid and charming
account of the transit. The poet was the practical
member of the party: the "brave Browning" struggled with the baggage, and the customs, and the
train arrangements; while the Scot philosopher
smoked infinite tobacco.

The best account of the domestic life of the
Brownings at Casa Guidi in Florence was written
by Nathaniel Hawthorne, and published in his *Italian Note-Books*. On a June evening, Mr. and Mrs.
Browning, William Cullen Bryant, and Nathaniel
Hawthorne ate strawberries and talked spiritualism.
Hawthorne and Browning stood on the little balcony overlooking the street, and heard the priests
chanting in the church of San Felice, the chant heard
only in June, which Browning was to hear again
on the night of the June day when he found the old
yellow book. Both chant and terrace were to be
immortalised in Browning's epic. Hawthorne said
that Browning had an elfin wife and an elf child.
"I wonder whether he will ever grow up, whether
it is desirable that he should." Like all visitors at
Casa Guidi, the American was impressed by the extraordinary sweetness, gentleness, and charity of
Elizabeth Browning, and by the energy, vivacity,
and conversational powers of her husband. Hawthorne said he seemed to be in all parts of the room
at once.

Mr. Barrett Browning told me in 1904 that he
remembered his mother, Elizabeth Barrett Browning, as clearly as though he had seen her yesterday.
He was eleven years old at the time of her death.

He would have it that her ill health had been greatly exaggerated. She was an invalid, but did not give the impression of being one. She was able to do many things, and had considerable power of endurance. One day in Florence she walked from her home out through the Porta Romana, clear up on the heights, and back to Casa Guidi. "That was pretty good, wasn't it?" said he. She was of course the idol of the household, and everything revolved about her. She was "intensely loved" by all her friends. Her father was a "very peculiar man." The son's account of her health differs radically from that written by the mother of E. C. Stedman, who said that Mrs. Browning was kept alive only by opium, which she had to take daily. This writer added, however, that in spite of Mrs. Browning's wretched health, she had never heard her speak ill of any one, though she talked with her many times.

After the death of his wife, Browning never saw Florence again. He lived in London, and after a few years was constantly seen in society. Tennyson, who hated society, said that Browning would die in a dress suit. His real fame did not begin until the year 1864, with the publication of *Dramatis Personæ*. During the first thirty years of his career, from the publication of *Pauline* in 1833 to the appearance of *Dramatis Personæ,* he received always tribute from the few, and neglect, seasoned with ridicule, from the many. *Pauline, Paracelsus, Pippa Passes, A Blot in the 'Scutcheon, Christmas-Eve, Men and Women*—each of these volumes was greeted enthusiastically by men and women whose own literary fame is permanent. But the world knew him not. How utterly obscure he was may be seen by the fact that so late as 1860, when the publisher's statement came in for *Men and Women,* it appeared that during the preceding six months not a single copy had been sold! The best was yet to be. The *Dramatis Personæ* was the first of his books to go into a genuine second edition. Then four years later came *The Ring and the Book,* which a contemporary review pronounced to be the "most precious and profound spiritual treasure which England has received since the days of Shakespeare."

Fame, which had shunned him for thirty years, came to him in extraordinary measure during the last part of his life: another exact parallel between him and the great pessimist Schopenhauer. It was naturally sweet, its sweetness lessened only by the thought that his wife had not lived to see it. Each had always believed in the superiority of the other: and the only cloud in Mrs. Browning's mind was the (to her) incomprehensible neglect of her husband by the public. At the time of the marriage, it was commonly said that a young literary man had eloped with a great poetess: during their married life, her books went invariably into many editions, while his did not sell at all. And even to the last day of Browning's earthly existence, her poems far outsold his, to his unspeakable delight. "The demand for my poems is nothing like so large," he wrote cheerfully, in correcting a contrary opinion that had been printed. Even so late as 1885, I found this passage in an account of Mrs. Browning's life, published that year. It appears that "she was married in 1846 to Robert Browning, who was also a poet and dramatic writer of some note, though his fame seems to have been almost totally eclipsed by the superior endowments of his gifted wife." This reminds us of the time when Mr. and Mrs. Schumann were presented to a Scandinavian King: Mrs. Schumann played on the piano, and His Majesty, turning graciously to the silent husband, enquired "Are you also musical?"

The last summer of Browning's life, the summer of 1889, was passed at Asolo: in the autumn he moved into his beautiful house in Venice, the Palazzo Rezzonico, which had the finest situation of

all Venetian residences, built at an angle in the
Grand Canal. Although seventy-seven years old,
he was apparently as vigorous as ever: no change
had taken place in his appearance, manner or habits.
One day he caught a bad cold walking on the Lido
in a bitter wind; and with his usual vehement energy
declined to take any proper care of his throat. Instead of staying in, he set out for long tramps with
friends, constantly talking in the raw autumn air.
In order to prove to his son that nothing was the
matter with him, he ran rapidly up three flights of
stairs, the son vainly trying to restrain him. Nothing is more characteristic of the youthful folly of
aged folk than their impatient resentment of prof-
fered hygienic advice. When we are children, we
reject with scorn the suggestions of our parents;
when we are old, we reject with equal scorn the advice of our children. Man is apparently an animal
more fit to give advice than to take it. Browning's
impulsive rashness proved fatal. Bronchitis with
heart trouble finally sent him to bed, though on the
last afternoon of his life he rose and walked about
the room. During the last few days he told many
good stories and talked with his accustomed eagerness. He died at ten o'clock in the evening of the
twelfth of December, 1889. A few moments be-

fore his death came a cablegram from London an-
nouncing that his last volume of poems had been
published that day, and that the evening papers were
speaking in high terms of its contents. "That is
very gratifying," said he.

Browning's life was healthy, comfortable, and
happy. With the exception of frequent headaches
in his earlier years, he never knew sickness or
physical distress. His son said that he had never
seen him in bed in the daytime until the last illness.
He had a truly wonderful digestion; it was his firm
belief that one should eat only what one really enjoyed, desire being the infallible sign that the food
was healthful. "My father was a man of *bonne
fourchette*," said Barrett Browning to me; "he was
not very fond of meat, but liked all kinds of Italian
dishes, especially with rich sauces. He always ate
freely of rich and delicate things. He could make
a whole meal off mayonnaise." It is pleasant to
remember that Emerson, the other great optimist
of the century, used to eat pie for breakfast. Unlike Carlyle and Tennyson, who smoked constantly,
Browning never used tobacco; he drank wine with
his meals, but sparingly, and never more than one
kind of wine at a dinner. While physically robust,
fond of riding and walking, never using a cab or

public conveyance if he could help it, he was like most first-class literary men in caring nothing whatever for competitive sports. He did not learn to swim until late in life; his son taught him at Pornic, in Brittany. He was venturesome for a man well on in years, swimming far out with boyish delight, as he has himself described it in the *Prologue* to *Fifine at the Fair*.

Browning's eyes were peculiar, one having a long focus, the other very short. He had the unusual accomplishment (try it and prove) of closing either eye without "squinching," and without any apparent effort, though sometimes on the street in strong sunshine his face would be a bit distorted. He did all his reading and writing with one eye, closing the long one as he sat down at his desk. He never wore glasses, and was proud of his microscopic eye. He often wrote minutely, to show off his powers. When he left the house to go for a walk, he shut the short eye and opened the long one, with which he could see an immense distance. He never suffered with any pain in his eyes except once, when a boy, he was trying to be a vegetarian in imitation of his youthful idol, Shelley.

Contrary to the oft-repeated statement, Browning was not a really fine pianist. As a very young man,

he used to play several instruments, and once he
had been able to play all of Beethoven's sonatas on
the piano. In later life he became ambitious to improve his skill with this instrument, and had much
trouble, for his fingers were clumsy and stiff. He
therefore used to rise at six, and practise finger-
exercises for an hour!

He loved first-class music ardently, had a profound knowledge of it, and was a good judge. If
the performance was fine, he would express his
praise with the utmost enthusiasm; but bad work
caused him acute pain. Sometimes at a concert he
would put his fingers in his ears, his suffering being
apparently uncontrollable.

The salient feature of his character was his boy-
ish vivacity and enthusiasm. If he looked out of
the window and saw a friend coming along the
street to call, he would often rush out and embrace
him. In conversation he was extraordinarily eager
and impulsive, with a great flow of talk on an enormous range of subjects. If he liked anything, he
spoke of it in the heartiest manner, laughing aloud
with delight. He was very generous in his appreciation and praise of other men's work, being beautifully free from that jealousy which is one of the
besetting sins of artists. He always tried to see

what was good. Occasionally he was enraged at reading a particularly hostile criticism of himself, but on the whole he stood abuse very well, and had abundant opportunity to exercise the gift of patience. A great admirer of Tennyson's poetry and of Tennyson's character—they were dear and intimate friends—he never liked the stock comparison. "Tennyson and I are totally unlike," he used to say. No letter from one rival to another was ever more beautiful than the letter Browning wrote to Tennyson on the occasion of the Laureate's eightieth birthday:

"MY DEAR TENNYSON—To-morrow is your birthday—indeed, a memorable one. Let me say I associate myself with the universal pride of our country in your glory, and in its hope that for many and many a year we may have your very self among us —secure that your poetry will be a wonder and delight to all those appointed to come after. And for my own part, let me further say, I have loved you dearly. May God bless you and yours.

"At no moment from first to last of my acquaintance with your works, or friendship with yourself, have I had any other feeling, expressed or kept silent, than this which an opportunity allows me to utter—that I am and ever shall be, my dear Tennyson, admiringly and affectionately yours,

"ROBERT BROWNING."

What I have said of Browning's impulsiveness is

borne out not only by the universal testimony of those who knew him well, but particularly by a letter of Mrs. Browning to Mrs. Jameson. The manuscript of this letter was bought in London by an American, and went down with the *Titanic* in 1912. An extract from it appeared in a bookseller's catalogue—"You must learn Robert—he is made of moods—chequered like a chess-board; and the colour goes for too much—till you learn to treat it as a game."

No man—little or great—was ever more free from pose. His appearance, in clothes and in hair, was studiously normal. No one in his later years would ever have guessed that he was a poet, either in seeing him on the street, or in meeting him at dinner. He was interested in multitudinous things, but never spoke of poetry—either in general or in his own particular—if he could avoid doing so. The fact that strangers who were presented to him and talked with him did not guess that he was *the* Mr. Browning, gave rise to numberless humorous situations.

Perhaps the best thing that can be said of his personal character is the truthful statement that he stood in the finest manner two searching tests of manhood—long neglect and sudden popularity. The

long years of oblivion, during which he was pro-
ducing much of his best work, made him neither
angry nor sour, though he must have suffered deeply.
On the other hand, when his fame reached prodigious proportions, he was neither conceited nor affected. He thoroughly believed in himself, and in
his work; and he cared more about it than he did
for its reception.

The crushing grief that came to him in the death
of his wife he bore with that Christian resignation
of which we hear more often than perhaps we see
in experience. For Browning was a Christian, not
only in faith but in conduct; it was the mainspring
of his art and of his life. There are so many writers
whose lives show so painful a contrast with the
ideal tone of their written work, that it is refreshing
and inspiring to be so certain of Browning; to know
that the author of the poems which thrill us was
as great in character as he was in genius.

II

WITH one exception, the economic law of supply and demand governs the production of literature exactly as it determines the price of wheat. For many years the Novel has been the chief channel of literary expression, the dominant literary form: in the days of Queen Elizabeth, the Drama was supreme. During the early part of the eighteenth century, theological poetry enjoyed a great vogue; Pope's *Essay on Man* circulated with the rapidity of a modern detective story. Consider the history of the English sonnet. This form of verse was exceedingly popular in 1600. By 1660 it had vanished, and remained obsolete for nearly a hundred years; about the middle of the eighteenth century it was revived by Thomas Edwards and others; in the nineteenth century it became fashionable, and still holds its place, as one may see by opening current magazines. Why is it that writers put their ideas on God, Nature, and Woman in the form

34

of a drama in 1600, and in the form of a novel in
1900? Why is it that an inspired man should make
poems of exactly fourteen lines in 1580 and in 1880,
and not do it in 1680? If we do not attempt an
ultimate metaphysical analysis, the answer is clear.
The bookseller supplies the public, the publisher supplies the bookseller, the author supplies the publisher. A bookseller has in his window what the
people want, and the publisher furnishes material
in response to the same desire; just as a farmer
plants in his fields some foodstuffs for which there
is a sharp demand. Authors are compelled to write
for the market, whether they like it or not, otherwise their work can not appear in print. The reason why the modern novel, with all its shortcomings,
is the mirror of ideas on every conceivable topic in
religious, educational, economic, and sociological
thought, is because the vast majority of writers are
at this moment compelled by the market to put their
reflections into the form of novels, just as Mar-
lowe and Chapman were forced to write plays.
With one exception, the law of supply and demand
determines the metrical shape of the poet's frenzy,
and the prose mould of the philosopher's ideas.

The exception is so rare that it establishes the
rule. The exception is Genius—next to radium the

scarcest article on earth. And even Genius often
follows the market—it takes the prevailing literary
fashion, and adapts itself to the form in vogue in a
more excellent way. Such genius—the Genius for
Adaptation—never has to wait long for recognition,
simply because it supplies a keen popular demand.
Such a genius was Shakespeare: such a genius was
Pope: such a genius was Scott: such a genius was
Byron: such a genius was Tennyson. But the true
exception to the great economic law is seen in the
Man of Original Genius, who cares not at all for
the fashion except perhaps to destroy it. This man
is outside the law of supply and demand, because
he supplies no demand, and there exists no demand
for him. He therefore has to create the demand
as well as the supply. Such a man in Music was
Wagner: such a man in Drama was Ibsen: such a
man in Poetry was Browning.

These three men were fortunate in all reaching
the age of seventy, for had they died midway in
their careers, even after accomplishing much of
their best work, they would have died in obscurity.
They had to wait long for recognition, because nobody was looking for them, nobody wanted them.
There was no demand for Wagner's music—but
there is now, and he made it. There was no de-

mand for plays like those of Ibsen; and there was
not the slightest demand for poetry like *Pauline* and
the *Dramatic Lyrics.* The reason why the public
does not immediately recognise the greatness of a
work of original genius, is because the public at
first—if it notices the thing at all—apprehends not
its greatness, but its strangeness. It is so unlike the
thing the public is seeking, that it seems grotesque
or absurd—many indeed declare that it is exactly
the opposite of what it professes to be. Thus, many
insisted that Ibsen's so-called dramas were not really
plays: they were merely conversations on serious
and unpleasant themes. In like manner, the critics
said that Wagner, whatever he composed, did not
compose music; for instead of making melodies, he
made harsh and discordant sounds. For eighty years,
many men of learning and culture have been loudly
proclaiming that Browning, whatever he was, was
not a poet; he was ingenious, he was thoughtful, a
philosopher, if you like, but surely no poet. When
The Ring and the Book was published, a thoroughly
respectable British critic wrote, "Music does not
exist for him any more than for the deaf." On the
other hand, the accomplished poet, musician, and
critic, Sidney Lanier, remarked:

"Have you seen Browning's *The Ring and the*

Book? I am confident that at the birth of this man, among all the good fairies who showered him with magnificent endowments, one bad one—as in the old tale—crept in by stealth and gave him a constitutional twist i' the neck, whereby his windpipe became, and has ever since remained, a marvellous tortuous passage. Out of this glottis-labyrinth his words won't, and can't, come straight. A hitch and a sharp crook in every sentence bring you up with a shock. But what a shock it is! Did you ever see a picture of a lasso, in the act of being flung? In a thousand coils and turns, inextricably crooked and involved and whirled, yet, if you mark the noose at the end, you see that it is directly in front of the bison's head, there, and is bound to catch him! That is the way Robert Browning catches you. The first sixty or seventy pages of *The Ring and the Book* are altogether the most doleful reading, in point either of idea or of music, in the English language; and yet the monologue of Giuseppe Caponsacchi, that of Pompilia Comparini, and the two of Guido Franceschini, are unapproachable, in their kind, by any living or dead poet, *me judice.* Here Browning's jerkiness comes in with inevitable effect. You get lightning glimpses—and, as one naturally expects from lightning, zigzag glimpses—into the intense night of the passion of these souls. It is entirely wonderful and without precedent."[1]

One of the most admirable things about Browning's admirable career as poet and man is that he wrote not to please the critics, as Tennyson often did, not to please the crowd, as the vast horde of ephemeral writers do, but to please himself. The critics and the crowd professed that they could not understand him; but he had no difficulty in understanding them. He knew exactly what they wanted, and declined to supply it. Instead of giving them what he thought they wanted, he gave them what he thought they needed. That illustrates the difference between the literary caterer and the literary master. Some poets, critics, dramatists, and novelists are born to be followers of the public taste; they have their reward. Only a few, and one at a time, are leaders. This is entirely as it should be, for, with followers, the more the merrier; with leaders it is quite otherwise.

In the case of a man of original genius, the first evidence of approaching fame is seen in the dust raised by contempt, scorn, ridicule, and various forms of angry resistance from those who will ulti-

---

[1] *Life of Sidney Lanier,* by Professor Edwin Mims.

mately be converts. People resist him as they resist the Gospel. He comes unto his own, and his own receive him not. The so-called reading public have the stupid cruelty of schoolboys, who will not tolerate on the part of any newcomer the slightest divergence in dress, manners, or conversation from the established standard. Conformity is king; for schoolboys are the most conservative mass of inertia that can be found anywhere on earth. And they are thorough masters of ridicule—the most powerful weapon known to humanity. But as in schoolboy circles the ostracising laughter is sometimes a sign that a really original boy has made his appearance, so the unthinking opposition of the conventional army of readers is occasionally a proof that the new man has made a powerful impression which can not be shaken off.

This is what Browning did with his "lasso" style. It was suitably adapted to his purposes, and the public behaved somewhat like the buffalo. They writhed, kicked, struggled, plunged, and the greater the uproar, the more evident it was that they were caught. Shortly before his death, Professor F. J. Child, a scholar of international fame, told me angrily that Wagner was no musician at all; that he was a colossal fraud; that the growing enthusiasm for him was mere affectation, which would soon pass away. He spoke with extraordinary passion. I wondered at his rage, but I understand it now. It was the rage of a king against the incoming and inexorable tide.

Nothing is more singular to contemplate than the variations in form of what the public calls melody, both in notation and in language. What delights the ears of one generation distresses or wearies the ears of another. Elizabethan audiences listened with rapture to long harangues in bombastic blank verse: a modern audience can not endure this. The senses of Queen Anne Englishmen were charmed by what they called the melody of Pope's verse—by its even regularity and steady flow. To us Pope's verse is full of wit and cerebration, but we find the measure intolerably monotonous. Indeed, by a curious irony of fate, Pope, who regarded himself as a supreme poet, has since frequently been declared to be no poet at all. Keats wrote *Endymion* in the heroic couplet—the very measure employed by Pope. But his use of it was so different that this poem would have seemed utterly lacking in melody to Augustan ears—Pope would have attempted to "versify" it. And yet we enjoy it. It seems ridiculous to say that the man who wrote *Der fliegende*

Holländer and *Tannhäuser* could not write melody, and yet it was almost universally said. It seems strange that critics should have declared that the man who wrote *Love Among the Ruins* could not write rhythmical verse, yet such was once almost the general opinion. Still, the rebellious instinct of the public that condemned Wagner in music and Browning in poetry was founded on something genuine; for Wagner was unlike other musicians, and Browning was unlike other poets.

Fraser's Magazine, for December, 1833, contained a review of Browning's first poem, *Pauline,* which had been published that year. The critic decided that the new poet was mad: "you being, beyond all question, as mad as Cassandra, without any of the power to prophesy like her, or to construct a connected sentence like anybody else. We have already had a Monomaniac; and we designate you 'The Mad Poet of the Batch;' as being mad not in one direction only, but in all. A little lunacy, like a little knowledge, would be a dangerous thing."

Yet it was in this despised and rejected poem that a great, original genius in English poetry was first revealed. It is impossible to understand Browning or even to read him intelligently without firmly fixing in the mind his theory of poetry, and comprehending fully his ideal and his aim. All this he set forth clearly in *Pauline,* and though he was only twenty years old when he wrote it, he never wavered from his primary purpose as expressed in two lines of the poem, two lines that should never be forgotten by those who really wish to enjoy the study of Browning:

> And then thou said'st a perfect bard was one
> Who chronicled the stages of all life.

What is most remarkable about this definition of poetry is what it omits. The average man regards poetry as being primarily concerned with the creation of beauty. Not a word is said about beauty in Browning's theory. The average man regards poetry as being necessarily melodious, rhythmical, tuneful, above all, pleasing to the senses; but Browning makes no allusion here to rime or rhythm, nor to melody or music of any sort. To him the bard is a Reporter of Life, an accurate Historian of the Soul, one who observes human nature in its various manifestations, and gives a faithful record. Sound, rhythm, beauty are important, because they are a part of life; and they are to be found in Browning's works like wild flowers in a field; but they are not in themselves the main things. The main thing is human life in its totality. Exactly in proportion to the poet's power of portraying life, is the poet great; if he correctly describes a wide range of life, he is greater than if he has succeeded only in a narrow stretch; and the Perfect Bard would be the one who had chronicled the stages of all life. Shakespeare is the supreme poet because he has approached nearer to this ideal than any one else—he has actually chronicled most phases of humanity, and has truthfully painted a wide variety of character. Browning therefore says of him in *Christmas-Eve*—

> As I declare our Poet, him
> Whose insight makes all others dim:
> A thousand poets pried at life,
> And only one amid the strife
> Rose to be Shakespeare.

Browning's poetry, as he elsewhere expresses it, was always dramatic in principle, always an attempt to interpret human life. With that large number of highly respectable and useful persons who do not care whether they understand him or not, I have here no concern: but to those who really wish to learn his secret, I insist that his main intention must ever be kept in mind. Much of his so-called obscurity, harshness, and uncouthness falls immediately into its proper place, is indeed necessary. The proof of his true greatness not as a philosopher, thinker, psychologist, but as a poet, lies in the simple fact that when the subject-matter he handles is beautiful or sublime, his style is usually adequate to the situation.   Browning had no difficulty in writing melodiously when he placed the posy in the Ring,

> O lyric Love, half angel and half bird
> And all a wonder and a wild desire,

although just a moment before, when he was joking about his lack of readers, he was anything but musical.   *The Ring and the Book* is full of exquisite beauty, amazing felicity of expression, fluent rhythm and melody; full also of crudities, jolts, harshness, pedantry, wretched witticisms, and coarseness.   Why these contrasts?   Because it is a study of human testimony.   The lawyers in this work speak no radiant or spiritual poetry; they talk like tiresome, conceited pedants because they were tiresome, conceited pedants; Pompilia's dying speech of adoring passion for Caponsacchi is sublime music, because she was a spiritual woman in a glow of exaltation.   Guido speaks at first with calm, smiling irony, and later rages like a wild beast caught in a spring-trap; in both cases the verse fits his mood.   If Pompilia's tribute to Caponsacchi had been expressed in language as dull and flat as the pleas of the lawyers, then we should be quite sure that Browning, whatever he was, was no poet. For it would indicate that he could not create the right diction for the right situation and character. Now, his picture of the triple light of sunset in *The Last Ride Together* is almost intolerably beautiful, because such a scene fairly overwhelms the senses. I hear the common and unintelligent comment, "Ah, if he had only always written like that!" He would have done so, if he had been interested in only the beautiful aspects of this world. "How could the man who wrote such lovely music as that have also written such harsh stuff as *Mr. Sludge, the Medium?*" The answer is that in the former he was chronicling a stage of life that in its very essence was beauty: in the latter, something exactly the opposite. Life has its trivialities and its ugliness, as well as its sublime aspirations. In Browning's poetry, whenever the thought rises, the style automatically rises with it.

Compare the diction of *Holy Cross Day* with that in *Love Among the Ruins*. Cleon is an old Greek poet, and he speaks noble, serene verse: Bishop Blougram is a subtle dialectician, a formidable antagonist in a joint debate, and he has the appropriate manner and language. Would you have him talk like the lover in *Evelyn Hope?*

Browning was a great artist, and the grotesque is an organic part of his structures. To find fault with the grotesque excrescences in Browning's poetry is exactly like condemning a cathedral because it has gargoyles. How could the architect that dreamed those wonderful columns and arches have made those hideous gargoyles? Did he flatter himself they were beautiful? When *Macbeth* was translated into German, the translator was aghast at the coarse language of the drunken porter. How could the great Shakespeare, who had proved so often his capacity as an artist, have made such an appalling blunder? So the translator struck out the offensive words, and made the porter sing a sweet hymn to the dawn.

The theory of poetry originally stated in *Pauline* Browning not only endeavored to exemplify in his work; he often distinctly repeated it. In *The Glove,* all the courtiers, hide-bound by conventional ideas, unite in derisive insults howled at the lady. She goes out 'mid hooting and laughter. Only two men follow her: one, because he loves her; the other, for purely professional reasons. To-day, he would of course be a society reporter. "I beg

your pardon, Madam, but would you kindly grant
me an interview? I represent the *New York Flash,*
and we shall be glad to present your side of this
story in our next Sunday issue." With equal professional zeal, Peter Ronsard is keenly interested in
discovering the motives that underlay the lady's
action. He simply must know, and in defense of
his importunity, he presents his credentials. He is a
poet, and therefore the strange scene that has just
been enacted comes within his special domain.

> I followed after,
> And asked, as a grace, what it all meant?
> If she wished not the rash deed's recallment?
> "For I"—so I spoke—"am a poet:
> Human nature,—behoves that I know it!"

In *Transcendentalism,* a poem which is commonly
misunderstood, Browning informs us that the true
poet must deal, not with abstract thought, but with
concrete things. A young poet informs an elder col-
league that he has just launched a huge philosophical
poem, called *Transcendentalism: a Poem in Twelve
Books.* His wiser critic tells him that he is on the
wrong track altogether; what he has written is prose,
not poetry. Poetry is not a discussion of abstract
ideas, but the creation of individual things. Transcendentalism is not a fit subject for poetry, because

it deals with metaphysical thought, instead of discussing men and women. To illustrate his point, he makes a comparison between botany and roses. Which is the more interesting, to read a heavy treatise on botany, or to behold roses? A few pedants may like botany better, but ordinary humanity is quite right in preferring flowers. Browning indicates that the poet should not compose abstract treatises, but should create individual works of art, like the stout Mage of Halberstadt,

> John, who made things Boehme wrote thoughts about.
> He with a "look you!" vents a brace of rhymes,
> And in there breaks the sudden rose herself,
> Over us, under, round us every side,
> Nay, in and out the tables and the chairs
> And musty volumes, Boehme's book and all,—
> Buries us with a glory, young once more,
> Pouring heaven into this shut house of life.

Many have failed to understand this poem, because they think that Browning himself is constantly guilty of the sin specifically condemned here. Browning has indeed often been called a thinker, a philosopher: but a moment's serious reflection will prove that of all English poetry outside of the drama, Browning's is the least abstract and the most concrete. Poetry is not condemned because it arouses thought, but only when it is abstract in method. Browning often deals

with profound ideas, but always by concrete illustrations. For example, he discusses the doctrine of
predestination by giving us the individual figure of
Johannes-Agricola in meditation: the royalist point
of view in the seventeenth century by cavaliers singing three songs: the damnation of indecision by two
Laodicæan lovers in *The Statue and the Bust*.
When Browning is interested in any doctrine, idea,
or system of thought, he creates a person to illustrate it.

Browning's theory of poetry is further reen-
forced by his poem *How It Strikes a Contemporary,*
which, in the final rearrangement of his works, he
placed directly after *Transcendentalism,* as though
to drive his doctrine home. Here is a picture of a
real poet. Where does he live, whence does he get
his sources of inspiration, and how does he pass his
time? The poem answers these questions in a most
instructive manner, if only we keep in mind the original definition given in *Pauline*. It is conventionally
believed that the country is more poetic than the
city: that an ideal residence for a poet would be in
lonely, lovely, romantic scenery; and that in splendid
solitude and isolation he should clothe his thoughts
in forms of beauty. Now Browning's own life and
methods of work were in exact contrast to these pop-

ular ideas; because his theory of poetry requires the poet to live in the very midst of human activities, and to draw his inspiration not from a mountain or the stars, but from all sorts and conditions of men. Thus, in the poem, *How It Strikes a Contemporary*, the poet lives in a noisy city, spends his time walking the streets, and instead of being lost in a trance, he is intensely aware of everything that happens in the town. The poet is an observer, not a dreamer. Indeed, the citizens think this old poet is a royal spy, because he notices people and events with such sharp attention. Browning would seem to say that the mistake is a quite natural one; the poet ought to act like a spy, for, if he be a true poet, he is a spy—a spy on human life. He takes upon himself the mystery of things, as if he were God's spy.

> He walked and tapped the pavement with his cane,
> Scenting the world, looking it full in face. . . .
> He glanced o'er books on stalls with half an eye,
> And fly-leaf ballads on the vendor's string,
> And broad-edge bold-print posters by the wall.
> He took such cognizance of men and things,
> If any beat a horse, you felt he saw;
> If any cursed a woman, he took note.

This is an exact description of the way Robert Browning walked the streets of Florence. Only a few years after this poem was printed, he was glancing o'er the books on stalls in the square of San Lorenzo, and found the old yellow volume which he turned into an epic of humanity. The true poet "scents" the world, smells it out, as a dog locates game. A still stronger expression is used in *Christmas-Eve,* where the poets "pried" at life, turned up its surface in order to disclose all its hidden treasures of meaning.

"TRANSCENDENTALISM: A POEM IN TWELVE BOOKS"

1855

Stop playing, poet! May a brother speak?
'Tis you speak, that's your error. Song's our art:
Whereas you please to speak these naked thoughts
Instead of draping them in sights and sounds.
—True thoughts, good thoughts, thoughts fit to treasure up!
But why such long prolusion and display,
Such turning and adjustment of the harp,
And taking it upon your breast, at length,
Only to speak dry words across its strings?
Stark-naked thought is in request enough:
Speak prose and hollo it till Europe hears!
The six-foot Swiss tube, braced about with bark,
Which helps the hunter's voice from Alp to Alp—
Exchange our harp for that,—who hinders you?

But here's your fault; grown men want thought,
    you think;
Thought's what they mean by verse, and seek in verse.
Boys seek for images and melody.

Men must have reason—so, you aim at men.
Quite otherwise! Objects throng our youth, 'tis true;
We see and hear and do not wonder much:
If you could tell us what they mean, indeed!
As German Boehme never cared for plants
Until it happed, a-walking in the fields,
He noticed all at once that plants could speak,
Nay, turned with loosened tongue to talk with him.
That day the daisy had an eye indeed—
Colloquized with the cowslip on such themes!
We find them extant yet in Jacob's prose.
But by the time youth slips a stage or two
While reading prose in that tough book he wrote
(Collating and emendating the same
And settling on the sense most to our mind),
We shut the clasps and find life's summer past.
Then, who helps more, pray, to repair our loss—
Another Boehme with a tougher book
And subtler meanings of what roses say,—
Or some stout Mage like him of Halberstadt,
John, who made things Boehme wrote thoughts about?
He with a "look you!" vents a brace of rhymes,
And in there breaks the sudden rose herself,
Over us, under, round us every side,
Nay, in and out the tables and the chairs
And musty volumes, Boehme's book and all,—
Buries us with a glory, young once more,
Pouring heaven into this shut house of life.

So come, the harp back to your heart again!
You are a poem, though your poem's naught.
The best of all you showed before, believe,
Was your own boy-face o'er the finer chords
Bent, following the cherub at the top
That points to God with his paired half-moon wings.

HOW IT STRIKES A CONTEMPORARY

1855

I only knew one poet in my life:
And this, or something like it, was his way.

  You saw go up and down Valladolid,
A man of mark, to know next time you saw.
His very serviceable suit of black
Was courtly once and conscientious still,
And many might have worn it, though none did:
The cloak, that somewhat shone and showed the threads,
Had purpose, and the ruff, significance.
He walked and tapped the pavement with his cane,
Scenting the world, looking it full in face,
An old dog, bald and blindish, at his heels.
They turned up, now, the alley by the church,
That leads nowhither; now, they breathed themselves
On the main promenade just at the wrong time:
You'd come upon his scrutinizing hat,
Making a peaked shade blacker than itself
Against the single window spared some house
Intact yet with its mouldered Moorish work,—
Or else surprise the ferrel of his stick
Trying the mortar's temper 'tween the chinks
Of some new shop a-building, French and fine.
He stood and watched the cobbler at his trade,
The man who slices lemons into drink,
The coffee-roaster's brazier, and the boys
That volunteer to help him turn its winch.
He glanced o'er books on stalls with half an eye,
And fly-leaf ballads on the vendor's string,
And broad-edge bold-print posters by the wall.
He took such cognizance of men and things,

If any beat a horse, you felt he saw;
If any cursed a woman, he took note;
Yet stared at nobody,—you stared at him,
And found, less to your pleasure than surprise,
He seemed to know you and expect as much.
So, next time that a neighbour's tongue was loosed,
It marked the shameful and notorious fact,
We had among us, not so much a spy,
As a recording chief-inquisitor,
The town's true master if the town but knew!
We merely kept a governor for form,
While this man walked about and took account
Of all thought, said and acted, then went home,
And wrote it fully to our Lord the King
Who has an itch to know things, he knows why,
And reads them in his bedroom of a night.
Oh, you might smile! there wanted not a touch,
A tang of . . . well, it was not wholly ease
As back into your mind the man's look came.
Stricken in years a little,—such a brow
His eyes had to live under!—clear as flint
On either side the formidable nose
Curved, cut and coloured like an eagle's claw.
Had he to do with A.'s surprising fate?
When altogether old B. disappeared
And young C. got his mistress,—was't our friend,
His letter to the King, that did it all?
What paid the bloodless man for so much pains?
Our Lord the King has favourites manifold,
And shifts his ministry some once a month;
Our city gets new governors at whiles,—
But never word or sign, that I could hear,
Notified to this man about the streets
The King's approval of those letters conned
The last thing duly at the dead of night.

Did the man love his office? Frowned our Lord,
Exhorting when none heard—"Beseech me not!
"Too far above my people,—beneath me!
"I set the watch,—how should the people know?
"Forget them, keep me all the more in mind!"
Was some such understanding 'twixt the two?

   I found no truth in one report at least—
That if you tracked him to his home, down lanes
Beyond the Jewry, and as clean to pace,
You found he ate his supper in a room
Blazing with lights, four Titians on the wall,
And twenty naked girls to change his plate!
Poor man, he lived another kind of life
In that new stuccoed third house by the bridge,
Fresh-painted, rather smart than otherwise!
The whole street might o'erlook him as he sat,
Leg crossing leg, one foot on the dog's back,
Playing a decent cribbage with his maid
(Jacynth, you're sure her name was) o'er the cheese
And fruit, three red halves of starved winter-pears,
Or treat of radishes in April. Nine,
Ten, struck the church clock, straight to bed went he.

   My father, like the man of sense he was,
Would point him out to me a dozen times;
"'St—'St," he'd whisper, "the Corregidor!"
I had been used to think that personage
Was one with lacquered breeches, lustrous belt,
And feathers like a forest in his hat,
Who blew a trumpet and proclaimed the news,
Announced the bull-fights, gave each church its turn,
And memorized the miracle in vogue!
He had a great observance from us boys;
We were in error; that was not the man.

I'd like now, yet had haply been afraid,
To have just looked, when this man came to die,
And seen who lined the clean gay garret-sides
And stood about the neat low truckle-bed,
With the heavenly manner of relieving guard.
Here had been, mark, the general-in-chief,
Thro' a whole campaign of the world's life and death,
Doing the King's work all the dim day long,
In his old coat and up to knees in mud,
Smoked like a herring, dining on a crust,—
And, now the day was won, relieved at once!
No further show or need for that old coat,
You are sure, for one thing! Bless us, all the while
How sprucely we are dressed out, you and I!
A second, and the angels alter that.
Well, I could never write a verse,—could you?
Let's to the Prado and make the most of time.

In common with all English poets—there is no
exception—Browning loved nature. But he loved
human nature so much more that when he contemplates natural objects he thinks of them *in terms of
humanity*. This is exactly contrary to the conventional method. Most poets and novelists describe
human faces in terms of outdoor nature: the heroine
has "stormy eyes," "rainy eyes," her face is swept
by "gusts of passion," and so on, *ad infinitum*. I
do not say that Browning's is the better way; I say
it is his way, because he was obsessed by humanity.
To take instances only from his first poem:

Thou wilt remember one warm morn when winter
Crept aged from the earth, and spring's first breath
Blew soft from the moist hills; the blackthorn boughs,
So dark in the bare wood, when glistening
In the sunshine were white with coming buds,
Like the bright side of a sorrow, and the banks
Had violets opening from sleep like eyes.

Autumn has come like Spring returned to us
Won from her girlishness.

             . . . the trees bend
O'er it as wild men watch a sleeping girl.

             So, when Spring comes
With sunshine back again like an old smile.

I am to sing whilst ebbing day dies soft,
As a lean scholar dies worn o'er his book,
And in the heaven stars steal out one by one
As hunted men steal to their mountain watch.

Browning's love for the dramatic was so intense
that he carried it into every kind of poetry that he
wrote. Various classes of his works he called
*Dramas, Dramatic Lyrics, Dramatic Romances,
Dramatic Idyls, Dramatis Personæ.* In one of her
prefaces, Elizabeth Barrett had employed—for the
first time in English literature, I think—the term
Dramatic Lyric. This naturally appealed to Browning, and he gave the title in 1842 to his first published collection of short poems. At first blush

"dramatic lyric" sounds like a contradiction in terms, like "non-mathematical algebra." Drama is the most objective branch of poetry, and the lyric the most subjective: but Browning was so intent upon the chronicling of all stages of life that he carried the methods of the drama into the lyric form, of which *Meeting at Night* may serve as an excellent example. Many of his short poems have the lyrical beauty of Shelley and Heine; but they all represent the soul of some historical or imaginary person.

At the very end of *The Ring and the Book*, Browning declared that human testimony was false, a statement that will be supported by any lawyer or judge of much court experience. Human testimony being worthless, there remains but one way for the poet to tell the truth about humanity, and that is through his art. The poet should use his skill not primarily with the idea of creating something beautiful, but with the main purpose of expressing the actual truth concerning human life and character. The highest art is the highest veracity, and this conforms to Browning's theory of poetry. This was his ideal, and by adhering to this he hoped to save his soul. Browning believed that by living up to our best capacity we attained unto salvation. The man who hid his talent in the earth was really a lost soul. Like many truly

great artists, Browning felt deeply the responsibility
of his splendid endowment. In one of his letters to
Miss Barrett, he said, "I must write poetry and save
my soul." In the last lines of *The Ring and the
Book* we find this thought repeated:

> So, British public, who may like me yet,
> (Marry and amen!) learn one lesson hence
> Of many which whatever lives should teach:
> This lesson, that our human speech is naught,
> Our human testimony false, our fame
> And human estimation words and wind.
> Why take the artistic way to prove so much?
> Because, it is the glory and good of Art,
> That Art remains the one way possible
> Of speaking truth, to minds like mine at least. . . .
> But Art,—wherein man nowise speaks to men,
> Only to mankind,—Art may tell a truth
> Obliquely, do the thing shall breed the thought,
> Nor wrong the thought, missing the mediate word.
> So may you paint your picture, twice show truth,
> Beyond mere imagery on the wall,—
> So, note by note, bring music from your mind,
> Deeper than ever e'en Beethoven dived,—
> So write a book shall mean beyond the facts,
> Suffice the eye and save the soul beside.
> And save the soul!

From first to last Browning understood the prevailing criticism of his poetry, directed against its
so-called lack of musical rhythm. He commented on
it more than once. But he answered it always in the

same way, in *Pippa Passes,* in the last stanzas of
Pacchiarotto, and in the *Epilogue* to the same volume. He insisted that what the critics meant by
melody was a childish jingle of rimes like Mother
Goose. Referring to *Sordello,* he makes the Second
Student in *Pippa Passes* remark, "Instead of cramp
couplets, each like a knife in your entrails, he should
write, says Bluphocks, both classically and intelligi-
bly. . . . One strip Cools your lip. . . .
One bottle Clears your throttle." In *Pacchiarotto,*
he calls to critics:

> And, what with your rattling and tinkling,
> Who knows but you give me an inkling
> How music sounds, thanks to the jangle
> Of regular drum and triangle?
> Whereby, tap-tap, chink-chink, 'tis proven
> I break rule as bad as Beethoven.
> "That chord now—a groan or a grunt is't?
> Schumann's self was no worse contrapuntist.
> No ear! or if ear, so tough-gristled—
> He thought that he sung while he whistled!"

Browning felt that there was at times a certain
virtue in mere roughness: that there were ideas,
which, if expressed in harsh phrase, would make a
deeper impression, and so be longer remembered.
The opening stanza of *The Twins* was meant to
emphasise this point:

> Grand rough old Martin Luther
> Bloomed fables—flowers on furze,
> The better the uncouther:
> Do roses stick like burrs?

Such a theory may help to explain the powerful
line in *Rabbi Ben Ezra:*

> Irks care the cropfull bird? Frets doubt the maw-crammed
> beast?

Of course Browning's theory of poetry does not
justify or explain all the unmusical passages in his
works. He felt, as every poet must, the difficulty of
articulation—the disparity between his ideas and the
verbal form he was able to give them. Browning
had his trials in composition, and he placed in the
mouth of the Pope his own ardent hope that in the
next world there will be some means of communica-
tion better than language:

> Expect nor question nor reply
> At what we figure as God's judgment bar!
> None of this vile way by the barren words
> Which, more than any deed, characterise
> Man as made subject to a curse: no speech.

Over and over again, however, Browning declared
that poetry should not be all sweetness. Flowers
growing naturally here and there in a pasture are
much more attractive than cut and gathered into a

nosegay. As Luther's long disquisitions are adorned
with pretty fables, that bloom like flowers on furze,
so, in the *Epilogue* to *Pacchiarotto,* Browning insisted that the wide fields of his verse are not without cowslips:

> And, friends, beyond dispute
>   I too have the cowslips dewy and dear.
> Punctual as Springtide forth peep they:
> But I ought to pluck and impound them, eh?
>   Not let them alone, but deftly shear
> And shred and reduce to—what may suit
> Children, beyond dispute?

Now, there are many law-abiding and transpar-
ently honest persons who prefer anthologies to
"works," who love to read tiny volumes prettily
bound, called "Beauties of Ruskin," and who have
substituted for the out-of-fashion "Daily Food"
books, painted bits of cardboard with sweet sayings
culled from popular idols of the day, with which
they embellish the walls of their offices and bed-
rooms, in the hope that they may hoist themselves
into a more hallowed frame of mind. This is the
class—always with us, though more prosperous than
the poor—who prefer a cut bouquet to the natural
flowers in wood and meadow, and for whose comfort and convenience Browning declined to work.
His poetry is too stiff for these readers, partly be-

cause they start with a preconceived notion of the
function of poetry. Instead of being charmed, their
first sensation is a shock. They honestly believe
that the attitude of the mind in apprehending poetry
should be passive, not active: is not the poet a public
entertainer? Did we not buy the book with the ex-
pectation of receiving immediate pleasure? The anticipated delight of many persons when they open a
volume of poems is almost physical, as it is when
they settle themselves to hear certain kinds of music.
They feel presumably as a comfortable cat does
when her fur is fittingly stroked. The torture that
many listeners suffered when they heard Wagner
for the first time was not imaginary, it was real;
"Oh, if somebody would only play a tune!" Yet
Wagner converted thousands of these quondam sufferers, and conquered them without making any
compromises. He simply enlarged their conception
of what opera-music might mean. He gave them
new sources of happiness without robbing them of
the old. For my part, although I prefer Wagner's
to all other operas, I keenly enjoy Mozart's *Don
Giovanni,* Charpentier's *Louise,* Gounod's *Faust,*
Strauss's *Salomé,* Verdi's *Aida,* and I never miss an
opportunity to hear Gilbert and Sullivan. Almost

all famous operas have something good in them except the works of Meyerbeer.

We all have moods when the mind wishes to be lulled, soothed, charmed, hypnotised with agreeable melody, and in English literature we fortunately have many great poets who can perform this service.

That strain again! it had a dying fall.

Tennyson was a veritable magician, who charmed with his genius hundreds and thousands of people. No arduous mental effort is necessary for the enjoyment of his verse, which is one reason why he is and will remain a popular poet. Browning can not be taken in just that way, any more than a man completely exhausted with the day's work can enjoy *Siegfried* or *Hedda Gabler*. Active, constant cerebration on the part of the listener or the reader is essential. This excludes at once a considerable number to whom the effort of real thinking is as strange as it is oppressive. Browning is a stimulus, not a sedative; his poetry is like an electric current which naturally fails to affect those who are non-conductors of poetry. As one of my undergraduate students tersely expressed it, "Tennyson soothes our senses: Browning stimulates our thoughts." Poetry

is in some ways like medicine. Tennyson quiets the
nerves: Browning is a tonic: some have found
Thomson's *Seasons* invaluable for insomnia: the
poetry of Swift is an excellent emetic.

I do not quite understand the intense anger of
many critics and readers over the eternal question of
Browning's obscurity. They have been harping on
this theme for eighty years and show no more sign
of exhaustion than a dog barking in the night. Why
do the heathen rage? Why do they not let Browning alone, and read somebody they can understand?
Browning is still gravely rebuked by many critics
for having written *Sordello*. Over and over again
we have been informed that the publication of this
poem shattered his reputation for twenty-five years.
Well, what of it? what difference does it make now?
He seems to have successfully survived it. This
huge work, which William Sharp called "that colossal derelict upon the ocean of poetry," is destined to have an immortality all its own. From one
point of view, we ought to be grateful for its publication. It has aroused inextinguishable laughter
among the blessed gods. It is not witty in itself, but
it is the cause of wit in many. Douglas Jerrold and
Carlyle commented delightfully on it; even Tennyson succeeded for once in saying something funny.

One critic called it a fine house in which the architect had forgotten to put any stairs. Another called it a huge boil in which all the impurities in Browning's system came to an impressive head, after which the patient, pure from poison, succeeded in writing the clear and beautiful *Pippa Passes*. Besides innumerable parodies that have been forgotten, Browning's obscurity was the impenetrable flint that struck two mental flashes that belong to literature, Calverley's *Cock and the Bull,* and Swinburne's *John Jones,* a brilliant exposition of the perversities in that tedious poem, *James Lee's Wife*. Not long ago, a young man sat by the lamplight, studying a thick volume with evident discomfort. To the friend who asked what he was doing, he replied, "I'm studying Browning."

"Why, no, you idiot, that isn't Browning: you are reading the index of first lines to the works of Wordsworth."

"By Jove! you're right! But it sounds just like Browning."

Browning's place in English literature is not with the great verse-sculptors, not with the masters of imperishable beauty of form; he does not belong to the glorious company where reign supreme Milton, Keats, and Tennyson; his place is rather with the

Interpreters of Life, with the poets who use their
art to express the shine and shade of life's tragi-
comedy—to whom the base, the trivial, the frivo-
lous, the grotesque, the absurd seem worth reporting
along with the pure, the noble, and the sublime,
since all these elements are alike human. In this
wide field of art, with the exception of Shakespeare,
who is the exception to everything, the first-born
and the last-born of all the great English poets know
no equal in the five centuries that rolled between
them. The first person to say this publicly was himself a poet and a devoted student of Form—Walter
Savage Landor. When he said it, people thought it
was mere hyperbole, the stressed language of com-
pliment; but we know now that Landor's words are
as true as they are beautiful:

> Shakespeare is not our poet, but the world's,
> Therefore on him no speech! and brief for thee,
> Browning! Since Chaucer was alive and hale,
> No man hath walk'd along our roads with step
> So active, so enquiring eye, or tongue
> So varied in discourse.

Many critics who are now dead, and some that
are yet alive, have predicted the speedy death of
Browning's reputation. This prediction seems to
afford a certain class of critics a calm and holy joy.
Some years ago, Mr. James Douglas, of London,

solemnly announced the approaching demise.
Browning will die, said he, even as Donne is dead,
and for the same reason. But Donne is not quite
dead.

I must survive a thing ere know it dead.

I think Donne will survive all our contemporary
criticisms about him. Ben Jonson said that Donne,
for not keeping of accent, deserved hanging. But
Donne, though he forgot to keep step with the procession of poets, has survived many poets who tripped
a regular measure. He has survived even Pope's
"versification" of his poems, one of the most unconsciously humorous things in English literature. Accent alone will not keep a man alive. Which poet
of these latter days stands the better chance to remain, Francis Thompson, whose spiritual flame occasionally burned up accent, or Alfred Austin, who
studied to preserve accent through a long life? Accent is indeed important; but raiment is of little
value unless it clothes a living body. Does Browning's best poetry smell of mortality? Nearly every
new novel I read in English has quotations from
Browning without the marks, sure evidence that the
author has read him and assumes that the readers
of the novel have a like acquaintance. When

Maeterlinck wrote his famous play, *Monna Vanna,* he took one of the scenes directly from Browning's *Luria* : he said that he had been inspired by Browning : that Browning is one of the greatest poets that England has ever produced : that to take a scene from him is a kind of public homage, such as we pay to Homer, Æschylus, and Shakespeare.

With the exception of Shakespeare, any other English poet could now be spared more easily than Browning. For, owing to his aim in poetry, and his success in attaining it, he gave us much vital truth and beauty that we should seek elsewhere in vain ; and, as he said in the *Epilogue* to *Pacchiarotto,* the strong, heady wine of his verse may become sweet in process of time.

III

LYRICS

A PURE lyric, as distinguished from other kinds of poetry, narrative, descriptive, epic, dramatic, should have three characteristic qualities, immediately evident on the first reading: it should be short, it should be melodious, it should express only one mood. A very long lyrical poem has never been written, and probably could not be: a lyric without fluent melody is unthinkable: and a poem representing a great variety of moods would more properly be classed as descriptive or dramatic than lyrical. Examples of the perfect lyric in nineteenth century English poetry are Shelley's *I Arise From Dreams of Thee:* Keats's *Bright Star:* Byron's *She Walks in Beauty:* Tennyson's *Break, Break, Break.* In each one of these notable illustrations the poem is a brief song of passion, representing the mood of the singer at that moment.

There are innumerable *lyrical* passages in Browning's long poems, and in his dramatic monologues:

there are splendid outbursts of melody. He could
not be ranked among the greatest English poets if
he had not been one of our greatest singers. But
we do not go to Browning primarily for song. He
is not one of our greatest lyrical poets. It is certain,
however, that he could have been had he chosen to
be. He wrote a sufficient number of pure lyrics to
prove his quality and capacity. But he was so much
more deeply interested in the study of the soul than
in the mere expression of beauty—he was so essentially, from *Pauline* to *Asolando*—a dramatic poet,
that his great contribution to literature is seen in
profound and subtle interpretations of the human
heart. It is fortunate that he made the soul his
specialty, because English literature is wonderfully
rich in song: there are many poets who can thrill us
with music: but there is only one Browning, and
there is no group of writers in any literature among
which he can be classed.

Browning's dramatic lyrics differ from Tennyson's short poems as the lyrics of Donne differed
from those of Campion; but Browning occasionally
tried his hand at the composition of a pure lyric,
as if to say, "You see I can write like this when I
choose." Therein lies his real superiority to almost
all other English poets: he could do their work, but

they could not do his. It is significant that his first poem, *Pauline,* should have deeply impressed two men of precisely opposite types of mind. These two were John Stuart Mill and Dante Gabriel Rossetti —their very names illustrating beautifully the difference in their mental tastes and powers. Carlyle called Mill a "logic-chopping engine," because his intellectual processes were so methodical, systematic, hard-headed: Rossetti was a master of color and harmony. Yet Mill found in *Pauline* the workings of a powerful mind: and Rossetti's sensitive temperament was charmed with the wonderful pictures and lovely melodies it contained.

I like to think that Mill read, paused, re-read and meditated on this passage:

> I am made up of an intensest life,
> Of a most clear idea of consciousness
> Of self, distinct from all its qualities,
> From all affections, passions, feelings, powers;
> And thus far it exists, if tracked, in all:
> But linked, in me, to self-supremacy
> Existing as a centre to all things,
> Most potent to create and rule and call
> Upon all things to minister to it;
> And to a principle of restlessness
> Which would be all, have, see, know, taste, feel, all—
> This is myself; and I should thus have been
> Though gifted lower than the meanest soul.

I like to think that Rossetti was thrilled with this picture of Andromeda:

> Andromeda!
> And she is with me: years roll, I shall change,
> But change can touch her not—so beautiful
> With her fixed eyes, earnest and still, and hair
> Lifted and spread by the salt-sweeping breeze,
> And one red beam, all the storm leaves in heaven,
> Resting upon her eyes and hair, such hair,
> As she awaits the snake on the wet beach
> By the dark rock and the white wave just breaking
> At her feet; quite naked and alone; a thing
> I doubt not, nor fear for, secure some god
> To save will come in thunder from the stars.

It is rather singular, in view of the great vogue of the sonnet in the nineteenth century, that neither Tennyson nor Browning should have succeeded in this form. The two men wrote very few sonnets— Browning fewer than Tennyson—and neither ever wrote a great one. Longfellow, so inferior in most respects to his two great English contemporaries, was an incomparably superior sonnetteer. Tennyson's sonnets are all mediocre: Browning did not publish a single sonnet in the final complete edition of his works. He did however print a very few on special occasions, and when he was twenty-two years old, between the composition of *Pauline* and *Paracelsus,* there appeared in the *Monthly Repository* a sonnet beginning which is the best example from his pen that has been preserved. Although he did not think much of it in later years, it has been frequently reprinted, and is worth keeping; both for the ardor of its passion, and because it is extraordinary that he should have begun so very early in his career a form of verse that he practically abandoned. This sonnet may have been addressed to a purely imaginary ideal; but it is possible that the young man had in mind Eliza Flower, for whom he certainly had a boy-ish love, and who was probably the original of Pauline. She and her sister, Sarah Flower, the au-thor of *Nearer, My God, to Thee,* were both older than Browning, and both his intimate friends dur-ing the period of his adolescence.

SONNET
1834

Eyes calm beside thee (Lady, could'st thou know!)
May turn away thick with fast-gathering tears:
I glance not where all gaze: thrilling and low
Their passionate praises reach thee—my cheek wears
Alone no wonder when thou passest by;
Thy tremulous lids bent and suffused reply
To the irrepressible homage which doth glow
On every lip but mine: if in thine ears
Their accents linger—and thou dost recall
Me as I stood, still, guarded, very pale,

> Beside each votarist whose lighted brow
> Wore worship like an aureole, "O'er them all
> My beauty," thou wilt murmur, "did prevail
> Save that one only:"—Lady, could'st thou know!

It is perhaps characteristic of Browning that this early sonnet should be so irregular in its rime-scheme.

The songs in *Paracelsus* (1835) prove that Browning was a genuine lyrical poet: the best of them, *Over the Sea Our Galleys Went,* is more properly a dramatic monologue: but the song in the second act, by Aprile (who I think stands for Keats) is a pure lyric, and so are the two stanzas sung by Paracelsus in the fourth act. There are lines here which suggest something of the drowsy music of Tennyson's *Lotos-Eaters,* published in 1832:

> . . . . such balsam falls
> Down sea-side mountain pedestals,
> From tree-tops where tired winds are fain,
> Spent with the vast and howling main,
> To treasure half their island-gain.

SONGS FROM *PARACELSUS*

1835

(Aprile sings)

> I hear a voice, perchance I heard
> Long ago, but all too low,
> So that scarce a care it stirred
> If the voice were real or no:

I heard it in my youth when first
The waters of my life outburst:
But, now their stream ebbs faint, I hear
That voice, still low, but fatal-clear—
As if all poets, God ever meant
Should save the world, and therefore lent
Great gifts to, but who, proud, refused
To do his work, or lightly used
Those gifts, or failed through weak endeavour,
So, mourn cast off by him for ever,—
As if these leaned in airy ring
To take me; this the song they sing.

"Lost, lost! yet come,
With our wan troop make thy home.
Come, come! for we
Will not breathe, so much as breathe
Reproach to thee,
Knowing what thou sink'st beneath.
So sank we in those old years,
We who bid thee, come! thou last
Who, living yet, hast life o'erpast.
And altogether we, thy peers,
Will pardon crave for thee, the last
Whose trial is done, whose lot is cast
With those who watch but work no more,
Who gaze on life but live no more.
Yet we trusted thou shouldst speak
The message which our lips, too weak,
Refused to utter,—shouldst redeem
Our fault: such trust, and all a dream!
Yet we chose thee a birthplace
Where the richness ran to flowers:
Couldst not sing one song for grace?
Not make one blossom man's and ours?

Must one more recreant to his race
Die with unexerted powers,
And join us, leaving as he found
The world, he was to loosen, bound?
Anguish! ever and for ever;
Still beginning, ending never.
Yet, lost and last one, come!
How couldst understand, alas,
What our pale ghosts strove to say,
As their shades did glance and pass
Before thee night and day?
Thou wast blind as we were dumb:
Once more, therefore, come, O come!
How should we clothe, how arm the spirit
Shall next thy post of life inherit—
How guard him from thy speedy ruin?
Tell us of thy sad undoing
Here, where we sit, ever pursuing
Our weary task, ever renewing
Sharp sorrow, far from God who gave
Our powers, and man they could not save!"

(Paracelsus sings)

Heap cassia, sandal-buds and stripes
    Of labdanum, and aloe-balls,
Smeared with dull nard an Indian wipes
    From out her hair: such balsam falls
    Down sea-side mountain pedestals,
From tree-tops where tired winds are fain,
Spent with the vast and howling main,
To treasure half their island-gain.

And strew faint sweetness from some old
    Egyptian's fine worm-eaten shroud
Which breaks to dust when once unrolled;
    Or shredded perfume, like a cloud

From closet long to quiet vowed,
With mothed and dropping arras hung,
Mouldering her lute and books among,
As when a queen, long dead, was young.

(Song by Festus)

Thus the Mayne glideth
Where my Love abideth.
Sleep's no softer: it proceeds
On through lawns, on through meads,
On and on, whate'er befall,
Meandering and musical,
Though the niggard pasturage
Bears not on its shaven ledge
Aught but weeds and waving grasses
To view the river as it passes,
Save here and there a scanty patch
Of primroses too faint to catch
A weary bee.
          And scarce it pushes
Its gentle way through strangling rushes
Where the glossy kingfisher
Flutters when noon-heats are near,
Glad the shelving banks to shun,
Red and steaming in the sun,
Where the shrew-mouse with pale throat
Burrows, and the speckled stoat;
Where the quick sandpipers flit
In and out the marl and grit
That seems to breed them, brown as they:
Nought disturbs its quiet way,
Save some lazy stork that springs,
Trailing it with legs and wings,
Whom the shy fox from the hill
Rouses, creep he ne'er so still.

The songs in *Pippa Passes* (1841) are all exquisite works of art. The one on the King had been printed in the *Monthly Repository* in 1835 : the others appeared for the first time in the published drama. All of them are vitally connected with the action of the plot, differing in this respect from the Elizabethan custom of simple interpolation. The song sung in the early morning by the girl in her chamber

All service ranks the same with God

contains the philosophy of the play—human lives are inextricably intertwined, and all are dependent on the will of God. No individual can separate himself either from other men and women, or can sever the connection between himself and his Father in Heaven. The first stanza repeats the teaching of Milton in the sonnet on his blindness : the second is more definitely connected with Pippa's professional work.

Untwine me from the mass
Of deeds which make up life,

refers to her daily duty as a girl in the silk-mill, for she naturally thinks of the complexity of life as a tangled skein.

All service ranks the same with God:
If now, as formerly he trod
Paradise, his presence fills
Our earth, each only as God wills
Can work—God's puppets, best and worst,
Are we; there is no last nor first.

Say not "a small event!" Why "small"?
Costs it more pain that this, ye call
A "great event," should come to pass,
Than that? Untwine me from the mass
Of deeds which make up life, one deed
Power shall fall short in or exceed!

OTHER SONGS FROM *PIPPA PASSES*

1841

You'll love me yet!—and I can tarry
  Your love's protracted growing:
June reared that bunch of flowers you carry,
  From seeds of April's sowing.

I plant a heartful now: some seed
  At least is sure to strike,
And yield—what you'll not pluck indeed,
  Not love, but, may be, like.

You'll look at least on love's remains,
  A grave's one violet:
Your look?—that pays a thousand pains.
  What's death? You'll love me yet!

Overhead the tree-tops meet,
Flowers and grass spring 'neath one's feet;
There was nought above me, nought below,
My childhood had not learned to know:

> For, what are the voices of birds
> —Ay, and of beasts,—but words, our words,
> Only so much more sweet?
> The knowledge of that with my life begun.
> But I had so near made out the sun,
> And counted your stars, the seven and one,
> Like the fingers of my hand:
> Nay, I could all but understand
> Wherefore through heaven the white moon ranges;
> And just when out of her soft fifty changes
> No unfamiliar face might overlook me—
> Suddenly God took me.

The most famous song in the play, which simply sings itself, is:

> The year's at the spring
> And day's at the morn;
> Morning's at seven;
> The hill-side's dew-pearled;
> The lark's on the wing;
> The snail's on the thorn:
> God's in his heaven—
> All's right with the world!

The last line is unfortunately very often misquoted

> All's well with the world!

a remark never made either by Pippa or by Browning. In Browning's philosophy all may be right with the world, and yet far from well. Perhaps it is too prosaically minute to point out in so beautiful a

poem, a scientific error, but at seven o'clock on the
first of January in Asolo the sun is still below
the horizon.

MERTOUN'S SONG FROM *A BLOT IN THE 'SCUTCHEON*

1843

There's a woman like a dew-drop, she's so purer than the
    purest;
And her noble heart's the noblest, yes, and her sure faith's the
    surest:
And her eyes are dark and humid, like the depth on depth of
    lustre
Hid i' the harebell, while her tresses, sunnier than the wild-
    grape cluster,
Gush in golden-tinted plenty down her neck's rose-misted
    marble:
Then her voice's music . . . call it the well's bubbling, the
    bird's warble!
And this woman says, "My days were sunless and my nights
    were moonless,
"Parched the pleasant April herbage, and the lark's heart's
    outbreak tuneless,
"If you loved me not!" And I who—(ah, for words of
    flame!) adore her,
Who am mad to lay my spirit prostrate palpably before her—
I may enter at her portal soon, as now her lattice takes me,
And by noontide as by midnight make her mine, as hers she
    makes me!

The two lyrics, *Home-Thoughts, from the Sea* and
Home-Thoughts, from Abroad, were written dur-

ing Browning's first Italian journey in 1838; and it
seems strange that he did not print them among the
Dramatic Lyrics of 1842 but reserved them for the
Dramatic Romances of 1845; especially as he sub-
sequently transferred them to the *Lyrics*. They are
both notable on account of the strong feeling for
England which they express. No great English
poet has said so little of England as Browning,
though his own feelings were always keenly patriotic. Even in *Pauline,* a poem without a country,
there occur the two lines

> . . . and I cherish most
> My love of England—how her name, a word
> Of hers in a strange tongue makes my heart beat!

The allusion to the English thrush has given immortality to *Home-Thoughts, from Abroad.* Many
had observed that the thrush sings a lilt, and immediately repeats it: but Browning was the first to give
a pretty reason for it. The thrush seems to say,
"You think that beautiful melody is an accident?
Well, I will show you it is no fluke, I will sing it
correctly right over again." Browning was not in
Italy in April—perhaps he wrote the first stanza on
the voyage, as he wrote *Home-Thoughts, from
the Sea,* and added the second stanza about May and
June after he had reached the country of his quest.

HOME-THOUGHTS, FROM THE SEA

1845

Nobly, nobly Cape Saint Vincent to the North-west died away;
Sunset ran, one glorious blood-red, reeking into Cadiz Bay;
Bluish 'mid the burning water, full in face Trafalgar lay;
In the dimmest North-east distance dawned Gibraltar grand
     and gray;
"Here and here did England help me: how can I help Eng-
     land?"—say,
Whoso turns as I, this evening, turn to God to praise and pray,
While Jove's planet rises yonder, silent over Africa.

HOME-THOUGHTS, FROM ABROAD

1845

I

Oh, to be in England
Now that April's there,
And whoever wakes in England
Sees, some morning, unaware,
That the lowest boughs and the brushwood sheaf
Round the elm-tree bole are in tiny leaf,
While the chaffinch sings on the orchard bough
In England—now!

II

And after April, when May follows,
And the whitethroat builds, and all the swallows!
Hark, where my blossomed pear-tree in the hedge
Leans to the field and scatters on the clover
Blossoms and dewdrops—at the bent spray's edge—
That's the wise thrush; he sings each song twice over,
Lest you should think he never could recapture
The first fine careless rapture!

And though the fields look rough with hoary dew,
All will be gay when noontide wakes anew
The buttercups, the little children's dower
—Far brighter than this gaudy melon-flower!

The collection of poems called *James Lee's Wife*, published in the *Dramatis Personæ* (1864), seems to me illustrative of Browning's worst faults; it is obscure, harsh, and dull. But it contains one fine lyric descriptive of an autumn morning, a morning, by the way, much commoner in America during autumn than anywhere in Europe. The second stanza is nobly ethical in its doctrine of love—that we should not love only those persons whom we can respect, for true love seeks no profit. It must be totally free from the prospect of gain. A beautiful face inspired another lyric in this volume, and Browning drew upon his memories of Correggio to give the perfect tone to the poem.

FROM JAMES LEE'S WIFE

1864

I

Oh, good gigantic smile o' the brown old earth,
    This autumn morning! How he sets his bones
To bask i' the sun, and thrusts out knees and feet
For the ripple to run over in its mirth;
    Listening the while, where on the heap of stones
The white breast of the sea-lark twitters sweet.

II

That is the doctrine, simple, ancient, true;
  Such is life's trial, as old earth smiles and knows.
If you loved only what were worth your love,
Love were clear gain, and wholly well for you:
  Make the low nature better by your throes!
Give earth yourself, go up for gain above!

A FACE

1864

If one could have that little head of hers
  Painted upon a background of pale gold,
Such as the Tuscan's early art prefers!
  No shade encroaching on the matchless mould
Of those two lips, which should be opening soft
  In the pure profile; not as when she laughs,
For that spoils all: but rather as if aloft
  Yon hyacinth, she loves so, leaned its staff's
Burthen of honey-coloured buds to kiss
And capture 'twixt the lips apart for this.
Then her lithe neck, three fingers might surround,
How it should waver on the pale gold ground
Up to the fruit-shaped, perfect chin it lifts!
I know, Correggio loves to mass, in rifts
Of heaven, his angel faces, orb on orb
Breaking its outline, burning shades absorb:
But these are only massed there, I should think,
  Waiting to see some wonder momently
  Grow out, stand full, fade slow against the sky
  (That's the pale ground you'd see this sweet face by),
  All heaven, meanwhile, condensed into one eye
Which fears to lose the wonder, should it wink.

One of the most original and powerful of Browning's lyrical pieces comes just where we should least expect it, at the end of that dark, dreary, and all but impenetrable wilderness of verse, *Fifine at the Fair*. It serves as an *Epilogue,* but it would be difficult and unprofitable to attempt to discover its connection with the poem to which is is appended. Its metre is unique in Browning, and stirs the heart with inexpressible force. In music it most closely resembles the swift thrilling roll of a snare drum, and can be read aloud in exact accord with that instrument. Browning calls it *The Householder,* and of course it represents in his own life the anticipated moment when the soul leaves its house to unite with its mate. Out of the catastrophe of death appears a radiant vision which really seems too good to be true.

> "What, and is it really you again?" quoth I:
> "I again, what else did you expect?" quoth She.

The man is weary of his old patched up body, now no longer needed: weary of the noisy nuisances of life, and the tiresome and futile gabble of humanity: resentful, now that his spirit has actually survived death, when he remembers the scientific books he had read which almost struck despair in him. He petulantly says,

"If you knew but how I dwelt down here!" quoth I:
"And was I so better off up there?" quoth She.

He is for immediate departure, leaving his empty
carcass where it lies; but she reminds him of
the necessity for decent burial.   Much is to be
done before they can begin to enjoy together
their new and freer existence.   There is the body
to be buried; the obituary notices to be written
for the papers: the parson and undertaker to be
summoned: the formalities of the funeral: the selection of a proper tombstone, with care for the
name and accurate carving of the date of death
thereupon: and finally a bit of verse in the way of
final flourish.   So these two spirits look on with im-
patience at the funeral exercises, at the weeping
friends left behind, and not until the coffin is under
ground, are they at liberty to depart from terrestial
scenes.   If we do survive the death of the body, with
what curious sensations must we regard the solemn ceremonies of its interment!

EPILOGUE TO *FIFINE*

1872

The Householder

I

Savage I was sitting in my house, late, lone:
Dreary, weary with the long day's work:

Head of me, heart of me, stupid as a stone:
    Tongue-tied now, now blaspheming like a Turk;
When, in a moment, just a knock, call, cry,
    Half a pang and all a rapture, there again were we!—
"What, and is it really you again?" quoth I:
    "I again, what else did you expect?" quoth She.

II

"Never mind, hie away from this old house—
    Every crumbling brick embrowned with sin and shame!
Quick, in its corners ere certain shapes arouse!
    Let them—every devil of the night—lay claim,
Make and mend, or rap and rend, for me! Good-bye!
    God be their guard from disturbance at their glee,
Till, crash, comes down the carcass in a heap!" quoth I:
    "Nay, but there's a decency required!" quoth She.

III

"Ah, but if you knew how time has dragged, days, nights!
    All the neighbour-talk with man and maid—such men!
All the fuss and trouble of street-sounds, window-sights:
    All the worry of flapping door and echoing roof; and then,
All the fancies . . . Who were they had leave, dared try
    Darker arts that almost struck despair in me?
If you knew but how I dwelt down here!" quoth I:
    "And was I so better off up there?" quoth She.

IV

"Help and get it over! *Re-united to his wife*
    (How draw up the paper lets the parish-people know?)
Lies M., or N., departed from this life,
    Day the this or that, month and year the so and so.
What i' the way of final flourish? Prose, verse? Try!
    Affliction sore long time he bore, or, what is it to be?
Till God did please to grant him ease. Do end!" quoth I:
    "I end with—Love is all and Death is nought!" quoth She.

The same thought—the dramatic contrast between
the free spirit and its prison-house—is the basis of
the two lyrics that serve as prologues to *Pacchiarotto*
and to *La Saisiaz*. As Dryden's prefaces are far
better than his plays, so Browning's *Prologues* to
Pacchiarotto, to *La Saisiaz,* to *The Two Poets of
Croisic,* to *Jocoseria* are decidedly superior in poetic
art and beauty to the volumes they introduce. Indeed the prologue to *The Two Poets of Croisic* is
one of the most beautiful and perfect lyrics in the
English language.

PROLOGUE

1878

I

Such a starved bank of moss
  Till that May-morn,
Blue ran the flash across:
  Violets were born!

II

Sky—what a scowl of cloud
  Till, near and far,
Ray on ray split the shroud
  Splendid, a star!

III

World—how it walled about
  Life with disgrace
Till God's own smile came out:
  That was thy face!

PROLOGUE TO *PACCHIAROTTO*

1876

I

O the old wall here! How I could pass
　　Life in a long Midsummer day,
My feet confined to a plot of grass,
　　My eyes from a wall not once away!

II

And lush and lithe do the creepers clothe
　　Yon wall I watch, with a wealth of green:
Its bald red bricks draped, nothing loth,
　　In lappets of tangle they laugh between.

III

Now, what is it makes pulsate the robe?
　　Why tremble the sprays? What life o'erbrims
The body,—the house, no eye can probe,—
　　Divined as, beneath a robe, the limbs?

IV

And there again! But my heart may guess
　　Who tripped behind; and she sang perhaps:
So, the old wall throbbed, and its life's excess
　　Died out and away in the leafy wraps.

V

Wall upon wall are between us: life
　　And song should away from heart to heart.
I—prison-bird, with a ruddy strife
　　At breast, and a lip whence storm-notes start—

VI

Hold on, hope hard in the subtle thing
  That's spirit: though cloistered fast, soar free;
Account as wood, brick, stone, this ring
  Of the rueful neighbours, and—forth to thee!

PROLOGUE TO *LA SAISIAZ*

1878

I

Good, to forgive;
  Best, to forget!
  Living, we fret;
Dying, we live.
Fretless and free,
  Soul, clap thy pinion!
  Earth have dominion,
Body, o'er thee!

II

Wander at will,
  Day after day,—
  Wander away,
Wandering still—
Soul that canst soar!
  Body may slumber:
  Body shall cumber
Soul-flight no more.

III

Waft of soul's wing!
  What lies above?
  Sunshine and Love,
Skyblue and Spring!

Body hides—where?
   Ferns of all feather,
   Mosses and heather,
Yours be the care!

PROLOGUE TO *JOCOSERIA*

1883

   Wanting is—what?
   Summer redundant,
   Blueness abundant,
   —Where is the blot?
Beamy the world, yet a blank all the same,
—Framework which waits for a picture to frame:
What of the leafage, what of the flower?
Roses embowering with nought they embower!
Come then, complete incompletion, O comer,
Pant through the blueness, perfect the summer!
    Breathe but one breath
    Rose-beauty above,
    And all that was death
    Grows life, grows love,
     Grows love!

NEVER THE TIME AND THE PLACE

1883

Never the time and the place
   And the loved one all together!
This path—how soft to pace!
   This May—what magic weather!
Where is the loved one's face?
In a dream that loved one's face meets mine,
   But the house is narrow, the place is bleak
Where, outside, rain and wind combine

With a furtive ear, if I strive to speak,
  With a hostile eye at my flushing cheek,
With a malice that marks each word, each sign!
O enemy sly and serpentine,
  Uncoil thee from the waking man!
      Do I hold the Past
      Thus firm and fast
  Yet doubt if the Future hold I can?
This path so soft to pace shall lead
Thro' the magic of May to herself indeed!
Or narrow if needs the house must be,
Outside are the storms and strangers: we—
Oh, close, safe, warm sleep I and she,
—I and she!

IV

DRAMATIC LYRICS

BROWNING'S poetic career extended from 1833 to 1889, nearly sixty years of fairly continuous composition. We may make a threefold division: first, the thirteen years before his marriage in 1846; second, the fifteen years of married life, closing in 1861; third, the remaining twenty-eight years. During the first period he published twelve works; during the second, two; during the third, eighteen. The fact that so little was published during the years when his wife was alive may be accounted for by the fact that the condition of her health required his constant care, and that after the total failure of *Men and Women* (1855) to attract any popular attention, Browning for some time spent most of his energy in clay-modelling, giving up poetry altogether. Not long before the death of Mrs. Browning, he was busy writing *Prince Hohenstiel-Schwangau,* although he did not publish it until the right moment, which came in 1871. After the appearance of *Dramatis Personæ* (1864), and *The Ring and the Book* (1868-9), Browning's fame spread like a prairie fire; and it was quite natural that his immense reputation was a sharp spur to composition. One is more ready to speak when one is sure of an audience. Capricious destiny, however, willed that the books which sold the fastest after publication, were, with few exceptions, the least interesting and valuable of all the poet's performances. Perhaps he did not take so much care now that his fame was assured; perhaps the fires in his own mind were dying; perhaps the loss of his wife robbed him of necessary inspiration, as it certainly robbed him of the best critic he ever had, and the only one to whom he paid any serious attention. When we remember that some of the *Dramatic Romances, Luria, A Soul's Tragedy, Christmas-Eve, Men and Women,* and some of the *Dramatis Personæ* were read by her in manuscript, and that *The Ring and the Book* was written in the shadow of her influence, we begin to realise how much she helped him. Their love-letters during the months that preceded their marriage indicate the excellence of her judgment, her profound and sympathetic understanding of his genius and his willingness to listen to her advice. He did not intend to publish

A Soul's Tragedy at all, though it is one of his most
subtle and interesting dramas, and only did so at her
request; part of the manuscript of *Christmas-Eve*
is in her handwriting.

It is worth remembering too that in later years
Browning hated to write poetry, and nothing but a
sense of duty kept him during the long mornings at
his desk. He felt the responsibility of genius without its inspiration.

Browning has given a little trouble to bibliogra-
phers by redistributing the poems originally published in the three works, *Dramatic Lyrics* (1842),
Dramatic Romances and Lyrics (1845), and *Men
and Women* (1855). The *Dramatic Lyrics* at first
contained sixteen pieces; the *Dramatic Romances
and Lyrics* twenty-three; the *Men and Women* fifty-
one. In the final arrangement the first of these in-
cluded fifty; the second, called simply *Dramatic Romances,* twenty-five; whilst the last was reduced to
thirteen. He also changed the titles of many of the
poems, revised the text somewhat, classified two separate poems under one title, *Claret and Tokay,* and
Here's to Nelson's Memory, under the heading *Nationality in Drinks,* and united the two sections of
Saul in one poem. It is notable that he omitted not
one, and indeed it is remarkable that with the excep-

tion of *The Boy and the Angel, A Lover's Quarrel, Mesmerism,* and *Another Way of Love,* every poem in the long list has the indubitable touch of genius; and even these four are not the worst of Browning's compositions.

It would have seemed to us perhaps more fitting if Browning had grouped the contents of all three works under the one heading *Men and Women;* for that would fairly represent the sole subject of his efforts. Perhaps he felt that the title was too general, and as a matter of fact, it would apply equally well to his complete poetical works. I think, however, that he especially loved the appellation *Dramatic Lyrics,* for he put over half of the poems finally under that category. The word "dramatic" obsessed Browning.

What is a dramatic lyric? When Tennyson published in 1842 his *Ulysses,* a Yankee farmer in America made in one sentence three remarks about it: a statement and two prophecies. He said that *Ulysses* belonged to a high class of poetry, destined to be the highest, and to be more cultivated in the next generation. Now *Ulysses* is both a dramatic lyric and a dramatic monologue, and Tennyson never wrote anything better than this poem. As it became increasingly evident that the nineteenth century was not going to have a great literary dramatic movement on the stage, while at the same time the interest in human nature had never been keener, the poets began to turn their attention to the interpretation of humanity by the representation of historical or imaginary individuals speaking: and their speech was to reveal the secrets of the human soul, in its tragedy and comedy, in its sublimity and baseness, in its nobility and folly. Later in life Tennyson cultivated sedulously the dramatic monologue; and Browning, the most original force in literature that the century produced, after abandoning his early attempts at success on the stage, devoted practically the entire strength of his genius to this form of poetry. Emerson was a wise man.

In reshuffling the short poems in the three works mentioned above, it is not always easy to see the logic of the distribution and it would be interesting if we could know the reasons that guided the poet in the classification of particular poems. Thus it is perfectly clear why *Incident of the French Camp, Count Gismond,* and *In a Gondola* were taken from the *Dramatic Lyrics* and placed among the *Dramatic Romances;* it is easy to see why *The Lost Leader* and *Home-Thoughts, from Abroad* were taken from the *Romances* and placed among the *Lyrics;* it is not quite so clear why *Rudel* and *Artemis Prologizes* were taken from the *Lyrics* and classed among *Men and Women,* when nearly all the poems originally published under the latter head were changed to *Lyrics* and *Romances.* In changing *How They Brought the Good News* from the *Dramatic Romances,* where it was originally published, to *Dramatic Lyrics,* Browning probably felt that the lyrical sound of the piece was more important than the story: but it really is a dramatic romance. Furthermore, *My Last Duchess* would seem to fall more properly under the heading *Men and Women;* Browning, however, took it from the *Dramatic Lyrics* and placed it among the *Dramatic Romances.* In most cases, however, the reason for the transfer of individual poems is clear; and a study of the classification is of positive assistance toward the understanding of the piece.

In the eight volumes published from 1841 to 1846, which Browning called *Bells and Pomegranates,* meaning simply Sound and Sense, Meat and Music, only two are collections of short poems and the other six contain exclusively plays—seven in all, two being printed together in the last volume. Browning intended the whole *Bells and Pomegranates* series to be devoted to the drama, as one may see by the original preface to *Pippa Passes:* but that drama and the next did not sell, and the publisher suggested that he include some short poems. This explains why the third volume is filled with lyrics; and in a note published with it, Browning half apologised for what might seem a departure from his original plan, saying these two might properly fall under the head of dramatic pieces; being, although lyrical in expression, "always dramatic in principle, and so many utterances of so many imaginary persons, not mine."

He means then by a dramatic lyric a poem that is short, that is musical, but that is absolutely not subjective—does not express or betray the writer's own ideas nor even his mood, as is done in Tennyson's ideal lyric, *Crossing the Bar.* A dramatic lyric is a composition lyrical in form, and dramatic in subject-matter; remembering all the time that by dramatic we do not necessarily mean anything exciting but simply something objective, something entirely apart from the poet's own feelings. On the stage this is accomplished by the creation of separate characters who *in propria persona* express views that may or may not be in harmony with the poet's own. Thus, Macbeth's speech, beginning

Out, out, brief candle!

is really a dramatic lyric; because it is lyrical in form, and it expresses views on the value of life which could hardly have been held by Shakespeare, though they seem eminently fitting from the lips of a man who had tried to gain the whole world by losing his soul, and had succeeded in losing both.

In view of Browning's love for this form of verse, it is interesting to remember that the first two independent short poems that he ever wrote and retained in his works are both genuine dramatic lyrics. These are *Porphyria's Lover* and *Johannes Agricola,* printed in the *Monthly Repository* in 1836, when Browning was twenty-four years old. Thus early did he show both aptitude for this form and excellence in it, for each of these pieces is a work of genius. They were meant to be studies in abnormal psychology, for they were printed together in the *Dramatic Lyrics* under the caption *Madhouse Cells.* Browning was very young then, and naturally thought a man who believed in predestination and a man who killed the woman he loved were both insane; but after a longer experience of life, and seeing how many strange creatures walk the streets, he ceased to call these two men, obsessed by religion and obsessed by love, mad. If Porphyria's lover is mad, there is method in his madness. Her superior

social rank has stifled hitherto the instincts of the
heart; she has never given her lover any favors;
but to-night, at the dinner-dance, by one of those
strange and inexplicable caprices that make Woman
the very Genius of the Unexpected, she has a vision.
In the midst of the lights and the laughter, she sees
her lonely lover sitting dejectedly in his cold and
cheerless cottage, thinking of her.   She slips away
from the gay company, trips through the pouring
rain, and enters the dark room like an angel of light.
After kindling a blazing fire in the grate, she kindles her lover's hope-dead heart; she draws him to
her and places his head on her naked shoulder.   Suddenly a thought comes to him; one can see the light
of murder in his eyes.   At this moment she is
sublime, fit for Heaven: for the first time in her life,
a noble impulse has triumphed over the debasing
conventions of society; if he lets her go, she will
surely fall from grace, and become a lost soul.   He
strangles her with her yellow hair, risking damnation for her salvation.   So the quick and the dead
sit together through the long night.

PORPHYRIA'S LOVER

1836

The rain set early in to-night,
The sullen wind was soon awake,

It tore the elm-tops down for spite,
   And did its worst to vex the lake:
   I listened with heart fit to break.
When glided in Porphyria; straight
   She shut the cold out and the storm,
And kneeled and made the cheerless grate
   Blaze up, and all the cottage warm;
   Which done, she rose, and from her form
Withdrew the dripping cloak and shawl,
   And laid her soiled gloves by, untied
Her hat and let the damp hair fall,
   And, last, she sat down by my side
   And called me.　When no voice replied,
She put my arm about her waist,
   And made her smooth white shoulder bare,
And all her yellow hair displaced,
   And, stooping, made my cheek lie there,
   And spread, o'er all, her yellow hair,
Murmuring how she loved me—she
   Too weak, for all her heart's endeavour,
To set its struggling passion free
   From pride, and vainer ties dissever,
   And give herself to me for ever.
But passion sometimes would prevail,
   Nor could to-night's gay feast restrain
A sudden thought of one so pale
   For love of her, and all in vain:
   So, she was come through wind and rain.
Be sure I looked up at her eyes
   Happy and proud; at last I knew
Porphyria worshipped me; surprise
   Made my heart swell, and still it grew
   While I debated what to do.
That moment she was mine, mine, fair,
   Perfectly pure and good: I found

A thing to do, and all her hair
   In one long yellow string I wound
   Three times her little throat around,
And strangled her. No pain felt she;
   I am quite sure she felt no pain.
As a shut bud that holds a bee,
   I warily oped her lids: again
   Laughed the blue eyes without a stain.
And I untightened next the tress
   About her neck; her cheek once more
Blushed bright beneath my burning kiss:
   I propped her head up as before,
   Only, this time my shoulder bore
Her head, which droops upon it still:
   The smiling rosy little head,
So glad it has its utmost will,
   That all it scorned at once is fled,
   And I, its love, am gained instead!
Porphyria's love: she guessed not how
   Her darling one wish would be heard.
And thus we sit together now,
   And all night long we have not stirred,
   And yet God has not said a word!

What is the meaning of that last enigmatical line?
Does it mean that the expected bolt from the sky
has not fallen, that God approves of the murder?
Or does it mean that the man is vaguely disap-
pointed, that he had hoped to hear a voice from
Heaven, saying, "This is my beloved son, in whom
I am well pleased"? Or does it mean that the

Power above is wholly indifferent, "when the sky, which noticed all, makes no disclosure"?

In *Johannes Agricola,* Browning wrote a lyric setting forth the strange and yet largely accepted doctrine that Almighty God before the foundations of the earth were laid, predestined a few of the coming population to everlasting bliss and the vast majority to eternal torture. This is by no means a meditation in a madhouse cell, as Browning first believed; but might logically be the reflections of a nineteenth century Presbyterian clergyman, seated in his comfortable library. It is the ecstatic mystical joy of one who realises, that through no merit of his own, he is numbered among the elect. Sir Thomas Browne quaintly pictured to himself the surprise of the noble, upright men of antiquity, when they wake up in hell simply because they did not believe on One of whom they had never heard; so Johannes speculates on the ironical fate of monks, ascetics, women and children, whose lives were full of innocence and purity, who nevertheless reach ultimately the lake of fire. Praise God for it! for if I could understand Him, I could not praise Him. How much more noble this predestinating God is than one who should reward virtue, and thus make eternal bliss a matter of calculation and bargain!

JOHANNES AGRICOLA IN MEDITATION

1836

There's heaven above, and night by night
  I look right through its gorgeous roof;
No suns and moons though e'er so bright
    Avail to stop me; splendour-proof
    I keep the broods of stars aloof:
For I intend to get to God,
  For 'tis to God I speed so fast,
For in God's breast, my own abode,
    Those shoals of dazzling glory passed,
    I lay my spirit down at last.
I lie where I have always lain,
  God smiles as he has always smiled;
Ere suns and moons could wax and wane,
    Ere stars were thundergirt, or piled
    The heavens, God thought on me his child;
Ordained a life for me, arrayed
  Its circumstances every one
To the minutest; ay, God said
    This head this hand should rest upon
    Thus, ere he fashioned star or sun.
And having thus created me,
  Thus rooted me, he bade me grow,
Guiltless for ever, like a tree
    That buds and blooms, nor seeks to know
    The law by which it prospers so:
But sure that thought and word and deed
  All go to swell his love for me,
Me, made because that love had need
    Of something irreversibly
    Pledged solely its content to be.
Yes, yes, a tree which must ascend,
    No poison-gourd foredoomed to stoop!

I have God's warrant, could I blend
   All hideous sins, as in a cup,
   To drink the mingled venoms up;
Secure my nature will convert
   The draught to blossoming gladness fast:
While sweet dews turn to the gourd's hurt,
   And bloat, and while they bloat it, blast,
   As from the first its lot was cast.
For as I lie, smiled on, full-fed
   By unexhausted power to bless,
I gaze below on hell's fierce bed,
   And those its waves of flame oppress,
   Swarming in ghastly wretchedness;
Whose life on earth aspired to be
   One altar-smoke, so pure!—to win
If not love like God's love for me,
   At least to keep his anger in;
   And all their striving turned to sin.
Priest, doctor, hermit, monk grown white
   With prayer, the broken-hearted nun,
The martyr, the wan acolyte,
   The incense-swinging child,—undone
   Before God fashioned star or sun!
God, whom I praise; how could I praise,
   If such as I might understand,
Make out and reckon on his ways,
   And bargain for his love, and stand,
   Paying a price, at his right hand?

The religious exaltation of the opening lines

There's heaven above, and night by night
   I look right through its gorgeous roof; . . .
For I intend to get to God,
   For 'tis to God I speed so fast,
For in God's breast, my own abode,

> Those shoals of dazzling glory, passed,
> I lay my spirit down at last

reminds one infallibly of Tennyson's beautiful dramatic lyric, *St. Agnes' Eve:*

> Deep on the convent roof the snows
>   Are sparkling to the moon:
> My breath to heaven like vapour goes,
>   May my soul follow soon!

It is interesting to remember that the former was published in 1836, the latter in 1837, and each in a periodical.

Perhaps Browning attempted to show the dramatic quality of his lyrics by finally placing at the very beginning the *Cavalier Tunes* and *The Lost Leader;* for the former voice in eloquent language the hatred of democratic ideas, and the latter, in language equally strenuous, is a glorification of democracy. Imagine Browning himself saying what he places in the mouth of his gallant cavaliers—"Hampden to hell!" In the second, *The Lost Leader,* nothing was farther from Browning's own feelings than a personal attack on Wordsworth, whom he regarded with reverence; in searching for an example of a really great character who had turned from the popular to the aristocratic party, he happened to think of the change from radicalism to conservatism exhibited by Wordsworth. Love for the lost leader is still strong in the breasts of his quondam followers who now must fight him; in Heaven he will not only be pardoned, he will be first there as he was always first here. In the following lines, the prepositions are interesting:

> Shakespeare was *of* us, Milton was *for* us,
> Burns, Shelley, were *with* us.

Shakespeare was indeed of the common people, but so far as we can conjecture, certainly not for them; Milton was not of them, but was wholly for them, being indeed regarded as an anarchist; Burns was a peasant, and Shelley a blue-blood, but both were with the popular cause. Browning himself, as we happen to know from one of his personal sonnets, was an intense Liberal in feeling.

CAVALIER TUNES

1842

I. MARCHING ALONG

I

Kentish Sir Byng stood for his King,
Bidding the crop-headed Parliament swing:
And, pressing a troop unable to stoop
And see the rogues flourish and honest folk droop,
Marched them along, fifty-score strong,
Great-hearted gentlemen, singing this song.

II

God for King Charles! Pym and such carles
To the Devil that prompts 'em their treasonous parles!
Cavaliers, up! Lips from the cup,
Hands from the pasty, nor bite take nor sup
Till you're—

    CHORUS.—*Marching along, fifty-score strong,*
            Great-hearted gentlemen, singing this song.

III

Hampden to hell, and his obsequies' knell
Serve Hazelrig, Fiennes, and young Harry as well!
England, good cheer! Rupert is near!
Kentish and loyalists, keep we not here

    CHORUS.—*Marching along, fifty-score strong,*
            Great-hearted gentlemen, singing this song?

IV

Then, God for King Charles! Pym and his snarls
To the Devil that pricks on such pestilent carles!
Hold by the right, you double your might;
So, onward to Nottingham, fresh for the fight,

    CHORUS.—*March we along, fifty-score strong,*
            Great-hearted gentlemen, singing this song!

II. GIVE A ROUSE

I

King Charles, and who'll do him right now?
King Charles, and who's ripe for fight now?
Give a rouse: here's, in hell's despite now,
King Charles!

II

Who gave me the goods that went since?
Who raised me the house that sank once?

Who helped me to gold I spent since?
Who found me in wine you drank once?
  CHORUS.—*King Charles, and who'll do him right now?*
    King Charles, and who's ripe for fight now?
    Give a rouse: here's, in hell's despite now,
    King Charles!

III

To whom used my boy George quaff else,
By the old fool's side that begot him?
For whom did he cheer and laugh else,
While Noll's damned troopers shot him?
  CHORUS.—*King Charles, and who'll do him right now?*
    King Charles, and who's ripe for fight now?
    Give a rouse: here's, in hell's despite now,
    King Charles!

III. BOOT AND SADDLE

I

Boot, saddle, to horse, and away!
Rescue my castle before the hot day
Brightens to blue from its silvery grey,
  CHORUS.—*Boot, saddle, to horse, and away!*

II

Ride past the suburbs, asleep as you'd say;
Many's the friend there, will listen and pray
"God's luck to gallants that strike up the lay—
  CHORUS.—*"Boot, saddle, to horse, and away!"*

III

Forty miles off, like a roebuck at bay,
Flouts Castle Brancepeth the Roundheads' array:
Who laughs, "Good fellows ere this, by my fay,
  CHORUS.—*"Boot, saddle, to horse, and away!"*

IV

Who? My wife Gertrude; that, honest and gay,
Laughs when you talk of surrendering, "Nay!
"I've better counsellors; what counsel they?
    CHORUS.—*"Boot, saddle, to horse, and away!"*

THE LOST LEADER

1845

I

Just for a handful of silver he left us,
    Just for a riband to stick in his coat—
Found the one gift of which fortune bereft us,
    Lost all the others she lets us devote;
They, with the gold to give, doled him out silver,
    So much was theirs who so little allowed:
How all our copper had gone for his service!
    Rags—were they purple, his heart had been proud!
We that had loved him so, followed him, honoured him,
    Lived in his mild and magnificent eye,
Learned his great language, caught his clear accents,
    Made him our pattern to live and to die!
Shakespeare was of us, Milton was for us,
    Burns, Shelley, were with us,—they watch from their
        graves!
He alone breaks from the van and the freemen,
    —He alone sinks to the rear and the slaves!

II

We shall march prospering,—not thro' his presence;
    Songs may inspirit us,—not from his lyre;
Deeds will be done,—while he boasts his quiescence,
    Still bidding crouch whom the rest bade aspire:
Blot out his name, then, record one lost soul more,
    One task more declined, one more footpath untrod,

One more devils'-triumph and sorrow for angels,
 One wrong more to man, one more insult to God!
Life's night begins: let him never come back to us!
 There would be doubt, hesitation and pain,
Forced praise on our part—the glimmer of twilight,
 Never glad confident morning again!
Best fight on well, for we taught him—strike gallantly,
 Menace our heart ere we master his own;
Then let him receive the new knowledge and wait us,
 Pardoned in heaven, the first by the throne!

The poem *Cristina* (1842), while not very remarkable as poetry, is notable because it contains
thus early in Browning's career, four of his most
important doctrines. The more one studies Browning, the more one is convinced that the poet's astonishing mental vigor is shown not in the number
and variety of his ideas, but rather in the number
and variety of illustrations of them. I can not at
this moment think of any poet, dramatist or novelist
who has invented so many plots as Browning. He
seems to present to us a few leading ideas in a vast
series of incarnations. Over and over again the
same thoughts, the same doctrines are repeated; but
the scenery, the situations, and the characters are
never alike. Here is where he remains true to the
theory set forth in *Transcendentalism;* the poet
should not produce thoughts but rather concrete
images of them; or, as he says in the closing lines

of *The Ring and the Book,* Art must do the thing that breeds the thought.

In *Cristina,* four of Browning's fundamental articles of faith are expressed: the doctrine of the elective affinities; the doctrine of success through failure; the doctrine that time is measured not by the clock and the calendar, but by the intensity of spiritual experiences; the doctrine that life on earth is a trial and a test, the result of which will be seen in the higher and happier development when the soul is freed from the limitations of time and space.

The expression "elective affinities" as applied to human beings was first brought into literature, I believe, by no less a person than Goethe, who in his novel, published in 1809, which he called *Elective Affinities (Wahlverwandschaften),* showed the tremendous force which tends to draw together certain persons of opposite sexes. The term was taken from chemistry, where an elective affinity means the "force by which the atoms of bodies of dissimilar nature unite"; elective affinity is then simply a chemical force.

In Goethe's novel, Charlotte thus addresses the Captain: "Would you tell me briefly what is meant here by Affinities?" The Captain replied, "In all natural objects with which we are acquainted, we

observe immediately that they have a certain relation." Charlotte: "Let me try and see whether I
can understand where you are bringing me. As
everything has a reference to itself, so it must have
some relation to others." Edward interrupts: "And
that will be different according to the natural differ-
ences of the things themselves. Sometimes they will
meet like friends and old acquaintances; they will
come rapidly together, and unite without either having to alter itself at all—as wine mixes with water."
Charlotte: "One can almost fancy that in these simple forms one sees people that one is acquainted
with." The Captain: "As soon as our chemical
chest arrives, we can show you a number of enter-
taining experiments, which will give you a clearer
idea than words, and names, and technical expressions." Charlotte: "It appears to me that if you
choose to call these strange creatures of yours re-
lated, the relationship is not so much a relationship
of blood as of soul or of spirit." The Captain: "We
had better keep to the same instances of which we
have already been speaking. Thus, what we call
limestone is a more or less pure calcareous earth in
combination with a delicate acid, which is familiar
to us in the form of a gas. Now, if we place a piece
of this stone in diluted sulphuric acid, this will

take possession of the lime, and appear with it in the form of gypsum, the gaseous acid at the same time going off in vapour. Here is a case of separation: a combination arises, and we believe ourselves now justified in applying to it the words 'Elective Affinity;' it really looks as if one relation had been deliberately chosen in preference to another." Charlotte: "Forgive me, as I forgive the natural philosopher. I can not see any choice in this; I see a natural necessity rather, and scarcely that. Opportunity makes relations as it makes thieves: and as long as the talk is only of natural substances, the choice appears to be altogether in the hands of the chemist who brings the creatures together. Once, however, let them be brought together, and then God have mercy on them." The scientific conversation is summed up by their all agreeing that the chemical term "elective affinities" can properly be applied in analogy to human beings.

An elective affinity as applied to men and women may result in happiness or misery; or may be frustrated by a still superior prudential or moral force. The law of elective affinity being a force, it is naturally unaware of any human artificial obstacles, such as a total difference in social rank, or the previous marriage of one or both of the parties. If two independent individuals meet and are drawn together by the law of elective affinities, they may marry and live happily forever after; if another marriage has already taken place, as in Goethe's story, the result may be tragedy. In *Cristina,* the elective affinities assert their force between a queen and a private individual; the result is, at least temporarily, unfortunate for the simple reason that the lady, although drawn toward the man by the workings of this mysterious force, is controlled even more firmly by the bondage of social convention; she behaves in a contrary manner to that shown by the stooping lady in Maurice Hewlett's story. This force needs only one moment, one glance, to assert its power:

> She should never have looked at me
> If she meant I should not love her!

Love in Browning is often love at first sight; no prolonged acquaintance is necessary; not even a spoken word, or any physical contact.

> Doubt you whether
> This she felt as, *looking at me,*
> Mine and her souls rushed together?

In Tennyson's *Locksley Hall* (published the same year), contact was important:

And our spirits rushed together at the touching of the lips.

Browning's portrayal of love shows that it can be a wireless telegraphy, that, in the instance of Cristina and her lover, exerted its force across a crowded room; in *The Statue and the Bust,* it is equally powerful across a public square in Florence. The glance, or as Donne expresses it, the "twisted eye-beams," is an important factor in Browning's poetry—sufficient to unite two souls throughout all eternity, as it does in *Tristan und Isolde.* Browning repeats his favorite doctrine of the elective affinities in *Evelyn Hope, Count Gismond, In a Gondola, Dis Aliter Visum, Youth and Art,* and other poems; and its noblest expression is perhaps in that wonderful scene in the crowded theatre at Arezzo; whilst the flippant audience are gazing at a silly musical comedy, the sad eyes of Pompilia encounter the grave, serious regard of Caponsacchi, and the two young hearts are united forever.

Another leading idea in Browning's philosophy is *Success in Failure.* This paradox is indeed a corner-stone in the construction of his thought. Every noble soul must fail in life, because every noble soul has an ideal. We may be encouraged by temporary successes, but we must be inspired by failure. Browning can forgive any daring criminal; but he

can not forgive the man who is selfishly satisfied
with his attainments and his position, and thus accepts compromises with life. The soul that ceases
to grow is utterly damned. The damnation of contentment is shown with beauty and fervor in one
of Browning's earliest lyrics, *Over the Sea Our
Galleys Went*. The voyagers were weary of the
long journey, they heeded not the voice of the pilot
Conscience, they accommodated their ideals to their
personal convenience. The reason why Browning
could not forgive Andrea was not because he was
Andrea del Sarto, the son of a tailor; it was because he was known as the Faultless Painter, because he could actually realise his dreams. The text
of that whole poem is found in the line

> Ah, but a man's reach should exceed his grasp.

In *Cristina,* the man's love is not rewarded here,
he fails; but he has aimed high, he has loved a queen.
He will always love her—in losing her he has found
a guiding principle for his own life, which will lead
him ever up and on.

> She has lost me, I have gained her;
> Her soul's mine: and thus, grown perfect,
> I shall pass my life's remainder.

Her body I have lost: some other man will possess that: but her soul I gained in the moment when our eyes met, and my life has reached a higher plane and now has a higher motive. In failure I reach real success.

This doctrine, illustrated repeatedly in Browning's works, is stated explicitly in *Rabbi Ben Ezra:*

> For thence,—a paradox
> Which comforts while it mocks,—
> Shall life succeed in that it seems to fail:
> What I aspired to be,
> And was not, comforts me:
> A brute I might have been, but would not sink i' the scale.

The thought that life is not measured by length of days is brought out clearly in *Cristina*. We constantly read in the paper interviews with centenarians, who tell us how to prolong our lives by having sufficient sleep, by eating moderately, by refraining from worry. But, as a writer in a southern journal expressed it, Why do these aged curiosities never tell us what use they have made of this prolonged existence? Mark Twain said cheerfully, "Methuselah lived nine hundred and sixty-nine years; but what of that? There was nothing doing." No drama on the stage is a success unless it has what we call a supreme moment; and the drama of our individual lives can not be really interesting or important un-

less it has some moments when we live intensely,
when we live longer than some persons live in years;
moments that settle our purpose and destiny.

> Oh, we're sunk enough here, God knows!
>   But not quite so sunk that moments,
> Sure, tho' seldom, are denied us,
>   When the spirit's true endowments
> Stand out plainly from its false ones,
>   And apprise it if pursuing
> Or the right way or the wrong way,
>   To its triumph or undoing.
> There are flashes struck from midnights,
>   There are fire-flames noondays kindle,
> Whereby piled-up honours perish,
>   Whereby swollen ambitions dwindle.

An American public man who one day fell in public esteem as far as Lucifer, said that it had taken
him fifty years to build up a great reputation, and
that he had lost it all in one forenoon. The dying
courtier in *Paracelsus* had such a moment.

Finally, in *Cristina,* we find that ardent belief in
a future life that lifts its head so often and so reso-
lutely in Browning's poetry, and on which, as we
shall see later, his optimism is founded. Science
tells us that the matter of which the universe is
composed is indestructible; Browning believes even
more strongly in the permanence of spirit. Aspiration, enthusiasm, love would not be given to us to

have their purposes broken off, not if this is a rational and economic universe; the important thing is not to have our hopes fulfilled here, the important thing is to keep hoping.   Such love as the man had for Cristina must eventually find its full satisfaction so long as it remains the guiding principle of his life, which will serve as a test of his tenacity.

> Life will just hold out the proving
> Both our powers, alone and blended:
> And then, come next life quickly!
> This world's use will have been ended.

Precisely the same situation and the same philosophical result of it are illustrated in the exquisite lyric, *Evelyn Hope*.   The lover is frustrated not by social distinctions, but by death.   The girl is lost to him here, but the power of love is not quenched nor even lessened by this disaster.   The man's ardor will steadily increase during the remaining years of his earthly existence; and then his soul will start out confident on its quest.

> God above
> Is great to grant, as mighty to make,
> And creates the love to reward the love:
> I claim you still, for my own love's sake!
> Delayed it may be for more lives yet,
> Through worlds I shall traverse, not a few:
> Much is to learn, much to forget,
> Ere the time be come for taking you.

This doctrine, that earthly existence is a mere test of the soul to determine its fitness for entering upon an eternal and freer stage of development, is frequently set forth in Browning. The apostle John makes it quite clear in *A Death in the Desert;* and in *Abt Vogler,* the inspired musician sings

And what is our failure here but a triumph's evidence
 For the fulness of the days? Have we withered or agonised?
Why else was the pause prolonged but that singing might issue
  thence?
 Why rushed the discords in but that harmony might be
  prized?

From the above discussion it should be plain that the short poem *Cristina* deserves patient and intense study, for it contains in the form of a dramatic lyric, some of Browning's fundamental ideas.

CRISTINA

1842

I

She should never have looked at me
 If she meant I should not love her!
There are plenty . . . men, you call such,
 I suppose . . . she may discover
All her soul to, if she pleases,
 And yet leave much as she found them:
But I'm not so, and she knew it
 When she fixed me, glancing round them.

II

What? To fix me thus meant nothing?
    But I can't tell (there's my weakness)
What her look said!—no vile cant, sure,
    About "need to strew the bleakness
"Of some lone shore with its pearl-seed.
    "That the sea feels"—no "strange yearning
"That such souls have, most to lavish
    "Where there's chance of least returning."

III

Oh, we're sunk enough here, God knows!
    But not quite so sunk that moments,
Sure tho' seldom, are denied us,
    When the spirit's true endowments
Stand out plainly from its false ones,
    And apprise it if pursuing
Or the right way or the wrong way,
    To its triumph or undoing.

IV

There are flashes struck from midnights,
    There are fire-flames noondays kindle,
Whereby piled-up honours perish,
    Whereby swollen ambitions dwindle,
While just this or that poor impulse,
    Which for once had play unstifled,
Seems the sole work of a life-time
    That away the rest have trifled.

V

Doubt you if, in some such moment,
    As she fixed me, she felt clearly,
Ages past the soul existed,
    Here an age 'tis resting merely,

And hence fleets again for ages,
  While the true end, sole and single,
It stops here for is, this love-way,
  With some other soul to mingle?

VI

Else it loses what it lived for,
  And eternally must lose it;
Better ends may be in prospect,
  Deeper blisses (if you choose it),
But this life's end and this love-bliss
  Have been lost here. Doubt you whether
This she felt as, looking at me,
  Mine and her souls rushed together?

VII

Oh, observe! Of course, next moment,
  The world's honours, in derision,
Trampled out the light for ever:
  Never fear but there's provision
Of the devil's to quench knowledge
  Lest we walk the earth in rapture!
—Making those who catch God's secret
  Just so much more prize their capture!

VIII

Such am I: the secret's mine now!
  She has lost me, I have gained her;
Her soul's mine: and thus, grown perfect,
  I shall pass my life's remainder.
Life will just hold out the proving
  Both our powers, alone and blended:
And then, come the next life quickly!
  This world's use will have been ended.

SONG FROM *PARACELSUS*
1835

Over the sea our galleys went,
With cleaving prows in order brave
To a speeding wind and a bounding wave,
    A gallant armament:
Each bark built out of a forest-tree
    Left leafy and rough as first it grew,
And nailed all over the gaping sides,
Within and without, with black bull-hides,
Seethed in fat and suppled in flame,
To bear the playful billows' game:
So, each good ship was rude to see,
Rude and bare to the outward view,
    But each upbore a stately tent
Where cedar pales in scented row
Kept out the flakes of the dancing brine,
And an awning drooped the mast below,
In fold on fold of the purple fine,
That neither noontide nor starshine
Nor moonlight cold which maketh mad,
    Might pierce the regal tenement.
When the sun dawned, oh, gay and glad
We set the sail and plied the oar;
But when the night-wind blew like breath,
For joy of one day's voyage more,
We sang together on the wide sea,
Like men at peace on a peaceful shore;
Each sail was loosed to the wind so free,
Each helm made sure by the twilight star,
And in a sleep as calm as death,
We, the voyagers from afar,
    Lay stretched along, each weary crew
In a circle round its wondrous tent

Whence gleamed soft light and curled rich scent,
   And with light and perfume, music too:
So the stars wheeled round, and the darkness past,
And at morn we started beside the mast,
And still each ship was sailing fast.

Now, one morn, land appeared—a speck
Dim trembling betwixt sea and sky:
"Avoid it," cried our pilot, "check
   "The shout, restrain the eager eye!"
But the heaving sea was black behind
For many a night and many a day,
And land, though but a rock, drew nigh;
So, we broke the cedar pales away,
Let the purple awning flap in the wind,
   And a statue bright was on every deck!
We shouted, every man of us,
And steered right into the harbour thus,
With pomp and pæan glorious.

A hundred shapes of lucid stone!
   All day we built its shrine for each,
A shrine of rock for every one,
Nor paused till in the westering sun
   We sat together on the beach
To sing because our task was done.
When lo! what shouts and merry songs!
What laughter all the distance stirs!
A loaded raft with happy throngs
Of gentle islanders!
"Our isles are just at hand," they cried,
   "Like cloudlets faint in even sleeping:
"Our temple-gates are opened wide,
   "Our olive-groves thick shade are keeping
"For these majestic forms"—they cried.

Oh, then we awoke with sudden start
From our deep dream, and knew, too late,
How bare the rock, how desolate,
Which had received our precious freight:
    Yet we called out—"Depart!
"Our gifts, once given, must here abide.
    "Our work is done; we have no heart
"To mar our work,"—we cried.

EVELYN HOPE

1855

I

Beautiful Evelyn Hope is dead!
    Sit and watch by her side an hour.
That is her book-shelf, this her bed;
    She plucked that piece of geranium-flower,
Beginning to die too, in the glass;
    Little has yet been changed, I think:
The shutters are shut, no light may pass
    Save two long rays thro' the hinge's chink.

II

Sixteen years old when she died!
    Perhaps she had scarcely heard my name;
It was not her time to love; beside,
    Her life had many a hope and aim,
Duties enough and little cares,
    And now was quiet, now astir,
Till God's hand beckoned unawares,—
    And the sweet white brow is all of her.

III

Is it too late then, Evelyn Hope?
    What, your soul was pure and true,
The good stars met in your horoscope,
    Made you of spirit, fire and dew—

And, just because I was thrice as old
   And our paths in the world diverged so wide,
Each was nought to each, must I be told?
   We were fellow mortals, nought beside?

IV

No, indeed! for God above
   Is great to grant, as mighty to make,
And creates the love to reward the love:
   I claim you still, for my own love's sake!
Delayed it may be for more lives yet,
   Through worlds I shall traverse, not a few:
Much is to learn, much to forget
   Ere the time be come for taking you.

V

But the time will come,—at last it will,
   When, Evelyn Hope, what meant (I shall say)
In the lower earth, in the years long still,
   That body and soul so pure and gay?
Why your hair was amber, I shall divine,
   And your mouth of your own geranium's red—
And what you would do with me, in fine,
   In the new life come in the old one's stead.

VI

I have lived (I shall say) so much since then,
   Given up myself so many times,
Gained me the gains of various men,
   Ransacked the ages, spoiled the climes;
Yet one thing, one, in my soul's full scope,
   Either I missed or itself missed me:
And I want and find you, Evelyn Hope!
   What is the issue? let us see!

VII

I loved you, Evelyn, all the while.
  My heart seemed full as it could hold?
There was place and to spare for the frank young smile,
  And the red young mouth, and the hair's young gold.
So, hush,—I will give you this leaf to keep:
  See, I shut it inside the sweet cold hand!
There, that is our secret: go to sleep!
  You will wake, and remember, and understand.

The dramatic lyric in two parts called *Meeting at Night* and *Parting at Morning* contains only sixteen lines and is a flawless masterpiece. Of the four dimensions of mathematics, one only has nothing to do with poetry. The length of a poem is of no importance in estimating its value. I do not fully understand what is meant by saying that a poem is too long or too short. It depends entirely on the art with which the particular subject is treated. A short poem of no value is too long; a long poem of genius is not too long. Richardson's *Clarissa* in eight volumes is not too long, as is proved by the fact that the numerous attempts to abridge it are all failures; whereas many short stories in our magazines are far too long. Browning's *Night and Morning* is not too short, because it contains in sixteen lines everything necessary; *The Ring and the Book* is not too long, because the twenty thousand and odd lines are all needed to make the study of testimony absolutely complete. But whilst the mathematical dimension of length is not a factor in poetry, the dimensions of breadth and depth are of vital importance, and the mysterious fourth dimension is the quality that determines whether or not a poem is a work of genius. Poems of the highest imagination can not be measured at all except in the fourth dimension. The first part of Browning's lyric is notable for its shortness, its breadth and its depth; the second part possesses these qualities even more notably, and also takes the reader's thoughts into a world entirely outside the limits of time and space.

Browning has often been called a careless writer and although he maintained that the accusation was untrue, the condition of some of the manuscripts he sent to the press—notably *Mr. Sludge, the Medium* —is proof positive that he did not work at each one of his poems at his highest level of patient industry. He was however in general a fastidious artist; much more so than is commonly supposed. He was one of our greatest impromptu poets, like Shakespeare, writing hot from the brain; he was not a polisher and reviser, like Chaucer and Tennyson. But he studied with care the sound of his words. Many years ago, Mrs. Le Moyne, who has done so much to increase the number of intelligent Browning

lovers in America, met the poet in Europe, and told
him she would like to recite to him one of his own
poems. "Go ahead, my dear." So she began to repeat in her beautiful voice *Meeting at Night;* she
spoke the third line

> And the little startled waves that leap

"Stop!" said Browning, "that isn't right." She
then learned from him the sharp difference between
"little startled waves" as she read it, and "startled
little waves" as he wrote it. He was trying to produce the effect of a warm night on the beach with
no wind, where the tiny wavelets simply crumble in
a brittle fashion on the sand. "Startled little waves"
produces this effect; "little startled waves" does not.

The impressionistic colors in this poem add much
to its effect; the grey sea, the black land, the yellow
moon, the fiery ringlets, the blue spurt of the match,
the golden light of morning. The sounds and smells
are realistic; one hears the boat cut harshly into the
slushy sand; the sharp scratch of the match; one in-
hales the thick, heavy odor radiating from the sea-
scented beach that has absorbed all day the hot
rays of the sun.

It is probable that the rendezvous is not at dusk,
as is commonly supposed, but at midnight. Owen

Wister, in his fine novel, *The Virginian,* speaks of the lover's journey as taking place at dusk. Now the half-moon could not scientifically be low at that early hour, and although most poets care nothing at all for the moon except as a decorative object, Browning was generally precise in such matters. An American poet submitted to the *Century Magazine* a poem that was accepted, the last line of each stanza reading

And in the west the waning moon hangs low.

One of the editorial staff remembered that the waning moon does not hang low in the west; he therefore changed the word to "weary," which made the poet angry. He insisted that he was a poet, not a man of science, and vowed that he would place his moon exactly where he chose. The editors replied, "You can have a waning moon in the west in some magazines, perhaps, but you can not have it there in the *Century.*" So it was published "weary," as any one may see who has sufficient time and patience.

Furthermore the contrast in this poem is not between evening and morning, but between night and morning. The English commonly draw a distinction between evening and night that we do not observe in America. *Pippa Passes* is divided into four

sections, Morning, Noon, Evening, Night. Furthermore the meeting is a clandestine one; not the
first one, for the man's soliloquy of his line of march
shows how often he has travelled this way before,
and now his eager mind, leaping far ahead of his
feet, repeats to him each stage of the journey. The
cottage is shrouded in absolute darkness until the
lover's tap is heard; then comes the sound and the
sight of the match, and the sudden thrill of the mad
embrace, when the wild heart-beats are louder than
the love-whispers.

The dramatic contrast in this poem is between the
man's feelings at night, and his mood in the morning. Both parts of the lyric, therefore, come from
the man's heart. It is absurd to suppose, as many
critics seem to think, that the second part is uttered
by the woman. Such a mistake could never have
arisen if it had not been for the word "him" in the
penultimate line, which does not of course, refer to
the man, but to the sun. To have the woman repeat
in her heart these lines not only destroys the true
philosophy of life set forth in the lyric, but the last
reflection,

> And the need of a world of men for me

would seem to make her taste rather catholic for
an ideal sweetheart.

The real meaning of the poem is simply this: The passionate intensity of love can not be exaggerated; in the night's meeting all other thoughts, duties, and pleasures are as though they were not; but with the day comes the imperious call of life and even if the woman could be content to live forever with her lover in the lonely cottage, he could not; he loves her honestly with fervor and sincerity, but he simply must go out into the world where men are, and take his share of the excitement and the struggle; he would soon be absolutely miserable if marooned from life, even with the woman he loves. Those novels that represent a man as having no interest in life but love are false to human nature. In this poem Browning represents facts as they are; it is not simply that the man wants to go out and live among other men, it is a natural law that he must, as truly a natural law as gravitation.

> And straight was a path of gold for him,
> And the need of a world of men for me.

Just as the sun must take his prescribed course through the sky, so must I run my circle of duties in the world of men. It is not a moral call of duty; it is the importunate pull of necessity.

There is still the possibility of another interpretation of the last line, though I think the one just given is correct, "I need the world of men; it is a natural law." Now it is just possible that we could interpret "need" in another sense, with an inversion; "the world of men needs me, and I must go to do my share." This would make the man perhaps nobler, but surely not so natural; indeed it would sound like a priggish excuse to leave his mistress. I have never quite surrendered to the cavalier's words

> I could not love thee, dear, so much,
> Loved I not Honour more.

Are we sure it is honor, and not himself, he loves more?

It is impossible to improve on the Cowboy's comment on these lines in Mr. Wister's *Virginian;* after Molly has read them aloud to the convalescing male, he remarks softly, "That is very, very true." Molly does not see why the Virginian admires these verses so much more than the others. "I could scarcely explain," says he, "but that man does know something." Molly wants to know if the lovers had quarrelled. "Oh, no! he will come back after he has played some more of the game." "The game?" "Life, ma'am. Whatever he was adoin' in the world of men. That's a bed-rock piece, ma'am."

The Virginian is much happier in his literary criticism of this lyric than he is of the *Good News* or of the *Incident of the French Camp;* in the latter instance, he misses the point altogether. The boy was not a poseur. The boy was so happy to think he had actually given his life for his master that he smilingly corrected Napoleon's cry "You're wounded!" It is as though one should congratulate an athletic contestant, and say "My felicitations! you won the second prize!" "No, indeed: I won the First."

Night and Morning suggests so many thoughts that we could continue our comments indefinitely; but time suffices for only one more. The nature picture of the dawn is absolutely perfect.

> Round the cape of a sudden came the sea.

He does not say that finally the cape became visible, but that the sea suddenly came round the cape. Any one who has stood on the ocean-shore before dawn, and gazed along the indented coast in the grey light, has observed the precise effect mentioned in these words. At first one sees only the blur of land where the cape is, and nothing beyond it; suddenly the light increases, and the sea actually appears to come around the point.

MEETING AT NIGHT
1845

The grey sea and the long black land;
And the yellow half-moon large and low;
And the startled little waves that leap
In fiery ringlets from their sleep,
As I gain the cove with pushing prow,
And quench its speed i' the slushy sand.

Then a mile of warm sea-scented beach;
Three fields to cross till a farm appears;
A tap at the pane, the quick sharp scratch
And blue spurt of a lighted match,
And a voice less loud, through its joys and fears,
Than the two hearts beating each to each!

PARTING AT MORNING

Round the cape of a sudden came the sea,
And the sun looked over the mountain's rim:
And straight was a path of gold for him,
And the need of a world of men for me.

It is interesting to remember that Browning, of
all poets most intellectual, should be so predom-
inantly the poet of Love. This passion is the motive
power of his verse, as he believed it to be the motive
power of the universe. He exhibits the love of men
and women in all its manifestations, from baseness
and folly to the noblest heights of self-renuncia-
tion. It is natural that the most masculine and the
most vigorous and the most intellectual of all our

poets should devote his powers mainly to the representation of love. For love is the essence of force, and does not spring from effeminate weakness or febrile delicacy. Any painter can cover a huge canvas, but, as has been observed, only the strong hand can do the fine and tender work. To discuss at length the love-poems of Browning would take us far beyond the limits of this volume; but certain of the dramatic lyrics may be selected to illustrate salient characteristics. As various poets in making portraits emphasise what is to them the most expressive features, the eyes or the lips, so Browning, the poet of the mind, loves best of all in his women and men, the Brow.

In *Evelyn Hope,*

> And the sweet white brow is all of her.

In *The Last Ride Together,*

> My mistress bent that brow of hers.

In *By the Fireside,*

> Reading by firelight, that great brow
> And the spirit-small hand propping it.

In *The Statue and the Bust,*

> Hair in heaps lay heavily
> Over a pale brow spirit-pure.

In *Count Gismond,*

> They, too, so beauteous! Each a queen
> By virtue of her brow and breast.

And the wonderful description of Pompilia by Caponsacchi:

> Her brow had not the right line, leaned too much,
> Painters would say; they like the straight-up Greek:
> This seemed bent somewhat with an invisible crown
> Of martyr and saint, not such as art approves.

In *Eurydice,*

> But give them me, the mouth, the eyes, the brow!

In *Count Gismond,*

> Our elder boy has got the clear
> Great brow.

In *The Statue and the Bust,*

> On his steady brow and quiet mouth.

His ideally beautiful women generally have yellow hair. The lady *In a Gondola* had coiled hair, "a round smooth cord of gold." In *Evelyn Hope,* the "hair's young gold:" in *Love Among the Ruins,* "eager eyes and yellow hair:" in *A Toccata,*

> Dear dead women, with such hair, too—what's become of all
>   the gold
> Used to hang and brush their bosoms?

And we must not forget his poem, *Gold Hair.*

His descriptions of women's faces are never conventional, rosy cheeks and bright eyes, but always definite and specific. In *Time's Revenges,* the unfortunate lover is maddened by the vision of the girl's face:

> So is my spirit, as flesh with sin,
> Filled full, eaten out and in
> With the face of her, the eyes of her,
> The lips, the little chin, the stir
> Of shadow round her mouth.

Browning's rejected lovers are such splendid fellows that one wonders at their ill luck. Tennyson's typical lovers, as seen in *Locksley Hall, Lady Clara Vere de Vere,* and the first part of *Maud,* behave in a manner that quite justifies the woman. They whine, they rave, and they seem most of all to be astonished at the woman's lack of judgment in not recognising their merits. Instead of a noble sorrow, they exhibit peevishness; they seem to say, "You'll be sorry some day." Browning's rejected lovers never think of themselves and their own defeat; they think only of the woman, who is now more adorable than ever. It never occurs to them that the woman is lacking in intelligence because of her refusal; nor that the man she prefers is a low-browed scoundrel. They are chivalrous; they do their best to win. When they lose, they would

rather have been rejected by this woman than accepted by any other; and they are always ready to
congratulate the man more fortunate than they.
They are in fact simply irresistible, and one can
not help believing in their ultimate success. In *The
Lost Mistress*, which Swinburne said was worth a
thousand *Lost Leaders*, the lover has just been rejected, and instead of thinking of his own misery,
he endeavours to make the awkward situation easier
for the girl by small-talk about the sparrows and the
leaf-buds. She has urged that their friendship continue; that this episode need not put an end to their
meetings, and that he can come to see her as often
as he likes, only there must be no nonsense; he must
promise to be sensible, and treat her only as a friend.
Instead of rejecting this suggestion with scorn, he
accepts, and agrees to do his best.

> Tomorrow we meet the same then, dearest?
>   May I take your hand in mine?
> Mere friends are we . . .
> Yet I will but say what mere friends say,
>   Or only a thought stronger;
> I will hold your hand but as long as all may,
>   Or so very little longer!

"I will do my best to please you, but remember I'm
made of flesh and blood."

In *One Way of Love,* the same kind of man appears. Pauline likes flowers, music, and fine speeches. He is just a mere man, who has never noticed a flower in his life, who is totally indifferent to music, and never could talk with eloquence. But if Pauline likes these things, he must endeavor to impress her, if not with his skill, at all events with his devotion. He sends her a beautiful bouquet; she does not even notice it. For months he tries to learn the instrument, until finally he can play "his tune." She does not even listen; he throws the lute away, for he cares nothing for music except for her sake. At last comes the supreme moment when he makes his declaration, on which the whole happiness of his life depends.

> This hour my utmost art I prove
> And speak my passion—heaven or hell?

Many lovers, on being rejected, would simply repeat the last word just quoted. This fine sportsman-like hero remarks,

> She will not give me heaven? 'Tis well!
> Lose who may—I still can say,
> Those who win heaven, blest are they!

"I can not reproach myself, for I did my best, and lost: still less can I reproach her; all I can say is, the man who gets her is lucky."

Finally, the same kind of character appears in one

of the greatest love-poems in all literature, *The Last Ride Together.* The situation just before the opening lines is an exact parallel to that of *The Lost Mistress.* Every day this young pair have been riding together. The man has fallen in love, and has mistaken the girl's camaraderie for a deeper feeling. He has just discovered his error, and without minimising the force of the blow that has wrecked his life's happiness, this is what he says:

> Then, dearest, since 'tis so,
> Since now at length my fate I know,
> Since nothing all my love avails,
> Since all, my life seemed meant for, fails,
> Since this was written and needs must be—
> My whole heart rises up to
>   (curse, oh, no!)
>   rises up to bless
> Your name in pride and thankfulness!
> Take back the hope you gave,—I claim
> Only a memory of the same,
> —And this beside, if you will not blame,
> Your leave for one more last ride with me.

What does the rejected lover mean by such brave words as "pride" and "thankfulness"? He means that it is a great honor to be rejected by such a woman, as Mr. Birrell says it is better to be knocked down by Doctor Johnson than to be picked up by Mr. Froude. He is thankful, too, to have known such a wonderful woman; and to show that he can control himself, and make the situation easier for her, he requests that to-day for the last time they ride just as usual—indeed they had met for that purpose, are properly accoutred, and were about to start, when he astonished her with his sudden and no longer controllable declaration. Right! We shall ride together. I am not yet banished from the sight of her. Perhaps the world will end to-night.

In the course of this poem, Browning develops one of his favorite ideas, that Life is always greater than Art. A famous poet may sit at his desk, and write of love in a way to thrill the hearts of his readers; but we should place him lower than rustic sweethearts meeting in the moonlight, because they are having in reality something which exists for the poet only in dreams. The same is true of sculpture and all pictorial art; men will turn from the greatest masterpiece of the chisel or the brush to look at a living woman.

> And you, great sculptor,—so, you gave
> A score of years to Art, her slave,
> And that's your Venus, whence we turn
> To yonder girl that fords the burn!

I was once seated in the square room in the gallery at Dresden that holds the most famous picture in the world, Rafael's Sistine Madonna. A number of tourists were in the place, and we were all gazing steadfastly at the immortal Virgin, when a pretty, fresh-colored young American girl entered the room. Every man's head twisted away from the masterpiece of art, and every man's eyes stared at the commonplace stranger, because she was alive! I was much amused, and could not help thinking of Browning's lines.

This doctrine, that Life is greater than Art, is repeated by Browning in *Cleon,* and it forms the whole content of Ibsen's last drama, *When We Dead Awaken.*

The lover's reasoning at the close of Browning's poem, that rejection may be better for him because now he has an unrealised ideal, and that the race itself is better than the victor's garland, reminds us of Lessing's noble saying, that if God gave him the choice between the knowledge of all truth and the search for it, he would humbly take the latter.

> One must lead some life beyond,
> Have a bliss to die with, *dim*-descried.

THE LOST MISTRESS
1845

All's over, then; does truth sound bitter
   As one at first believes?
Hark, 'tis the sparrows' good-night twitter
   About your cottage eaves!

And the leaf-buds on the vine are woolly,
   I noticed that, to-day;
One day more bursts them open fully
   —You know the red turns gray.

To-morrow we meet the same then, dearest?
   May I take your hand in mine?
Mere friends are we,—well, friends the merest
   Keep much that I resign:

For each glance of the eye so bright and black
   Though I keep with heart's endeavour,—
Your voice, when you wish the snowdrops back,
   Though it stay in my soul forever!—

Yet I will but say what mere friends say,
   Or only a thought stronger;
I will hold your hand but as long as all may,
   Or so very little longer!

ONE WAY OF LOVE
1855
I

All June I bound the rose in sheaves.
Now, rose by rose, I strip the leaves
And strew them where Pauline may pass.
She will not turn aside? Alas!

Let them lie. Suppose they die?
The chance was they might take her eye.

II.

How many a month I strove to suit
These stubborn fingers to the lute!
To-day I venture all I know.
She will not hear my music? So!
Break the string; fold music's wing:
Suppose Pauline had bade me sing!

III

My whole life long I learned to love.
This hour my utmost art I prove
And speak my passion—heaven or hell?
She will not give me heaven? 'Tis well!
Lose who may—I still can say,
Those who win heaven, blest are they!

THE LAST RIDE TOGETHER

1855

I

I said—Then, dearest, since 'tis so,
Since now at length my fate I know,
Since nothing all my love avails,
Since all, my life seemed meant for, fails,
    Since this was written and needs must be—
My whole heart rises up to bless
Your name in pride and thankfulness!
Take back the hope you gave,—I claim
Only a memory of the same,
—And this beside, if you will not blame,
    Your leave for one more last ride with me.

II

My mistress bent that brow of hers;
Those deep dark eyes where pride demurs
When pity would be softening through,
Fixed me a breathing-while or two
   With life or death in the balance: right!
The blood replenished me again;
My last thought was at least not vain:
I and my mistress, side by side
Shall be together, breathe and ride,
So, one day more am I deified.
   Who knows but the world may end to-night?

III

Hush! if you saw some western cloud
All billowy-bosomed, over-bowed
By many benedictions—sun's
And moon's and evening-star's at once—
   And so, you, looking and loving best,
Conscious grew, your passion drew
Cloud, sunset, moonrise, star-shine too,
Down on you, near and yet more near,
Till flesh must fade for heaven was here!—
Thus leant she and lingered—joy and fear!
   Thus lay she a moment on my breast.

IV

Then we began to ride. My soul
Smoothed itself out, a long-cramped scroll
Freshening and fluttering in the wind.
Past hopes already lay behind.
   What need to strive with a life awry?
Had I said that, had I done this,
So might I gain, so might I miss.

Might she have loved me? just as well
She might have hated, who can tell!
Where had I been now if the worst befell?
   And here we are riding, she and I.

V

Fail I alone, in words and deeds?
Why, all men strive and who succeeds?
We rode; it seemed my spirit flew,
Saw other regions, cities new,
   As the world rushed by on either side.
I thought,—All labour, yet no less
Bear up beneath their unsuccess.
Look at the end of work, contrast
The petty done, the undone vast,
This present of theirs with the hopeful past!
   I hoped she would love me; here we ride.

VI

What hand and brain went ever paired?
What heart alike conceived and dared?
What act proved all its thought had been?
What will but felt the fleshly screen?
   We ride and I see her bosom heave.
There's many a crown for who can reach.
Ten lines, a statesman's life in each!
The flag stuck on a heap of bones,
A soldier's doing! what atones?
They scratch his name on the Abbey-stones.
   My riding is better, by their leave.

VII

What does it all mean, poet? Well,
Your brains beat into rhythm, you tell
What we felt only; you expressed
You hold things beautiful the best,

And pace them in rhyme so, side by side.
'Tis something, nay 'tis much: but then,
Have you yourself what's best for men?
Are you—poor, sick, old ere your time—
Nearer one whit your own sublime
Than we who never have turned a rhyme?
    Sing, riding's a joy! For me, I ride.

VIII

And you, great sculptor—so, you gave
A score of years to Art, her slave,
And that's your Venus, whence we turn
To yonder girl that fords the burn!
    You acquiesce, and shall I repine?
What, man of music, you grown grey
With notes and nothing else to say,
Is this your sole praise from a friend,
"Greatly his opera's strains intend,
"Put in music we know how fashions end!"
    I gave my youth; but we ride, in fine.

IX

Who knows what's fit for us? Had fate
Proposed bliss here should sublimate
My being—had I signed the bond—
Still one must lead some life beyond,
    Have a bliss to die with, dim-descried.
This foot once planted on the goal,
This glory-garland round my soul,
Could I descry such? Try and test!
I sink back shuddering from the quest.
Earth being so good, would heaven seem best?
    Now, heaven and she are beyond this ride.

X

And yet—she has not spoke so long!
What if heaven be that, fair and strong

At life's best, with our eyes upturned
Whither life's flower is first discerned,
  We, fixed so, ever should so abide?
What if we still ride on, we two
With life for ever old yet new,
Changed not in kind but in degree,
The instant made eternity,—
And heaven just prove that I and she
  Ride, ride together, for ever ride?

Browning's lovers, as has been illustrated, are usually chivalrous, whether their passions have or have not the sanction of law. The poem *In a Gondola,* which has been more often translated into foreign languages than perhaps any other of Browning's works, gives us a picture of a night in Venice. The fluent rhythms of the verse indicate the lazy glide of the gondola through the dark waters of the canal. The lovers speak, sing, and muse; and their conversation is full of the little language characteristic of those who are in complete possession of each other, soul and body. They delight in passionate reminiscences: they love to recall their first chance meeting:

    Ah, the autumn day
I, passing, saw you overhead!

The wind blew out the curtains of her apartment, and her pet parrot escaped, giving the man his op-

portunity. They rehearse over again the advancing
stages of their drama. She asks him to kiss her like
a moth, then like a bee—in the attempt to recapture
the first shy sweetness of their dawning passion.
They play little love-games. He pretends he is a
Jew, carrying her away from her family to a
tribal feast; then that they twain are spirits of stars,
meeting in the thin air aloft. The intensity of their
bliss is sharpened by the black cloud of danger in
which they move: for if the Three, husband, father,
and brother of the lady become aware of this secret
liaison, there can be only one end to it—a tragedy
of blood. The lighted taper held in the window by
the trusted maid shows that they are "safe," and
for the last time they play again their little comedy
of formality. She pretends to be the formal *grande
dame,* the lady with the colder breast than snow: he
is the bashful gallant, who hardly dares touch the
tips of her fingers. In this laughing moment, the
dagger of the husband is driven deep into his back.
Like all of Browning's lovers, he gives, even on the
edge of the eternal darkness, no thought to himself,
but only to her. Gathering his dying energies, he
speaks in a loud tone, so that the conspirators, invisible in the Venetian night, may hear him:

> Care not for the cowards! Care
> Only to put aside thy beauteous hair
> My blood will hurt!

And in the last agony, he comforts her with the thought that all this, the joy of love and the separation by murder, have been ordained.

In *Love Among the Ruins,* with which *Men and Women* originally opened, and which some believe to be Browning's masterpiece, Love is given its place as the supreme fact in human history. This is a scene in the Roman Campagna at twilight, and the picture in the first stanza reminds us of Gray's *Elegy* in the perfection of its quiet silver tone. With a skill nothing short of genius, Browning has maintained in this poem a double parallel. Up to the fifth stanza, the contrast is between the present peace of the vast solitary plain, and its condition years ago when it was the centre of a city's beating heart: from the fifth stanza to the close, the contrast is between this same vanished civilisation and the eternal quality of Love. I do not remember any other work in literature where a double parallel is given with such perfect continuity and beauty; the first half of each stanza is in exact antithesis to the last. The parenthesis—*so they say*—is a delicate touch of dramatic irony. No one would dream that this

quiet plain was once the site of a great city, for no
proofs remain: we have to take the word of the
archæologists for it. Some day a Japanese shep-
herd may pasture his sheep on Manhattan Island.

After a poetic discourse on the text *Sic transit
gloria mundi*—the love motive is suddenly intro-
duced in the fifth stanza; and now the contrast
changes, and becomes a comparison between the
ephemeral nature of civilisation and the permanent
fact of Love. At the exact spot where the grand-
stand formerly stood at the finish of the horse-race,
where the King, surrounded by courtiers, watched
the whirling chariots, now remains motionless,
breathless, a yellow-haired girl. The proud King's
eyes looked over the stadium and beheld the domes
and pinnacles of his city, the last word of civilisation; the girl's eager eyes look over the silent plain
searching for the coming of her lover. And Browning would have us believe that this latter fact is far
more important historically than the former.

Suppose an American professor of archæology
is working on the grassy expanse, collecting material for his new book; he looks up for a moment and
sees a pair of rustic lovers kissing in the twilight;
he smiles, and resumes what seems to him his important labor. Little does he imagine that this

love-scene is more significant than all the broken bits
of pottery he digs out of the ground; yet such is the
fact.   For all he can do at his very best is to recon-
struct a vanished past, while the lovers are acting
a scene that belongs to eternity.   Love is best.

LOVE AMONG THE RUINS

1855

I

Where the quiet-coloured end of evening smiles,
   Miles and miles
On the solitary pastures where our sheep
   Half-asleep
Tinkle homeward thro' the twilight, stray or stop
   As they crop—
Was the site once of a city great and gay,
   (So they say)
Of our country's very capital, its prince
   Ages since
Held his court in, gathered councils, wielding far
   Peace or war.

II

Now,—the country does not even boast a tree
   As you see,
To distinguish slopes of verdure, certain rills
   From the hills
Intersect and give a name to, (else they run
   Into one)
Where the domed and daring palace shot its spires
   Up like fires

O'er the hundred-gated circuit of a wall
      Bounding all,
Made of marble, men might march on nor be pressed,
      Twelve abreast.

III

And such plenty and perfection, see, of grass
      Never was!
Such a carpet as, this summer-time, o'erspreads
      And embeds
Every vestige of the city, guessed alone,
      Stock or stone—
Where a multitude of men breathed joy and woe
      Long ago;
Lust of glory pricked their hearts up, dread of shame
      Struck them tame;
And that glory and that shame alike, the gold
      Bought and sold.

IV

Now,—the single little turret that remains
      On the plains,
By the caper overrooted, by the gourd
      Overscored,
While the patching houseleek's head of blossom winks
      Through the chinks—
Marks the basement whence a tower in ancient time
      Sprang sublime,
And a burning ring, all round, the chariots traced
      As they raced,
And the monarch and his minions and his dames
      Viewed the games.

V

And I know, while thus the quiet-coloured eve
Smiles to leave
To their folding, all our many-tinkling fleece
In such peace,
And the slopes and rills in undistinguished grey
Melt away—
That a girl with eager eyes and yellow hair
Waits me there
In the turret whence the charioteers caught soul
For the goal,
When the king looked, where she looks now, breathless,
dumb
Till I come.

VI

But he looked upon the city, every side,
Far and wide,
All the mountains topped with temples, all the glades'
Colonnades,
All the causeys, bridges, aqueducts,—and then,
All the men!
When I do come, she will speak not, she will stand,
Either hand
On my shoulder, give her eyes the first embrace
Of my face,
Ere we rush, ere we extinguish sight and speech
Each on each.

VII

In one year they sent a million fighters forth
South and North,
And they built their gods a brazen pillar high
As the sky,
Yet reserved a thousand chariots in full force—
Gold, of course,

Oh heart! oh blood that freezes, blood that burns!
  Earth's returns
For whole centuries of folly, noise and sin!
  Shut them in,
With their triumphs and their glories and the rest!
  Love is best.

In the poem *Respectability* Browning gives us a
more vulgar, but none the less vital aspect of love.
This is no peaceful twilit harmony; this scene is
set on a windy, rainy night in noisy Paris, on the
left bank of the Seine, directly in front of the Institute of France. Two reckless lovers—either old
comrades or picked-up acquaintances of this very
night, it matters not which—come tripping along
gaily, arm in arm. The man chaffs at worldly conventions, at the dullness of society, at the hypocrisy
of so-called respectable people, and congratulates
himself and his fair companion on the fun they are
having. What fools they would have been had they
waited through a long, formal courtship for the
sanction of an expensive marriage! The world, he
says, does not forbid kisses, only it says, you must
see the magistrate first. My finger must not touch
your soft lips until it is covered with the glove of
marriage. Bah! what do we care for the world's
good word? At this moment they reach the lighted
windows of the Institute, and like a pair of spar-

rows, they glance within at the highly proper but terribly tedious company. What do they see? They see Guizot compelled by political exigency to shake hands hypocritically with his enemy Montalembert. But before them down a dim court shine three lamps, an all-night dance resort. Come on! run for it! that's the place for us! no dull formalities, no hypocrisies there! Something doing!

RESPECTABILITY

1855

I

Dear, had the world in its caprice
　　Deigned to proclaim "I know you both,
　　"Have recognized your plighted troth,
"Am sponsor for you: live in peace!"—
How many precious months and years
　　Of youth had passed, that speed so fast,
　　Before we found it out at last,
The world, and what it fears?

II

How much of priceless life were spent
　　With men that every virtue decks,
　　And women models of their sex,
Society's true ornament,—
Ere we dared wander, nights like this,
　　Thro' wind and rain, and watch the Seine,
　　And feel the Boulevart break again
To warmth and light and bliss?

III

I know! the world proscribes not love;
   Allows my finger to caress
   Your lips' contour and downiness,
Provided it supply a glove.
The world's good word!—the Institute!
   Guizot receives Montalembert!
   Eh? Down the court three lampions flare:
Put forward your best foot!

In the list of *Dramatis Personæ,* Browning placed
Confessions shortly after *A Death in the Desert,* as
if to show the enormous contrast in two death-bed
scenes. After a presentation of the last noble, spiritual, inspired moments of the apostle John, we have
portrayed for us the dying delirium of an old
sinner, whose thought travels back to the sweetest
moments of his life, his clandestine meetings with
the girl he loved. The solemn voice of the priest
is like the troublesome buzzing of a fly.

     Do I view the world as a vale of tears?

Not much!

   Like Matthew Arnold's *Wish,* the brother-doctor
of the soul who is called in

     To canvass with official breath

is simply a nuisance in these last minutes of life.
The row of medicine bottles, all useless now for
practical purposes, represents to his fevered eyes the

topography of the scene where the girl used to come running to meet him. "I know, sir, it's improper,"—I ought not to talk this way to a clergyman, my mind isn't right, I'm dying, and this is all I can think of.

> How sad and bad and mad it was—
> But then, how it was sweet!

CONFESSIONS

1864

What is he buzzing in my ears?
　"Now that I come to die,
Do I view the world as a vale of tears?"
　Ah, reverend sir, not I!

What I viewed there once, what I view again
　Where the physic bottles stand
On the table's edge,—is a suburb lane,
　With a wall to my bedside hand.

That lane sloped, much as the bottles do,
　From a house you could descry
O'er the garden-wall; is the curtain blue
　Or green to a healthy eye?

To mine, it serves for the old June weather
　Blue above lane and wall;
And that farthest bottle labelled "Ether"
　Is the house o'ertopping all.

At a terrace, somewhere near the stopper,
　There watched for me, one June,
A girl: I know, sir, it's improper,
　My poor mind's out of tune.

Only, there was a way . . . you crept
  Close by the side, to dodge
Eyes in the house, two eyes except:
  They styled their house "The Lodge."

What right had a lounger up their lane?
  But, by creeping very close,
With the good wall's help,—their eyes might strain
  And stretch themselves to Oes,

Yet never catch her and me together,
  As she left the attic, there,
By the rim of the bottle labelled "Ether,"
  And stole from stair to stair,

And stood by the rose-wreathed gate. Alas,
  We loved, sir—used to meet:
How sad and bad and mad it was—
  But then, how it was sweet!

We may close our considerations of the dramatic
lyrics with three love-poems.   Whenever in his later
years Browning was asked to write a selection with
his autograph, he used to say playfully that the only
one of his poems that he could remember was *My
Star;* hence more copies of this exist in manuscript
than any other of his productions.   It was of course
a tribute to his wife; she shone upon his life like a
star of various colors; but the moment the world
attempted to pry into the secret of her genius, she
shut off the light altogether.   Let the world regard
Saturn, the most wonderful star in the heavens.   My
star shines for me alone.

The first and best of the series of *Bad Dreams* gives us again in Browning's last volume his doctrine of love. Love is its own reward: it may be sad not to have love returned, but the one unspeakable tragedy is to lose the capacity for loving. In a terrible dream, the face of the woman changes from its familiar tenderness to a glance of stony indifference, and in response to his agonised enquiry, she declares that her love for him is absolutely dead. Then comes a twofold bliss: one was in the mere waking from such desolation, but the other consisted in the fact that even if the dream were true, his love for her knew no diminution. Thank God, I loved on the same!

The most audacious poem of Browning's old age is *Summum Bonum*. Since the dawn of human speculative thought, philosophers have asked this question, What is the highest good? It has been answered in various ways. Omar Khayyam said it was Wine: John Stuart Mill said it was the greatest happiness of the greatest number: the Westminster Catechism said it was to glorify God and enjoy Him forever. Browning says it is the kiss of one girl. This kiss is the concentrated essence of all the glory, beauty, and sweetness of life. In order to understand such a paradox, we must remember that in

Browning's philosophy, Love is the engine of the
whole universe. I have no doubt that Love meant to
him more than it has ever meant to any other poet
or thinker; just as I am sure that the word Beauty
revealed to Keats a vision entirely beyond the range
of even the greatest seers. Love is the supreme fact;
and every manifestation of it on earth, from the Divine Incarnation down to a chance meeting of lovers,
is more important than any other event or idea. Now
we have seen that it is Browning's way invariably
to represent an abstract thought by a concrete illustration. Therefore in this great and daring lyric
we find the imaginary lover calling the kiss of the
woman he loves the highest good in life.

MY STAR
1855

All that I know
   Of a certain star
Is, it can throw
   (Like the angled spar)
Now a dart of red,
   Now a dart of blue;
Till my friends have said
   They would fain see, too,
My star that dartles the red and the blue!
Then it stops like a bird; like a flower, hangs furled:
   They must solace themselves with the Saturn above it.
What matter to me if their star is a world?
   Mine has opened its soul to me; therefore I love it.

BAD DREAMS
1889

Last night I saw you in my sleep:
　And how your charm of face was changed!
I asked "Some love, some faith you keep?"
　You answered "Faith gone, love estranged."

Whereat I woke—a twofold bliss:
　Waking was one, but next there came
This other: "Though I felt, for this,
　My heart break, I loved on the same."

SUMMUM BONUM
1889

All the breath and the bloom of the year in the bag of one
　　bee:
　All the wonder and wealth of the mine in the heart of one
　　gem:
In the core of one pearl all the shade and the shine of the sea:
　Breath and bloom, shade and shine,—wonder, wealth, and—
　　how far above them—
　　　　Truth, that's brighter than gem,
　　　　Trust, that's purer than pearl,—
Brightest truth, purest trust in the universe—all were for me
　　In the kiss of one girl.

V

DRAMATIC MONOLOGUES

ALTHOUGH Browning was not a failure as a dramatist—*A Blot in the 'Scutcheon* and *In a Balcony* are the greatest verse tragedies in the language since the Elizabethans—he found the true channel for his genius in the Dramatic Monologue. He takes a certain critical moment in one person's life, and by permitting the individual to speak, his character, the whole course of his existence, and sometimes the spirit of an entire period in the world's history are revealed in a brilliant searchlight. With very few exceptions, one of which will be given in our selections, a dramatic monologue is not a meditation nor a soliloquy; it is a series of remarks, usually confessional, addressed either orally or in an epistolary form to another person or to a group of listeners. These other figures, though they do not speak, are necessary to the understanding of the monologue; we often see them plainly, and see their faces change in expression as the monologue advances. At the dinner table of Bishop Blougram, the little man Gigadibs is conspicuously there; and Lucrezia is so vividly before us in *Andrea del Sarto,* that a clever actress has actually assumed this silent rôle on the stage, and exhibited simply by her countenance the effect of Andrea's monologue. This species of verse is perhaps the highest form of poetic art, as it is the most difficult; for with no stage setting, no descriptions, no breaks in the conversation, the depths of the human heart are exposed.

One of the greatest dramatic monologues in all literature is *My Last Duchess,* and it is astounding that so profound a life-drama should have been conceived and faultlessly expressed by so young a poet. The whole poem contains only fifty-six lines, but it could easily be expanded into a three-volume novel. Indeed it exhibits Browning's genius for condensation as impressively as *The Ring and the Book* proves his genius for expansion. The metre is interesting. It is the heroic couplet, the same form exactly in which Pope wrote his major productions. Yet the rime, which is as evident as the recurring strokes of a tack-hammer in Pope, is scarcely heard at all in *My Last Duchess.* Its effect is so muffled, so concealed, that I venture to say that many who are quite familiar with the poem, could not declare offhand whether it were written in rime or in blank verse. This technical trick is accomplished by what the French call overflow, the running on of the sense from one line to another, a device so dear to the heart of Milton. Some one has well said that Dryden's couplets are links in a chain, whilst Pope's are pearls on a string. Pope enclosed nearly every couplet, so that they are quite separate, which is one reason why he has given us such a vast number of aphorisms. To see how totally different in effect the heroic couplet is when it is closed and when it is open, one may compare almost any selection from Pope with the opening lines of Keats's *Endymion,* and then silently marvel that both poems are written in exactly the same measure.

POPE

Peace to all such! but were there one whose fires
True genius kindles, and fair fame inspires;
Blest with each talent and each art to please,
And born to write, converse, and live with ease:
Should such a man, too fond to rule alone,
Bear, like the Turk, no brother near the throne,
View him with scornful, yet with jealous eyes,
And hate for arts that caused himself to rise.

KEATS

A thing of beauty is a joy forever:
Its loveliness increases; it will never

Pass into nothingness; but still will keep
A bower quiet for us, and a sleep
Full of sweet dreams, and health, and quiet breathing.
Therefore, on every morrow, are we wreathing
A flowery band to bind us to the earth.

One has only to glance at the printed page of *My Last Duchess,* and see how few of the lines end in punctuation points, to discover the method employed when a poet wishes to write a very strict measure in a very free manner.

I have sometimes thought that George Eliot took a hint from this poem in the composition of *Daniel Deronda,* for the relations between Grandcourt and Gwendolen are exactly the same as existed between the Duke and his late wife; a more recent, though not so great an example, may be found in Mrs. Burnett's novel, *The Shuttle.* The poem is a study in cold, systematic torture of a warm human soul by an icy-hearted tyrant.

Browning adopts one of his favorite methods of character-revelation here. All that we know of the Duchess is the testimony given by her worst enemy, her husband; and yet, in attempting to describe her, he has succeeded in painting only his own narrow and hideous heart. Slander is often greater in the recoil than in the discharge; when a man attempts to give an unfavorable portrait of another, he usually gives us an exact likeness of himself. Pope meant his picture of Addison to be correct; but although he made the picture with immortal art, it is no more like Addison than it resembles St. Francis; it is, however, an absolutely faithful image of Pope himself. This is one reason why slander is such an exceedingly dangerous weapon to handle.

The Duke tells the envoy that his late Duchess was flirtatious, plebeian in her enthusiasm, not sufficiently careful to please her husband; but the evident truth is that he had a Satanic pride, that he was yellow with jealousy, that he was methodically cruel. His jealousy is shown by the fact that he would allow only a monk to paint her: "I said 'Frà Pandolf' by design," and he required the monk to do the whole task in one day. His pride is shown in the fact that although her expansive nature displeased him, he would never stoop to remonstrate with her. His cruelty is shown in the fact that he coldly repressed her little enthusiasms, and finally murdered her. I suppose she was really a frank, charming girl, who came from a happy home, a bright and eager bride; she was one of those lovely women whose kindness and responsiveness are as natural as the sunlight. She loved to watch the sunset from the terrace; she loved to pet the white

mule; she was delighted when some one brought her
a gift of cherries. Then she was puzzled, bewil-
dered, when she found that all her expressions of delight in life received a cold, disapproving glance of
scorn from her husband; her lively talk at dinner,
her return from a ride, flushed and eager, met invariably this icy stare of hatred. She smiled too
much to please him.

Then all smiles stopped together.

What difference does it make whether he deliberately poisoned her, or whether he simply broke
her heart by the daily chill of silent contempt? For
her, at all events, death must have been a release.
She would have been happier with a drunken husband, with a brute who kicked her, rather than with
this supercilious cold-hearted patrician. Toward
the end of the poem, in his remarks about the dowry,
we see that the Duke is as avaricious as he is cruel;
though he says with a disagreeable smile, that the
woman herself is his real object. The touch to
make this terrible man complete comes at the very
end. The Duke and the envoy prepare to descend
the staircase; the latter bows, to give precedence to
the man with the nine hundred years' old name: but
the Duke, with a purr like a tiger, places his arm

around the shoulder of the visitor, and they take the first step. Just then the master of the palace calls attention casually to a group of statuary. It is Neptune taming a sea-horse. That's the way I break them in!

Throughout the whole monologue, the Duke speaks in a quiet, steady, ironical tone; the line

The depth and passion of its earnest glance

is pronounced in intense irony, in ridicule of the conventional remark made by previous visitors. Only once or twice do we see the teeth of this monster flash, revealing his horrible heart. When he speaks of the "officious fool" who brought the cherries, and when he says "all smiles stopped together"; then the envoy looks at him with a fearful question in his eyes, but the Duke's face immediately resumes its mask of stone.

MY LAST DUCHESS

FERRARA

1842

That's my last Duchess painted on the wall,
Looking as if she were alive. I call
That piece a wonder, now: Frà Pandolf's hands
Worked busily a day, and there she stands.
Will't please you sit and look at her? I said
"Frà Pandolf" by design, for never read

Strangers like you that pictured countenance,
The depth and passion of its earnest glance,
But to myself they turned (since none puts by
The curtain I have drawn for you, but I)
And seemed as they would ask me, if they durst,
How such a glance came there; so, not the first
Are you to turn and ask thus. Sir, 'twas not
Her husband's presence only, called that spot
Of joy into the Duchess' cheek: perhaps
Frà Pandolf chanced to say "Her mantle laps
"Over my lady's wrist too much," or "Paint
"Must never hope to reproduce the faint
"Half-flush that dies along her throat:" such stuff
Was courtesy, she thought, and cause enough
For calling up that spot of joy. She had
A heart—how shall I say?—too soon made glad,
Too easily impressed; she liked whate'er
She looked on, and her looks went everywhere.
Sir, 'twas all one! My favour at her breast,
The dropping of the daylight in the West,
The bough of cherries some officious fool
Broke in the orchard for her, the white mule
She rode with round the terrace—all and each
Would draw from her alike the approving speech,
Or blush, at least. She thanked men,—good! but thanked
Somehow—I know not how—as if she ranked
My gift of a nine-hundred-years-old name
With anybody's gift. Who'd stoop to blame
This sort of trifling? Even had you skill
In speech—(which I have not)—to make your will
Quite clear to such an one, and say, "Just this
"Or that in you disgusts me; here you miss,
"Or there exceed the mark"—and if she let
Herself be lessoned so, nor plainly set
Her wits to yours, forsooth, and made excuse,

⸻E'en then would be some stooping; and I choose
Never to stoop. Oh sir, she smiled, no doubt,
Whene'er I passed her; but who passed without
Much the same smile? This grew; I gave commands;
Then all smiles stopped together. There she stands
As if alive. Will't please you rise? We'll meet
The company below, then. I repeat,
The Count your master's known munificence
Is ample warrant that no just pretence
Of mine for dowry will be disallowed;
Though his fair daughter's self, as I avowed
At starting, is my object. Nay, we'll go
Together down, sir. Notice Neptune, though,
Taming a sea-horse, thought a rarity,
Which Claus of Innsbruck cast in bronze for me!

To turn from *My Last Duchess* to *Count Gismond* is like coming out of a damp cellar into God's own sunshine. Originally Browning called these two poems *Italy* and *France;* but he later fell madly in love with Italy, and I suppose could not bear to have so cold-blooded a tragedy represent the country graven on his heart. The charm and brightness of *Count Gismond* are properly connected with one of the loveliest towns in the world, the old city of Aix in Provence, a jewel on the hills rising from the Mediterranean Sea.

Gismond is Browning's hero. He is the resolute man who does not hesitate, who makes himself instantly master of the situation, who appears like

Lohengrin in the moment of Elsa's sharp distress, a
messenger from Heaven.

> Or, if virtue feeble were,
> Heaven itself would stoop to her.

When the lady was publicly accused by the
scoundrel Gauthier, I suppose many men said, "What
a pity that so fair a woman should be so foul!"
Others said gravely, "This matter ought to be judi-
cially examined." Gismond was the only man who
realised that a defenseless orphan was insulted, and
the words were hardly out of Gauthier's mouth when
he received "the fist's reply to the filth." The lovers
walked away from the "shouting multitude," the
fickle, cowardly, contemptible public, who did not
dare to defend the lady in her need, but had lungs
enough for the victor, whoever he might be. It is
pleasant to notice the prayer of the lady for the
dead Gauthier. "I hope his soul is in heaven." This
is no mere Christian forgiveness. Gauthier had
proved to be the means of her life-happiness. Had
it not been for his shameful accusation, she would
never have met Gismond. Out of her agony came
her richest blessing.

All this happened years ago, but when her husband appears with the children she tells him a white
lie. "I have just been boasting to Adela about the

skill of my hunting hawk." She has been doing
nothing of the kind; but she can not talk about the
great event of her life before the children.

COUNT GISMOND

AIX IN PROVENCE

1842

I

Christ God who savest man, save most
    Of men Count Gismond who saved me!
Count Gauthier, when he chose his post,
    Chose time and place and company
To suit it; when he struck at length
My honour, 'twas with all his strength.

II

And doubtlessly ere he could draw
    All points to one, he must have schemed!
That miserable morning saw
    Few half so happy as I seemed,
While being dressed in queen's array
To give our tourney prize away.

III

I thought they loved me, did me grace
    To please themselves; 'twas all their deed;
God makes, or fair or foul, our face;
    If showing mine so caused to bleed
My cousins' hearts, they should have dropped
A word, and straight the play had stopped.

IV

They, too, so beauteous! Each a queen
   By virtue of her brow and breast;
Not needing to be crowned, I mean,
   As I do. E'en when I was dressed,
Had either of them spoke, instead
Of glancing sideways with still head!

V

But no: they let me laugh, and sing
   My birthday song quite through, adjust
The last rose in my garland, fling
   A last look on the mirror, trust
My arms to each an arm of theirs,
And so descend the castle-stairs—

VI

And come out on the morning-troop
   Of merry friends who kissed my cheek,
And called me queen, and made me stoop
   Under the canopy—(a streak
That pierced it, of the outside sun,
Powdered with gold its gloom's soft dun)—

VII

And they could let me take my state
   And foolish throne amid applause
Of all come there to celebrate
   My queen's-day—Oh I think the cause
Of much was, they forgot no crowd
Makes up for parents in their shroud!

VIII

However that be, all eyes were bent
   Upon me, when my cousins cast
Theirs down; 'twas time I should present
   The victor's crown, but . . . there, 'twill last

No long time . . . the old mist again
Blinds me as then it did. How vain!

IX

See! Gismond's at the gate, in talk
    With his two boys: I can proceed.
Well, at that moment, who should stalk
    Forth boldly—to my face, indeed—
But Gauthier, and he thundered "Stay!"
And all stayed. "Bring no crowns, I say!

X

"Bring torches! Wind the penance-sheet
    "About her! Let her shun the chaste,
"Or lay herself before their feet!
    "Shall she whose body I embraced
"A night long, queen it in the day?
"For honour's sake no crowns, I say!"

XI

I? What I answered? As I live,
    I never fancied such a thing
As answer possible to give.
    What says the body when they spring
Some monstrous torture-engine's whole
Strength on it? No more says the soul.

XII

Till out strode Gismond; then I knew
    That I was saved. I never met
His face before, but, at first view,
    I felt quite sure that God had set
Himself to Satan; who would spend
A minute's mistrust on the end?

XIII

He strode to Gauthier, in his throat
    Gave him the lie, then struck his mouth

With one back-handed blow that wrote
    In blood men's verdict there.   North, South,
East, West, I looked.   The lie was dead,
And damned, and truth stood up instead.

XIV

This glads me most, that I enjoyed
    The heart of the joy, with my content
In watching Gismond unalloyed
    By any doubt of the event:
God took that on him—I was bid
Watch Gismond for my part: I did.

XV

Did I not watch him while he let
    His armourer just brace his greaves,
Rivet his hauberk, on the fret
    The while!   His foot . . . my memory leaves
No least stamp out, nor how anon
He pulled his ringing gauntlets on.

XVI

And e'en before the trumpet's sound
    Was finished, prone lay the false knight,
Prone as his lie, upon the ground:
    Gismond flew at him, used no sleight
O' the sword, but open-breasted drove,
Cleaving till out the truth he clove.

XVII

Which done, he dragged him to my feet
    And said "Here die, but end thy breath
"In full confession, lest thou fleet
    "From my first, to God's second death!
"Say, hast thou lied?"   And, "I have lied
"To God and her," he said, and died.

XVIII

Then Gismond, kneeling to me, asked
  —What safe my heart holds, though no word
Could I repeat now, if I tasked
  My powers for ever, to a third
Dear even as you are. Pass the rest
Until I sank upon his breast.

XIX

Over my head his arm he flung
  Against the world; and scarce I felt
His sword (that dripped by me and swung)
  A little shifted in its belt:
For he began to say the while
How South our home lay many a mile.

XX

So 'mid the shouting multitude
  We two walked forth to never more
Return. My cousins have pursued
  Their life, untroubled as before
I vexed them. Gauthier's dwelling-place
God lighten! May his soul find grace!

XXI

Our elder boy has got the clear
  Great brow; tho' when his brother's black
Full eye shows scorn, it . . . Gismond here?
  And have you brought my tercel back?
I just was telling Adela
How many birds it struck since May.

The *Soliloquy of the Spanish Cloister* differs from
most of the Dramatic Monologues in not being ad-

dressed to a listener; but the difference is more apparent than real; for the other person is in plain view all the time, and the Soliloquy would have no point were it not for the peaceful activities of Friar Lawrence. This poem, while it deals ostensibly with the lives of only two monks, gives us a glimpse into the whole monastic system. When a number of men retired into a monastery and shut out the world forever, certain sins and ambitions were annihilated, while others were enormously magnified. All outside interests vanished; but sin remained, for it circulates in the human heart as naturally as blood in the body. The cloister was simply a little world, with the nobleness and meanness of human nature exceedingly conspicuous. When the men were once enclosed in the cloister walls, they knew that they must live in that circumscribed spot till the separation of death. Naturally therefore political ambitions, affections, envies, jealousies, would be writ large; human nature would display itself in a manner most interesting to a student, if only he could live there in a detached way. This is just what Browning tries to do; he tries to live imaginatively with the monks, and to practise his profession as the Chronicler of Life.

The only way to realise what the monastic life

really meant would be to imagine a small modern college situated in the country, and the passage of a decree that not a single student should leave the college grounds until his body was committed to the tomb. The outside interests of the world would quickly grow dim and eventually vanish; and everything would be concentrated within the community. I suppose that the passions of friendship, hatred, and jealousy would be prodigiously magnified. There must have been friendships among the monks of the middle ages compared to which our boasted college friendships are thin and pale; and there must have been frightful hatreds and jealousies. In all communities there are certain persons that get on the nerves of certain others; the only way to avoid this acute suffering is to avoid meeting the person who causes it. But imagine a cloister where dwells a man you simply can not endure: every word he says, every motion he makes, every single mannerism of walk and speech is intolerable. Now you must live with this man until one of you dies: you must sit opposite to him at meals, you can not escape constant contact. Your only resource is profane soliloquies: but if you have a sufficiently ugly disposition, you can revenge yourself upon him in a thousand secret ways.

Friar Lawrence unconsciously and innocently fans the flames of hatred in our speaker's heart, simply because he does not dream of the effect he produces. Every time he talks at table about the weather, the cork-crop, Latin names, and other trivialities, the man sitting opposite to him would like to dash his plate in his face: every time Friar Lawrence potters around among his roses, the other looking down from his window, with a face distorted with hate, would like to kill him with a glance. Poor Lawrence drives our soliloquist mad with his deliberate table manners, with his deliberate method of speech, with his care about his own goblet and spoon. And all the time Lawrence believes that his enemy loves him!

From another point of view, this poem resembles *My Last Duchess* in that it is a revelation of the speaker's heart. We know nothing about Friar Lawrence except what his deadly enemy tells us; but it is quite clear that Lawrence is a dear old man, innocent as a child; while the speaker, simply in giving his testimony against him, reveals a heart jealous, malicious, lustful; he is like a thoroughly bad boy at school, with a pornographic book carefully concealed. Just at the moment when his rage and hatred reach a climax, the vesper bell sounds; and the speaker, who is an intensely strict formalist and ritualist, presents to us an amusing spectacle; for out of the same mouth proceed blessing and cursing.

SOLILOQUY OF THE SPANISH CLOISTER
1842
I

Gr-r-r—there go, my heart's abhorrence!
    Water your damned flower-pots, do!
If hate killed men, Brother Lawrence,
    God's blood, would not mine kill you!
What? your myrtle-bush wants trimming?
    Oh, that rose has prior claims—
Needs its leaden vase filled brimming?
    Hell dry you up with its flames!

II

At the meal we sit together:
    Salve tibi! I must hear
Wise talk of the kind of weather,
    Sort of season, time of year:
Not a plenteous cork-crop: scarcely
    Dare we hope oak-galls, I doubt:
What's the Latin name for "parsley"?
    What's the Greek name for Swine's Snout?

III

Whew! We'll have our platter burnished,
    Laid with care on our own shelf!
With a fire-new spoon we're furnished,
    And a goblet for ourself,
Rinsed like something sacrificial
    Ere 'tis fit to touch our chaps—
Marked with L. for our initial!
    (He-he! There his lily snaps!)

IV

Saint, forsooth!   While brown Dolores
  Squats outside the Convent bank
With Sanchicha, telling stories,
  Steeping tresses in the tank,
Blue-black, lustrous, thick like horsehairs,
  —Can't I see his dead eye glow,
Bright as 'twere a Barbary corsair's?
  (That is, if he'd let it show!)

V

When he finishes refection,
  Knife and fork he never lays
Cross-wise, to my recollection,
  As do I, in Jesu's praise.
I the Trinity illustrate,
  Drinking watered orange-pulp—
In three sips the Arian frustrate;
  While he drains his at one gulp.

VI

Oh, those melons? If he's able
  We're to have a feast! so nice!
One goes to the Abbot's table,
  All of us get each a slice.
How go on your flowers? None double
  Not one fruit-sort can you spy?
Strange!—And I, too, at such trouble,
  Keep them close-nipped on the sly!

VII

There's a great text in Galatians,
  Once you trip on it, entails
Twenty-nine distinct damnations,
  One sure, if another fails:

If I trip him just a-dying,
   Sure of heaven as sure can be,
Spin him round and send him flying
   Off to hell, a Manichee?

VIII

Or, my scrofulous French novel
   On grey paper with blunt type!
Simply glance at it, you grovel
   Hand and foot in Belial's gripe:
If I double down its pages
   At the woeful sixteenth print,
When he gathers his greengages,
   Ope a sieve and slip it in't?

IX

Or, there's Satan!—one might venture
   Pledge one's soul to him, yet leave
Such a flaw in the indenture
   As he'd miss till, past retrieve,
Blasted lay that rose-acacia
   We're so proud of! *Hy, Zÿ, Hine* . . .
'St, there's Vespers! *Plena gratiâ*
   Ave, Virgo! Gr-r-r—you swine!

Everybody loves Browning's *Ghent to Aix* poem.
Even those who can not abide the poet make an exception here; and your thorough-going Browningite
never outgrows this piece. It is the greatest horseback poem in the literature of the world: compared
to this, *Paul Revere's Ride* is the amble of a splay-
footed nag. It sounds as though it had been written in the saddle: but it was really composed dur-

ing a hot day on the deck of a vessel in the Mediterranean, and written off on the flyleaf of a printed
book that the poet held in his hand. Poets are always most present with the distant, as Mrs. Browning said; and Browning, while at sea, thought with
irresistible longing of his good horse eating his
head off in the stable at home. Everything about
this poem is imaginary; there never had been any
such good news brought, and it is probable that no
horse could cover the distance in that time.

But the magnificent gallop of the verse: the change
from moonset to sunrise: the scenery rushing
by: the splendid spirit of horse and man: and the
almost insane joy of the rider as he enters Aix—
these are more true than history itself. Browning
is one of our greatest poets of motion—whether it
be the glide of a gondola, the swift running of the
Marathon professional Pheidippides, the steady advance of the galleys over the sea in *Paracelsus,* the
sharp staccato strokes of the horse's hoofs through
the Metidja, or the swinging stride of the students
as they carry the dead grammarian up the mountain. Not only do the words themselves express the
sound of movement; but the thought, in all these
great poems of motion, travels steadily and naturally
with the advance. It is interesting to compare a

madly-rushing poem like *Ghent to Aix* with the absolute calm of *Andrea del Sarto*. It gives one an appreciation of Browning's purely technical skill.

No one has ever, so far as I know, criticised *Ghent to Aix* adversely except Owen Wister's Virginian; and his strictures are hypercritical. As Roland threw his head back fiercely to scatter the spume-flakes, it would be easy enough for the rider to see the eye-sockets and the bloodfull nostrils. Every one has noticed how a horse will do the ear-shift, putting one ear forward and one back at the same moment. Browning has an imaginative reason for it. One ear is pushed forward to listen for danger ahead; the other bent back, to catch his master's voice. Was there ever a greater study in passionate coöperation between man and beast than this splendid poem?

"HOW THEY BROUGHT THE GOOD NEWS FROM GHENT TO AIX"

1845

I sprang to the stirrup, and Joris, and he;
I galloped, Dirck galloped, we galloped all three;
"Good speed!" cried the watch, as the gate-bolts undrew;
"Speed!" echoed the wall to us galloping through;
Behind shut the postern, the lights sank to rest,
And into the midnight we galloped abreast.

Not a word to each other; we kept the great pace
Neck by neck, stride by stride, never changing our place;
I turned in my saddle and made its girths tight,
Then shortened each stirrup, and set the pique right,
Rebuckled the cheek-strap, chained slacker the bit,
Nor galloped less steadily Roland a whit.

'Twas moonset at starting; but while we drew near
Lokeren, the cocks crew and twilight dawned clear;
At Boom, a great yellow star came out to see;
At Düffeld, 'twas morning as plain as could be;
And from Mecheln church-steeple we heard the half-chime,
So Joris broke silence with, "Yet there is time!"

At Aershot, up leaped of a sudden the sun,
And against him the cattle stood black every one,
To stare through the mist at us galloping past,
And I saw my stout galloper Roland at last,
With resolute shoulders, each butting away
The haze, as some bluff river headland its spray:

And his low head and crest, just one sharp ear bent back
For my voice, and the other pricked out on his track;
And one eye's black intelligence,—ever that glance
O'er its white edge at me, his own master, askance!
And the thick heavy spume-flakes which aye and anon
His fierce lips shook upwards in galloping on.

By Hasselt, Dirck groaned; and cried Joris, "Stay spur!
Your Roos galloped bravely, the fault's not in her,
We'll remember at Aix"—for one heard the quick wheeze
Of her chest, saw the stretched neck and staggering knees,
And sunk tail, and horrible heave of the flank,
As down on her haunches she shuddered and sank.

So, we were left galloping, Joris and I,
Past Looz and past Tongres, no cloud in the sky;

The broad sun above laughed a pitiless laugh,
'Neath our feet broke the brittle bright stubble like chaff;
Till over by Dalhem a dome-spire sprang white,
And "Gallop," gasped Joris, "for Aix is in sight!"

"How they'll greet us!"—and all in a moment his roan
Rolled neck and croup over, lay dead as a stone;
And there was my Roland to bear the whole weight
Of the news which alone could save Aix from her fate,
With his nostrils like pits full of blood to the brim,
And with circles of red for his eye-sockets' rim.

Then I cast loose my buffcoat, each holster let fall,
Shook off both my jack-boots, let go belt and all,
Stood up in the stirrup, leaned, patted his ear,
Called my Roland his pet-name, my horse without peer;
Clapped my hands, laughed and sang, any noise, bad or
        good,
Till at length into Aix Roland galloped and stood.

And all I remember is—friends flocking round
As I sat with his head 'twixt my knees on the ground;
And no voice but was praising this Roland of mine,
As I poured down his throat our last measure of wine,
Which (the burgesses voted by common consent)
Was no more than his due who brought good news from
        Ghent.

The monologue of the dying Bishop is as great
a masterpiece as *My Last Duchess;* it has not a superfluous word, and in only a few lines gives us the
spirit of the Italian Renaissance. Ruskin said that
Browning is "unerring in every sentence he writes
about the Middle Ages, always vital, right, and pro-

found." He added, "I know no other piece of modern English, prose or poetry, in which there is so much told, as in these lines, of the Renaissance spirit." Yet Browning had never seen Rome until a few months before this poem was published. It is an example, not of careful study, but of the inexplicable divination of genius. Browning permits a delirious old Bishop to talk a few lines, and a whole period of history is written.

The church of Saint Prassede is in a dirty little alley in Rome, hard by the great church of Saint Maria Maggiore. You push through the group of filthy, importunate beggars, open a leather door, and you drop from the twentieth to the sixteenth century. It is one of the most ornate churches in Rome; the mosaic angels in the choir are precisely as the poet describes them. The tomb of the imaginary Gandolf may be identified with a Bishop's tomb on the south side of the church, and the Latin inscription under it, while it does not contain the form "elucescebat," is not pure Tully, but rather belongs to the Latin of Ulpian's time. The recumbent figure is in exact accord with the description by Browning.

Skeptics are essential to the welfare of the Church; it is only in periods of sharp, skilful hostility that the Church becomes pure. In the Middle

Ages, when it ran riot with power, there were plenty of churchmen as corrupt as our dying man. His love for a Greek manuscript is as sensual as his love for his mistress; and having lived a life of physical delight, it is natural that his last thoughts should concern themselves with the abode of his body rather than with the destination of his soul. Of course his mind is wandering, or he would not speak with quite such shameless cynicism. Browning has made him talk of Saint Praxed at *his* sermon on the mount, in order to prove the delirium. S. Praxed was a female saint.

The constant confusion of Greek mythology with the ritual of the Christian church is a characteristic feature both of this poem and of the period of history it represents.

Kipling is particularly fond of this work, and it will be remembered what use he makes of it in *Stalky and Co.*

THE BISHOP ORDERS HIS TOMB AT SAINT PRAXED'S CHURCH

ROME, 15—

1845

Vanity, saith the preacher, vanity!
Draw round my bed: is Anselm keeping back?
Nephews—sons mine . . . ah God, I know not! Well—
She, men would have to be your mother once,

Old Gandolf envied me, so fair she was!
What's done is done, and she is dead beside,
Dead long ago, and I am Bishop since,
And as she died so must we die ourselves,
And thence ye may perceive the world's a dream.
Life, how and what is it? As here I lie
In this state-chamber, dying by degrees,
Hours and long hours in the dead night, I ask
"Do I live, am I dead?" Peace, peace seems all.
Saint Praxed's ever was the church for peace;
And so, about this tomb of mine. I fought
With tooth and nail to save my niche, ye know:
—Old Gandolf cozened me, despite my care;
Shrewd was that snatch from out the corner South
He graced his carrion with, God curse the same!
Yet still my niche is not so cramped but thence
One sees the pulpit o' the epistle-side,
And somewhat of the choir, those silent seats,
And up into the aery dome where live
The angels, and a sunbeam's sure to lurk:
And I shall fill my slab of basalt there,
And 'neath my tabernacle take my rest,
With those nine columns round me, two and two,
The odd one at my feet where Anselm stands:
Peach-blossom marble all, the rare, the ripe
As fresh-poured red wine of a mighty pulse.
—Old Gandolf with his paltry onion-stone,
Put me where I may look at him! True peach,
Rosy and flawless: how I earned the prize!
Draw close: that conflagration of my church
—What then? So much was saved if aught were
          missed!
My sons, ye would not be my death? Go dig
The white-grape vineyard where the oil-press stood,
Drop water gently till the surface sink,

And if ye find . . . Ah God, I know not, I! . . .
Bedded in store of rotten fig-leaves soft,
And corded up in a tight olive-frail,
Some lump, ah God, of *lapis lazuli,*
Big as a Jew's head cut off at the nape,
Blue as a vein o'er the Madonna's breast . . .
Sons, all have I bequeathed you, villas, all,
That brave Frascati villa with its bath,
So, let the blue lump poise between my knees,
Like God the Father's globe on both his hands
Ye worship in the Jesu Church so gay,
For Gandolf shall not choose but see and burst!
Swift as a weaver's shuttle fleet our years:
Man goeth to the grave, and where is he?
Did I say basalt for my slab, sons? Black—
'Twas ever antique-black I meant! How else
Shall ye contrast my frieze to come beneath?
The bas-relief in bronze ye promised me,
Those Pans and Nymphs ye wot of, and perchance
Some tripod, thyrsus, with a vase or so,
The Saviour at his sermon on the mount,
Saint Praxed in a glory, and one Pan
Ready to twitch the Nymph's last garment off,
And Moses with the tables . . . but I know
Ye mark me not! What do they whisper thee,
Child of my bowels, Anselm? Ah, ye hope
To revel down my villas while I gasp
Bricked o'er with beggar's mouldy travertine
Which Gandolf from his tomb-top chuckles at!
Nay, boys, ye love me—all of jasper, then!
'Tis jasper ye stand pledged to, lest I grieve.
My bath must needs be left behind, alas!
One block, pure green as a pistachio-nut,
There's plenty jasper somewhere in the world—
And have I not Saint Praxed's ear to pray

Horses for ye, and brown Greek manuscripts,
And mistresses with great smooth marbly limbs?
—That's if ye carve my epitaph aright,
Choice Latin, picked phrase, Tully's every word,
No gaudy ware like Gandolf's second line—
Tully, my masters? Ulpian serves his need!
And then how I shall lie through centuries,
And hear the blessed mutter of the mass,
And see God made and eaten all day long,
And feel the steady candle-flame, and taste
Good strong thick stupefying incense-smoke!
For as I lie here, hours of the dead night,
Dying in state and by such slow degrees,
I fold my arms as if they clasped a crook,
And stretch my feet forth straight as stone can point,
And let the bedclothes, for a mortcloth, drop
Into great laps and folds of sculptor's-work:
And as yon tapers dwindle, and strange thoughts
Grow, with a certain humming in my ears,
About the life before I lived this life,
And this life too, popes, cardinals and priests,
Saint Praxed at his sermon on the mount,
Your tall pale mother with her talking eyes,
And new-found agate urns as fresh as day,
And marble's language, Latin pure, discreet,
—Aha, ELUCESCEBAT quoth our friend?
No Tully, said I, Ulpian at the best!
Evil and brief hath been my pilgrimage.
All *lapis,* all, sons! Else I give the Pope
My villas! Will ye ever eat my heart?
Ever your eyes were as a lizard's quick,
They glitter like your mother's for my soul,
Or ye would heighten my impoverished frieze,

Piece out its starved design, and fill my vase
With grapes, and add a vizor and a Term,
And to the tripod ye would tie a lynx
That in his struggle throws the thyrsus down,
To comfort me on my entablature
Whereon I am to lie till I must ask
"Do I live, am I dead?" There, leave me, there!
For ye have stabbed me with ingratitude
To death—ye wish it—God, ye wish it! Stone—
Gritstone, a-crumble! Clammy squares which sweat
As if the corpse they keep were oozing through—
And no more *lapis* to delight the world!
Well go! I bless ye. Fewer tapers there,
But in a row: and, going, turn your backs
—Ay, like departing altar-ministrants,
And leave me in my church, the church for peace,
That I may watch at leisure if he leers—
Old Gandolf, at me, from his onion-stone,
As still he envied me, so fair she was!

Browning gives us a terrible study of jealousy in
The Laboratory. The chemist says nothing, but the
contrast between the placid face of the old scientist,
intent only upon his work, and the wildly passionate
countenance of the little woman with him, is sufficiently impressive. Those were the days when murder was a fine art. She plans the public death of
the woman she hates so that the lover will never
be able to forget the dying face. Radiant in queenly
beauty, with the smile of satisfaction that accom-

panies the inner assurance of beauty and power—
in a moment she will be convulsively rolling on the
floor, her swollen face purplish-black with the poison, her mouth emitting foam like a mad dog. There
is no doubt that the little murderess intends to follow her rival to the tomb. She has given the chemist her entire fortune as pay for the drop of poison;
he may kiss her, if he likes! All shame, all womanly
reserve are gone: what does anything matter now?
It is a true study of jealousy, because the little creature does not dream of attacking the *man* who de-
serted her; all her hellish energy is directed against
the woman. Indeed the poison that she buys will
not transform her rival more completely than the
dreadful poison of jealousy has already transformed her from what she was to what she is.

The language and metre fit the thought. Tennyson passed a severe judgment on the first line

Now that I, tying thy glass mask tightly

saying that it lacked smoothness, that it was a very
difficult mouthful. But is this not intentional and
absolutely right? The woman is speaking slowly
with compressed lips, her voice convulsed with terrible hatred and the terrible resolution for revenge.

THE LABORATORY

ANCIEN REGIME

1844

I

Now that I, tying thy glass mask tightly,
May gaze thro' these faint smokes curling whitely,
As thou pliest thy trade in this devil's-smithy—
Which is the poison to poison her, prithee?

II

He is with her, and they know that I know
Where they are, what they do: they believe my tears flow
While they laugh, laugh at me, at me fled to the drear
Empty church, to pray God in, for them!—I am here.

III

Grind away, moisten and mash up thy paste,
Pound at thy powder,—I am not in haste!
Better sit thus, and observe thy strange things,
Than go where men wait me and dance at the King's.

IV

That in the mortar—you call it a gum?
Ah, the brave tree whence such gold oozings come!
And yonder soft phial, the exquisite blue,
Sure to taste sweetly,—is that poison too?

V

Had I but all of them, thee and thy treasures,
What a wild crowd of invisible pleasures!
To carry pure death in an earring, a casket,
A signet, a fan-mount, a filigree basket!

VI

Soon, at the King's, a mere lozenge to give,
And Pauline should have just thirty minutes to live!
But to light a pastile, and Elise, with her head
And her breast and her arms and her hands, should drop
　　　dead!

VII

Quick—is it finished? The colour's too grim!
Why not soft like the phial's, enticing and dim?
Let it brighten her drink, let her turn it and stir,
And try it and taste, ere she fix and prefer!

VIII

What a drop! She's not little, no minion like me!
That's why she ensnared him: this never will free
The soul from those masculine eyes,—say, "no!"
To that pulse's magnificent come-and-go.

IX

For only last night, as they whispered, I brought
My own eyes to bear on her so, that I thought
Could I keep them one half minute fixed, she would fall
Shrivelled; she fell not; yet this does it all!

X

Not that I bid you spare her the pain;
Let death be felt and the proof remain:
Brand, burn up, bite into its grace—
He is sure to remember her dying face!

XI

Is it done? Take my mask off! Nay, be not morose;
It kills her, and this prevents seeing it close:
The delicate droplet, my whole fortune's fee!
If it hurts her, beside, can it ever hurt me?

XII

Now, take all my jewels, gorge gold to your fill,
You may kiss me, old man, on my mouth if you will!
But brush this dust off me, lest horror it brings
Ere I know it—next moment I dance at the King's!

Fra Lippo Lippi and *Andrea del Sarto* are both great art poems, and both in striking contrast. The former is dynamic, the latter static. The tumultuous vivacity of the gamin who became a painter contrasts finely with the great technician, a fellow almost damned in a fair wife. Fra Lippo Lippi was a street mucker, like Gavroche; he unconsciously learned to paint portraits by the absolute necessity of studying human faces on the street. Nothing sharpens observation like this. He had to be able to tell at a glance whether the man he accosted would give him food or a kick. When they took him to the cloister, he obtained a quite new idea about religion. He naturally judged that, as he judged everything else in life, from the practical point of view. Heretofore, like many small boys, he had rather despised religion, and thought the monks were fools. "Don't you believe it," he cries: "there is a lot in religion. You get free clothes, free shelter, three meals a day, and you don't have to work! Why, it's the easiest thing I know." The monks discovered his talent with pencil and brush, and they made him decorate the chapel. When the work was done, he called them in. To their amazement and horror, the saints and angels, instead of being ideal faces, were the living portraits of the familiar figures about the cloister. "Why, there's the iceman! there's the laundress!" He rebelled when they told him this was wicked: he said it was all a part of God's world, that the business of the artist was to interpret life; he wished they would let him enter the pulpit, take the Prior's place, and preach a sermon that would make them all sit up.

The philosophy of æsthetics has never been more truly or more succinctly stated than in these lines:

> Or say there's beauty with no soul at all—
> (I never saw it—put the case the same—)
> If you get simple beauty and nought else,
> You get about the best thing God invents:
> That's somewhat: and you'll find the soul you have
>   missed,
> Within yourself, when you return him thanks.

Contemplation of beautiful objects in nature, art, and literature, which perhaps at first sight have no significance, gradually awakens in our own hearts a dawning sense of what Beauty may mean; and thus enlarges and develops our minds, and makes them susceptible to the wonder and glory of life.

The relation of art to life—art being the teacher that makes us understand life—is perfectly well understood by Fra Lippo Lippi.

> For, don't you mark? we're made so that we love
> First when we see them painted, things we have passed
> Perhaps a hundred times nor cared to see.

If one stands to-day in the Ancient and Modern Gallery in Florence, and contemplates Fra Lippo Lippi's masterpiece, *The Coronation of the Virgin,* and reads the lines about it in this poem, one will get a new idea of the picture. It is a representation of the painter's whole nature, half genius, half mucker —the painting is a glory of form and color, and then in the corner the artist had the assurance to place himself in his monk's dress among the saints and angels, where he looks as much out of place as a Bowery Boy in a Fifth Avenue drawing-room. Not content with putting himself in the picture, he stuck a Latin tag on himself, which means, "This fellow did the job."

Browning loves Fra Lippo Lippi, in spite of the man's impudence and debauchery; because the painter loved life, had a tremendous zest for it, and was not ashamed of his enthusiasm. The words he speaks came from the poet's own heart:

> The world and life's too big to pass for a dream. . . .
> It makes me mad to see what men shall do
> And we in our graves! This world's no blot for us,
> Nor blank; it means intensely, and means good:
> To find its meaning is my meat and drink.

The change from *Fra Lippo Lippi* to *Andrea del Sarto* is the change from a blustering March day to a mild autumn twilight. The original picture in Florence which inspired the poem represents Andrea and his wife sitting together, while she is holding the letter from King Francis. This is a poem of acquiescence, as the other is a poem of protest, and never was language more fittingly adapted to the mood in each instance. One can usually recognise Andrea's pictures clear across the gallery rooms; he has enveloped them all in a silver-grey gossamer mist, and in some extraordinary manner Browning has contrived to clothe his poem in the same diaphanous garment. It is a poem of twilight, of calm, of failure in success. Andrea's pictures are superior technically to those of his great contemporaries— Rafael, Michel Angelo, Leonardo da Vinci—but their imperfect works have a celestial glory, the glory of aspiration, absent from his perfect productions. His work indeed is,

> Faultily faultless, icily regular, splendidly null,
> Dead perfection, no more.

It is natural, that he, whose paintings show perfection of form without spirit, should have married a woman of physical beauty devoid of soul. She has ruined him, but she could not have ruined him had he been a different man. He understands her, however, in the quiet light of his own failure. He tells her she must not treat him so badly that he can not paint at all; and adds the necessary explanation that his ceasing to paint would stop her supplies of cash. For although it is incomprehensible to her, people are willing to give large sums of money for her ridiculous husband's ridiculous daubs. His mind, sensitive to beauty, is drunk with his wife's loveliness of face and form; and like all confirmed drunkards, he can not conquer himself now, though otherwise he knows it means death and damnation. He has a complete knowledge of the whole range of his powers, and of his limitations. He can not help feeling pride in his marvellous technique, that he can do what other men dream of doing; but he knows that without aspiration the soul is dead.

Poor Andrea! History has treated him harshly. He is known throughout all time as "the tailor's son," and Browning has given him in this immortal poem a condemnation that much of his work does not really deserve. For there is inspiration in many of Andrea's Madonnas.   Browning, with his fixed idea of the glory of the imperfect, the divine evidence of perpetual development, could not forgive Andrea for being called the "faultless painter." Thus Browning has made of him a horrible example, has used him merely as the text for a sermon.

There was just enough truth to give Browning his opportunity.   The superiority of Rafael over Andrea lies precisely in the aspiration of the former's work.   Schopenhauer says the whole Christian religion is in the face of Rafael's *Saint Cecilia,* "an entire and certain gospel."   Andrea's virgins have more of the beauty of this world: Rafael's have the beauty of holiness.

ANDREA DEL SARTO

(CALLED "THE FAULTLESS PAINTER")

1855

But do not let us quarrel any more,
No, my Lucrezia; bear with me for once:
Sit down and all shall happen as you wish.
You turn your face, but does it bring your heart?
I'll work then for your friend's friend, never fear,
Treat his own subject after his own way,
Fix his own time, accept too his own price,
And shut the money into this small hand
When next it takes mine. Will it? tenderly?
Oh, I'll content him,—but to-morrow, Love!
I often am much wearier than you think,
This evening more than usual, and it seems

As if—forgive now—should you let me sit
Here by the window with your hand in mine
And look a half-hour forth on Fiesole,
Both of one mind, as married people use,
Quietly, quietly the evening through,
I might get up to-morrow to my work
Cheerful and fresh as ever. Let us try.
To-morrow, how you shall be glad for this!
Your soft hand is a woman of itself,
And mine the man's bared breast she curls inside.
Don't count the time lost, neither; you must serve
For each of the five pictures we require:
It saves a model. So! keep looking so—
My serpentining beauty, rounds on rounds!
—How could you ever prick those perfect ears,
Even to put the pearl there! oh, so sweet—
My face, my moon, my everybody's moon,
Which everybody looks on and calls his,
And, I suppose, is looked on by in turn,
While she looks—no one's: very dear, no less.
You smile? why, there's my picture ready made,
There's what we painters call our harmony!
A common greyness silvers everything,—
All in a twilight, you and I alike
—You, at the point of your first pride in me
(That's gone you know),—but I, at every point;
My youth, my hope, my art, being all toned down
To yonder sober pleasant Fiesole.
There's the bell clinking from the chapel-top;
That length of convent-wall across the way
Holds the trees safer, huddled more inside;
The last monk leaves the garden; days decrease,
And autumn grows, autumn in everything.
Eh? the whole seems to fall into a shape

As if I saw alike my work and self
And all that I was born to be and do,
A twilight-piece. Love, we are in God's hand.
How strange now, looks the life he makes us lead;
So free we seem, so fettered fast we are!
I feel he laid the fetter: let it lie!
This chamber for example—turn your head—
All that's behind us! You don't understand
Nor care to understand about my art,
But you can hear at least when people speak:
And that cartoon, the second from the door
—It is the thing, Love! so such things should be—
Behold Madonna!—I am bold to say.
I can do with my pencil what I know,
What I see, what at bottom of my heart
I wish for, if I ever wish so deep—
Do easily, too—when I say, perfectly,
I do not boast, perhaps: yourself are judge,
Who listened to the Legate's talk last week,
And just as much they used to say in France.
At any rate 'tis easy, all of it!
No sketches first, no studies, that's long past:
I do what many dream of, all their lives,
—Dream? strive to do, and agonize to do,
And fail in doing. I could count twenty such
On twice your fingers, and not leave this town,
Who strive—you don't know how the others strive
To paint a little thing like that you smeared
Carelessly passing with your robes afloat,—
Yet do much less, so much less, Someone says,
(I know his name, no matter)—so much less!
Well, less is more, Lucrezia: I am judged.
There burns a truer light of God in them,
In their vexed beating stuffed and stopped-up brain,
Heart, or whate'er else, than goes on to prompt

This low-pulsed forthright craftsman's hand of mine.
Their works drop groundward, but themselves, I know,
Reach many a time a heaven that's shut to me,
Enter and take their place there sure enough,
Though they come back and cannot tell the world.
My works are nearer heaven, but I sit here.
The sudden blood of these men! at a word—
Praise them, it boils, or blame them, it boils too.
I, painting from myself and to myself,
Know what I do, am unmoved by men's blame
Or their praise either. Somebody remarks
Morello's outline there is wrongly traced,
His hue mistaken; what of that? or else,
Rightly traced and well ordered; what of that?
Speak as they please, what does the mountain care?
Ah, but a man's reach should exceed his grasp,
Or what's a heaven for? All is silver-grey
Placid and perfect with my art: the worse!
I know both what I want and what might gain,
And yet how profitless to know, to sigh
"Had I been two, another and myself,
"Our head would have o'erlooked the world!" No doubt.
Yonder's a work now, of that famous youth
The Urbinate who died five years ago.
('Tis copied, George Vasari sent it me.)
Well, I can fancy how he did it all,
Pouring his soul, with kings and popes to see,
Reaching, that heaven might so replenish him,
Above and through his art—for it gives way;
That arm is wrongly put—and there again—
A fault to pardon in the drawing's lines,
Its body, so to speak: its soul is right,
He means right—that, a child may understand.
Still, what an arm! and I could alter it:
But all the play, the insight and the stretch—

Out of me, out of me! And wherefore out?
Had you enjoined them on me, given me soul,
We might have risen to Rafael, I and you!
Nay, Love, you did give all I asked, I think—
More than I merit, yes, by many times.
But had you—oh, with the same perfect brow,
And perfect eyes, and more than perfect mouth,
And the low voice my soul hears, as a bird
The fowler's pipe, and follows to the snare—
Had you, with these the same, but brought a mind!
Some women do so. Had the mouth there urged
"God and the glory! never care for gain.
"The present by the future, what is that?
"Live for fame, side by side with Agnolo!
"Rafael is waiting: up to God, all three!"
I might have done it for you. So it seems:
Perhaps not. All is as God over-rules.
Beside, incentives come from the soul's self;
The rest avail not. Why do I need you?
What wife had Rafael, or has Agnolo?
In this world, who can do a thing, will not;
And who would do it, cannot, I perceive:
Yet the will's somewhat—somewhat, too, the power—
And thus we half-men struggle. At the end,
God, I conclude, compensates, punishes.
'Tis safer for me, if the award be strict,
That I am something underrated here,
Poor this long while, despised, to speak the truth.
I dared not, do you know, leave home all day,
For fear of chancing on the Paris lords.
The best is when they pass and look aside;
But they speak sometimes; I must bear it all.
Well may they speak! That Francis, that first time,
And that long festal year at Fontainebleau!
I surely then could sometimes leave the ground,

Put on the glory, Rafael's daily wear,
In that humane great monarch's golden look,—
One finger in his beard or twisted curl
Over his mouth's good mark that made the smile,
One arm about my shoulder, round my neck,
The jingle of his gold chain in my ear,
I painting proudly with his breath on me,
All his court round him, seeing with his eyes,
Such frank French eyes, and such a fire of souls
Profuse, my hand kept plying by those hearts,—
And, best of all, this, this, this face beyond,
This in the background, waiting on my work,
To crown the issue with a last reward!
A good time, was it not, my kingly days?
And had you not grown restless . . . but I know—
'Tis done and past; 'twas right, my instinct said;
Too live the life grew, golden and not grey,
And I'm the weak-eyed bat no sun should tempt
Out of the grange whose four walls make his world.
How could it end in any other way?
You called me, and I came home to your heart.
The triumph was—to reach and stay there; since
I reached it ere the triumph, what is lost?
Let my hands frame your face in your hair's gold,
You beautiful Lucrezia that are mine!
"Rafael did this, Andrea painted that;
"The Roman's is the better when you pray,
"But still the other's Virgin was his wife—"
Men will excuse me. I am glad to judge
Both pictures in your presence; clearer grows
My better fortune, I resolve to think.
For, do you know, Lucrezia, as God lives,
Said one day Agnolo, his very self,
To Rafael . . . I have known it all these years . . .
(When the young man was flaming out his thoughts

Upon a palace-wall for Rome to see,
Too lifted up in heart because of it)
"Friend, there's a certain sorry little scrub
"Goes up and down our Florence, none cares how,
"Who, were he set to plan and execute
"As you are, pricked on by your popes and kings,
"Would bring the sweat into that brow of yours!"
To Rafael's!—And indeed the arm is wrong.
I hardly dare . . . yet, only you to see,
Give the chalk here—quick, thus the line should go!
Ay, but the soul! he's Rafael! rub it out!
Still, all I care for, if he spoke the truth,
(What he? why, who but Michel Agnolo?
Do you forget already words like those?)
If really there was such a chance, so lost,—
Is, whether you're—not grateful—but more pleased.
Well, let me think so. And you smile indeed!
This hour has been an hour! Another smile?
If you would sit thus by me every night
I should work better, do you comprehend?
I mean that I should earn more, give you more.
See, it is settled dusk now; there's a star;
Morello's gone, the watch-lights show the wall,
The cue-owls speak the name we call them by.
Come from the window, love,—come in, at last,
Inside the melancholy little house
We built to be so gay with. God is just.
King Francis may forgive me: oft at nights
When I look up from painting, eyes tired out,
The walls become illumined, brick from brick
Distinct, instead of mortar, fierce bright gold,
That gold of his I did cement them with!
Let us but love each other. Must you go?
That Cousin here again? he waits outside?
Must see you—you, and not with me? Those loans?

More gaming debts to pay? you smiled for that?
Well, let smiles buy me! have you more to spend?
While hand and eye and something of a heart
Are left me, work's my ware, and what's it worth?
I'll pay my fancy. Only let me sit
The grey remainder of the evening out,
Idle, you call it, and muse perfectly
How I could paint, were I but back in France,
One picture, just one more—the Virgin's face,
Not yours this time! I want you at my side
To hear them—that is, Michel Agnolo—
Judge all I do and tell you of its worth.
Will you? To-morrow, satisfy your friend.
I take the subjects for his corridor,
Finish the portrait out of hand—there, there,
And throw him in another thing or two
If he demurs; the whole should prove enough
To pay for this same Cousin's freak. Beside,
What's better and what's all I care about,
Get you the thirteen scudi for the ruff!
Love, does that please you? Ah, but what does he,
The Cousin! what does he to please you more?

I am grown peaceful as old age to-night.
I regret little, I would change still less.
Since there my past life lies, why alter it?
The very wrong to Francis!—it is true
I took his coin, was tempted and complied,
And built this house and sinned, and all is said.
My father and my mother died of want.
Well, had I riches of my own? you see
How one gets rich! Let each one bear his lot.
They were born poor, lived poor, and poor they died:
And I have laboured somewhat in my time
And not been paid profusely. Some good son

Paint my two hundred pictures—let him try!
No doubt, there's something strikes a balance. Yes,
You loved me quite enough, it seems to-night.
This must suffice me here. What would one have?
In heaven, perhaps, new chances, one more chance—
Four great walls in the New Jerusalem,
Meted on each side by the angel's reed,
For Leonard, Rafael, Agnolo and me
To cover—the three first without a wife,
While I have mine! So—still they overcome
Because there's still Lucrezia,—as I choose.

Again the Cousin's whistle! Go, my Love.

Karshish and *Cleon* are studies of the early days
of Christianity. Each man writes a letter—one to
a professor, one to a king—which reveals both his
own nature and the steady advance of the kingdom
of God. The contrast between the scientist and the
man of letters is not favorable to the latter. Karshish is an ideal scientist, with a naturally skeptical
mind, yet wide open, willing to learn from any and
every source, thankful for every new fact; Cleon is
an intellectual snob. His mind is closed by its own
culture, and he regards it as absurd that any man in
humble circumstances can teach him anything.
Learning, which has made the scientist modest, has
made Cleon arrogant. Such is the difference between the ideal man of science, and the typical man
of culture.

Young Karshish was the best student in his department at the university; he has won a travelling fellowship, and writes letters home to Professor Abib, the Dean of the Graduate School. This is the twenty-second letter, and although we have not seen the others, we may easily conjecture their style and contents. They resemble Darwin's method of composition describing his tour around the world—one fact is noted accurately and then another. This particular letter is entrusted to a messenger who had the pink-eye; the young doctor easily cured him, and the man having no money, begged to give some service. He winks his eyes gladly in the strong sunlight which had hurt him so cruelly until the doctor came to his relief. Very well! he shall run with an epistle.

Karshish has met Lazarus: and it is significant of Browning's method that it is not the resurrection from the grave which interests him, nor what happened to Lazarus in the tomb; it is the profound spiritual change in the man. Lazarus does not act like a faker; he is not sensational, does not care whether you believe his story or not, is a thoroughly quiet, intelligent, sensible man. Only his conduct has ceased to be swayed by any selfish interest, and there is some tremendous force working in his life that puzzles the physician. It is amusing how the latter tries to shake off his obsession, how he tries to persuade himself that Lazarus had a prolonged epileptic fit, or that he is now mad; how he tries to interest himself once more in the fauna and flora of the country. Impossible! the story of Lazarus dominates him.

His letter is naturally full of apologies for writing to the great Abib on such a theme. He is afraid Abib will be disgusted with him, will call him home, as a disgrace to the university he represents. What! my favorite student, carefully trained in science, to swallow the story of the first madman or swindler he meets? A man raised from the dead? Such cases are diurnal. What would a modern professor think if one of his travelling fellows wrote home from South America that he had met a man raised from the dead, and was really impressed by his story? His fellowship would be instantly taken away from him.

He anticipates Abib's suggestions. If you think there is really anything interesting in the yarn, why don't you seek out the magician who brought him back to life? Oh, naturally, I thought of that the first thing. But I discovered that the doctor who

meaningless is so repugnant not merely to his heart's
desire but to his mental sense of the fitness of things,
that it has sometimes seemed as if there must be a
future life where the soul can pursue its natural
course ahead. But he dismisses this thought as impossible; for if there were a future life, I should be
the first to know of it. It would certainly have been
revealed to a splendid mind like mine. It is the mountain peak that catches the first flush of the dawn,
not the valley: it is the topmost branch of the great
tree that gets the first whisper of the coming breeze.
It is a pity that Cleon had not heard the Gospel. I
thank thee, O Father, that Thou hast hidden these
things from the wise and prudent, and hast revealed
them unto babes. Even so, Father: for so it seemed
good in Thy sight. It was not through men like
Cleon that the Gospel made its first advance.

His postscript, like that of Karshish, is interesting, though strikingly different. The king had enclosed a letter to Paul, but as he did not know Paul's
address, he wondered if Cleon would not be kind
enough to see that the evangelist obtained the letter. Cleon was decidedly vexed. I neither know
nor care where Paul may be. You don't suppose
for a moment that Paul knows anything I don't
know? You don't suppose anything Paul could say

would have any weight for men like me? Oh, I
have heard of him; I was taking a constitutional one
day, and I saw a little group of persons listening to
an orator. I touched a man on the shoulder, and I
said, What is that idiot talking about? And he replied that the man said that a person named Jesus
Christ had risen from the dead, and could save all
those who believed on Him from death. What crazy
nonsense people swallow! So Cleon smiled in his
wisdom and went on his way. But through the lines
of his speech we feel the rising tide of Christianity,
where

> Far back, through creeks and inlets making,
> Comes silent, flooding in, the main.

AN EPISTLE

CONTAINING THE STRANGE MEDICAL EXPERIENCE OF KARSHISH,
THE ARAB PHYSICIAN

1855

Karshish, the picker-up of learning's crumbs,
The not-incurious in God's handiwork
(This man's-flesh he hath admirably made,
Blown like a bubble, kneaded like a paste,
To coop up and keep down on earth a space
That puff of vapour from his mouth, man's soul)
—To Abib, all-sagacious in our art,
Breeder in me of what poor skill I boast;
Like me inquisitive how pricks and cracks
Befall the flesh through too much stress and strain,
Whereby the wily vapour fain would slip

Back and rejoin its source before the term,—
And aptest in contrivance (under God)
To baffle it by deftly stopping such:—
The vagrant Scholar to his Sage at home
Sends greeting (health and knowledge, fame with
      peace)
Three samples of true snake-stone—rarer still,
One of the other sort, the melon-shaped,
(But fitter, pounded fine, for charms than drugs)
And writeth now the twenty-second time.

  My journeyings were brought to Jericho:
Thus I resume. Who studious in our art
Shall count a little labour unrepaid?
I have shed sweat enough, left flesh and bone
On many a flinty furlong of this land.
Also, the country-side is all on fire
With rumours of a marching hitherward:
Some say Vespasian cometh, some, his son.
A black lynx snarled and pricked a tufted ear;
Lust of my blood inflamed his yellow balls:
I cried and threw my staff and he was gone.
Twice have the robbers stripped and beaten me,
And once a town declared me for a spy;
But at the end, I reach Jerusalem,
Since this poor covert where I pass the night,
This Bethany, lies scarce the distance thence
A man with plague-sores at the third degree
Runs till he drops down dead. Thou laughest here!
'Sooth, it elates me, thus reposed and safe,
To void the stuffing of my travel-scrip
And share with thee whatever Jewry yields.
A viscid choler is observable
In tertians, I was nearly bold to say;
And falling-sickness hath a happier cure

Than our school wots of: there's a spider here
Weaves no web, watches on the ledge of tombs,
Sprinkled with mottles on an ash-gray back;
Take five and drop them . . . but who knows his mind,
The Syrian runagate I trust this to?
His service payeth me a sublimate
Blown up his nose to help the ailing eye.
Best wait: I reach Jerusalem at morn,
There set in order my experiences,
Gather what most deserves, and give thee all—
Or I might add, Judæa's gum-tragacanth
Scales off in purer flakes, shines clearer-grained,
Cracks 'twixt the pestle and the porphyry,
In fine exceeds our produce. Scalp-disease
Confounds me, crossing so with leprosy—
Thou hadst admired one sort I gained at Zoar—
But zeal outruns discretion. Here I end.

  Yet stay: my Syrian blinketh gratefully,
Protesteth his devotion is my price—
Suppose I write what harms not, though he steal?
I half resolve to tell thee, yet I blush,
What set me off a-writing first of all.
An itch I had, a sting to write, a tang!
For, be it this town's barrenness—or else
The Man had something in the look of him—
His case has struck me far more than 'tis worth.
So, pardon if—(lest presently I lose
In the great press of novelty at hand
The care and pains this somehow stole from me)
I bid thee take the thing while fresh in mind,
Almost in sight—for, wilt thou have the truth?
The very man is gone from me but now,
Whose ailment is the subject of discourse.
Thus then, and let thy better wit help all!

'Tis but a case of mania—subinduced
By epilepsy, at the turning-point
Of trance prolonged unduly some three days:
When, by the exhibition of some drug
Or spell, exorcization, stroke of art,
Unknown to me and which 'twere well to know,
The evil thing out-breaking all at once
Left the man whole and sound of body indeed,—
But, flinging (so to speak) life's gates too wide,
Making a clear house of it too suddenly,
The first conceit that entered might inscribe
Whatever it was minded on the wall
So plainly at that vantage, as it were,
(First come, first served) that nothing subsequent
Attaineth to erase those fancy-scrawls
The just-returned and new-established soul
Hath gotten now so thoroughly by heart
That henceforth she will read or these or none.
And first—the man's own firm conviction rests
That he was dead (in fact they buried him)
—That he was dead and then restored to life
By a Nazarene physician of his tribe:
—'Sayeth, the same bade "Rise," and he did rise.
"Such cases are diurnal," thou wilt cry.
Not so this figment!—not, that such a fume,
Instead of giving way to time and health,
Should eat itself into the life of life,
As saffron tingeth flesh, blood, bones and all!
For see, how he takes up the after-life.
The man—it is one Lazarus a Jew,
Sanguine, proportioned, fifty years of age,
The body's habit wholly laudable,
As much, indeed, beyond the common health
As he were made and put aside to show.
Think, could we penetrate by any drug

And bathe the wearied soul and worried flesh,
And bring it clear and fair, by three days' sleep!
Whence has the man the balm that brightens all?
This grown man eyes the world now like a child.
Some elders of his tribe, I should premise,
Led in their friend, obedient as a sheep,
To bear my inquisition. While they spoke,
Now sharply, now with sorrow,—told the case,—
He listened not except I spoke to him,
But folded his two hands and let them talk,
Watching the flies that buzzed: and yet no fool.
And that's a sample how his years must go.
Look, if a beggar, in fixed middle-life,
Should find a treasure,—can he use the same
With straitened habits and with tastes starved small,
And take at once to his impoverished brain
The sudden element that changes things,
That sets the undreamed-of rapture at his hand
And puts the cheap old joy in the scorned dust?
Is he not such an one as moves to mirth—
Warily parsimonious, when no need,
Wasteful as drunkenness at undue times?
All prudent counsel as to what befits
The golden mean, is lost on such an one:
The man's fantastic will is the man's law.
So here—we call the treasure knowledge, say,
Increased beyond the fleshly faculty—
Heaven opened to a soul while yet on earth,
Earth forced on a soul's use while seeing heaven:
The man is witless of the size, the sum,
The value in proportion of all things,
Or whether it be little or be much.
Discourse to him of prodigious armaments
Assembled to besiege his city now,
And of the passing of a mule with gourds—

'Tis one! Then take it on the other side,
Speak of some trifling fact,—he will gaze rapt
With stupour at its very littleness,
(Far as I see) as if in that indeed
He caught prodigious import, whole results;
And so will turn to us the bystanders
In ever the same stupour (note this point)
That we too see not with his opened eyes.
Wonder and doubt come wrongly into play,
Preposterously, at cross purposes.
Should his child sicken unto death,—why, look
For scarce abatement of his cheerfulness,
Or pretermission of the daily craft!
While a word, gesture, glance from that same child
At play or in the school or laid asleep
Will startle him to an agony of fear,
Exasperation, just as like. Demand
The reason why—"'tis but a word," object—
"A gesture"—he regards thee as our lord
Who lived there in the pyramid alone,
Looked at us (dost thou mind?) when, being young,
We both would unadvisedly recite
Some charm's beginning, from that book of his,
Able to bid the sun throb wide and burst
All into stars, as suns grown old are wont.
Thou and the child have each a veil alike
Thrown o'er your heads, from under which ye both
Stretch your blind hands and trifle with a match
Over a mine of Greek fire, did ye know!
He holds on firmly to some thread of life—
(It is the life to lead perforcedly)
Which runs across some vast distracting orb
Of glory on either side that meagre thread,
Which, conscious of, he must not enter yet—
The spiritual life around the earthly life:

The law of that is known to him as this,
His heart and brain move there, his feet stay here.
So is the man perplext with impulses
Sudden to start off crosswise, not straight on,
Proclaiming what is right and wrong across,
And not along, this black thread through the blaze—
"It should be" balked by "here it cannot be."
And oft the man's soul springs into his face
As if he saw again and heard again
His sage that bade him "Rise" and he did rise.
Something, a word, a tick o' the blood within
Admonishes: then back he sinks at once
To ashes, who was very fire before,
In sedulous recurrence to his trade
Whereby he earneth him the daily bread;
And studiously the humbler for that pride,
Professedly the faultier that he knows
God's secret, while he holds the thread of life.
Indeed the especial marking of the man
Is prone submission to the heavenly will—
Seeing it, what it is, and why it is.
'Sayeth, he will wait patient to the last
For that same death which must restore his being
To equilibrium, body loosening soul
Divorced even now by premature full growth:
He will live, nay, it pleaseth him to live
So long as God please, and just how God please.
He even seeketh not to please God more
(Which meaneth, otherwise) than as God please.
Hence, I perceive not he affects to preach
The doctrine of his sect whate'er it be,
Make proselytes as madmen thirst to do:
How can he give his neighbour the real ground,
His own conviction? Ardent as he is—
Call his great truth a lie, why, still the old

"Be it as God please" reassureth him.
I probed the sore as thy disciple should:
"How, beast," said I, "this stolid carelessness
Sufficeth thee, when Rome is on her march
To stamp out like a little spark thy town,
Thy tribe, thy crazy tale and thee at once?"
He merely looked with his large eyes on me.
The man is apathetic, you deduce?
Contrariwise, he loves both old and young,
Able and weak, affects the very brutes
And birds—how say I? flowers of the field—
As a wise workman recognises tools
In a master's workshop, loving what they make.
Thus is the man as harmless as a lamb:
Only impatient, let him do his best,
At ignorance and carelessness and sin—
An indignation which is promptly curbed:
As when in certain travel I have feigned
To be an ignoramus in our art
According to some preconceived design,
And happed to hear the land's practitioners,
Steeped in conceit sublimed by ignorance,
Prattle fantastically on disease,
Its cause and cure—and I must hold my peace!

  Thou wilt object—Why have I not ere this
Sought out the sage himself, the Nazarene
Who wrought this cure, inquiring at the source,
Conferring with the frankness that befits?
Alas! it grieveth me, the learned leech
Perished in a tumult many years ago,
Accused—our learning's fate—of wizardry,
Rebellion, to the setting up a rule
And creed prodigious as described to me.
His death, which happened when the earthquake fell

(Prefiguring, as soon appeared, the loss
To occult learning in our lord the sage
Who lived there in the pyramid alone)
Was wrought by the mad people—that's their wont!
On vain recourse, as I conjecture it,
To his tried virtue, for miraculous help—
How could he stop the earthquake? That's their way!
The other imputations must be lies:
But take one, though I loathe to give it thee,
In mere respect for any good man's fame.
(And after all, our patient Lazarus
Is stark mad; should we count on what he says?
Perhaps not: though in writing to a leech
'Tis well to keep back nothing of a case.)
This man so cured regards the curer, then,
As—God forgive me! who but God himself,
Creator and sustainer of the world,
That came and dwelt in flesh on it awhile!
—'Sayeth that such an one was born and lived,
Taught, healed the sick, broke bread at his own house,
Then died, with Lazarus by, for aught I know,
And yet was . . . what I said nor choose repeat,
And must have so avouched himself, in fact,
In hearing of this very Lazarus
Who saith—but why all this of what he saith?
Why write of trivial matters, things of price
Calling at every moment for remark?
I noticed on the margin of a pool
Blue-flowering borage, the Aleppo sort,
Aboundeth, very nitrous. It is strange!

Thy pardon for this long and tedious case,
Which, now that I review it, needs must seem
Unduly dwelt on, prolixly set forth!
Nor I myself discern in what is writ

Good cause for the peculiar interest
And awe indeed this man has touched me with.
Perhaps the journey's end, the weariness
Had wrought upon me first. I met him thus:
I crossed a ridge of short sharp broken hills
Like an old lion's cheek teeth. Out there came
A moon made like a face with certain spots
Multiform, manifold, and menacing:
Then a wind rose behind me. So we met
In this old sleepy town at unaware,
The man and I. I send thee what is writ.
Regard it as a chance, a matter risked
To this ambiguous Syrian—he may lose,
Or steal, or give it thee with equal good.
Jerusalem's repose shall make amends
For time this letter wastes, thy time and mine;
Till when, once more thy pardon and farewell!

The very God! think, Abib; dost thou think?
So, the All-Great, were the All-Loving too—
So, through the thunder comes a human voice
Saying, "O heart I made, a heart beats here!
Face, my hands fashioned, see it in myself!
Thou hast no power nor mayst conceive of mine,
But love I gave thee, with myself to love,
And thou must love me who have died for thee!"
The madman saith He said so: it is strange.

The poem *Childe Roland* is unique among Browning's monologues. His poetry usually is of the noon-day and the market-place; but this might have been written by Coleridge, or Maeterlinck, or Edgar Allan Poe. It has indeed the "wizard twilight Coleridge knew." The atmosphere is uncanny and ghoul-haunted: the scenery is a series of sombre and horrible imaginings. No consistent allegory can be made out of it, for which fact we should rejoice. It is a poem, not a sermon; it is intended to stimulate the imagination, rather than awaken the conscience. And as we accompany the knight on his lonely and fearful journey, we feel thrills caused only by works of genius.

The poem is an example of the power of creative imagination. Out of one line from an old ballad quoted by Shakespeare, Browning has built up a marvellous succession of vivid pictures. The twilight deepens as Childe Roland advances; one can feel the darkness coming on.

> . . . . hands unseen
> Were hanging the night around us fast.

Although the poem means nothing specifically except a triumphant close to a heart-shaking experience, the close is so solemnly splendid that it is difficult to repress a shout of physical exultation. One lonely man, in the presence of all the Powers of the Air, sends out an honest blast of defiance—the individual will against the malignant forces of the whole universe.

What happened when he blew his horn? Did the awful mountains in the blood-red sunset dissolve as the walls of Jericho fell to a similar sound? Did the round, squat Tower vanish like a dream-phantom? Or was the sound of the horn the last breath of the hero? If we believe the former, then Childe Roland is telling his experience to a listener; it is the song of the man "who came whither he went." If the latter, which seems to me more dramatic, and more like Browning, then the monologue is murmured by the solitary knight as he advances on his darkening path.

Three entirely different interpretations may be made of the poem. First, the Tower is the quest, and Success is found only in the moment of Failure. Second, the Tower is the quest, and when found is worth nothing : the hero has spent his life searching something that in the end is seen to be only a round, squat, blind turret—for such things do men throw away their lives! Third, the Tower is not the quest at all—it is damnation, and when the knight turns *aside* from the true road to seek the Tower, he is a lost soul steadily slipping through increasing darkness to hell.

Whilst I do not believe this third interpretation, for it seems to me contrary to the whole spirit of the piece, it is surprising that if one reads through the poem with that idea and none other in mind, how

much support can be found for it. The hoary cripple is the devil, meant to lead us into temptation; and
the third stanza seems for the moment to complete
this thought.

> If at his counsel I should turn aside
>   Into that ominous tract, which, all agree
>   Hides the Dark Tower. Yet acquiescingly
> I did turn as he pointed:

If all knew that the ominous tract contained the
Dark Tower, why was the knight outside of it, if
the Tower were his quest? He turns aside, acquiescingly: he has given up a life of noble aspiration, and now hands over his despairing heart in
surrender to the powers of darkness. He goes on
his way a beaten man, only hoping that the end may
not be long delayed.

Much in the letter of the poem may support this
view; but the whole spirit of it is opposed to such
an interpretation, and the ringing close does not
sound like spiritual failure. Nor do I believe in the
second interpretation; for it is quite unlike Browning
to write a magnificent poem with a cynical conclu-
sion.

No, I believe that once upon a time, Roland, Giles,
Cuthbert, and other knights in solemn assembly took
an oath to go on the quest of the Dark Tower: to

find it or perish on the way. All but these three have apparently kept their word; they have never returned, and when Roland is on the last stages of his journey, he sees why; they have died a horrible death. The quest is indeed an unspeakably perilous thing: for all but Giles and Cuthbert are dead, and these two suffered a fate worse than death—the awful fear inspired by something hideous on the march changed these splendid specimens of manhood into craven traitors. Roland remembers with cruel agony the ruddy young face of Cuthbert, glowing under its yellow hair: was there ever such a magnificent fellow? But the path to the Tower had shaken his manhood, and disgraced him forever. How well Roland remembers the morning when Giles took the oath to find the Tower! That was ten years ago. The frank, manly young knight stepped forth, and declared proudly that he dared do all that might become a man. But he had some awful experience in the course of the quest that changed him from the soul of honor to a whimpering coward. His own companions spat upon him and cursed him.

Roland alone is left. And he has experienced so many disappointments that now all hope of finding the Tower is dead in his breast. Just one spark of

manhood remains.   He can not succeed, but God
grant that he may be fit to fail.

> . . .   just to fail as they, seemed best,
> And all the doubt was now—should I be fit?

As he advances, the country becomes an abomina-
tion of desolation; then appear evidences of struggle, the marks of monsters: then the awful, boiling
river, with the nerve-shattering shriek from its
depths as he thrust in his spear.   On the other bank,
fresh evidences of fearful combats, followed farther along by the appearance of engines of torture.
Those of his companions who had survived the
beasts had there perished in this frightful manner.
Nevertheless, Roland advances, his eyes on the
ground.   Suddenly the wide wing of some dreadful
bird of the night brushed his cap, and he looked up
—to his overwhelming amazement, *he sees the
Tower!*   He sees it as the sailor sees the rocks on a
dark night, only when the ship is lost.   He sees it in
a sudden glare of hell; the air is full of mocking
laughter, the scorn of fiends mingling with the sound
of the names of their victims, his peers and comrades, all lost!   The ugly misshapen mountains look
like sinister giants, lying chin upon hand, lazily
awaiting his destruction.   But this atom of human-

ity, in the presence of all the material forces of this world and the supernatural powers of darkness, places the horn to his lips, and sends out on the evening air a shrill blast of utter defiance. He that endureth to the end shall be saved. Not his possessions, not his happiness, not his bodily frame—they all succumb: but *he* shall be saved.

Thus we may take this wholly romantic poem as one more noble illustration of Browning's favorite doctrine—Success in Failure.

"CHILDE ROLAND TO THE DARK TOWER CAME"

See Edgar's song in *Lear*

1855

My first thought was, he lied in every word,
  That hoary cripple, with malicious eye
  Askance to watch the working of his lie
On mine, and mouth scarce able to afford
Suppression of the glee, that pursed and scored
  Its edge, at one more victim gained thereby.

What else should he be set for, with his staff?
  What, save to waylay with his lies, ensnare
  All travellers who might find him posted there,
And ask the road? I guessed what skull-like laugh
Would break, what crutch 'gin write my epitaph
  For pastime in the dusty thoroughfare,

If at his counsel I should turn aside
  Into that ominous tract which, all agree,
  Hides the Dark Tower. Yet acquiescingly

I did turn as he pointed: neither pride
Nor hope rekindling at the end descried,
　　So much as gladness that some end might be.

For, what with my whole world-wide wandering,
　　What with my search drawn out through years, my
　　　　　hope
　　Dwindled into a ghost not fit to cope
With that obstreperous joy success would bring,—
I hardly tried now to rebuke the spring
　　My heart made, finding failure in its scope.

As when a sick man very near to death
　　Seems dead indeed, and feels begin and end
　　The tears, and takes the farewell of each friend,
And hears one bid the other go, draw breath
Freelier outside, ("since all is o'er," he saith,
　　"And the blow fallen no grieving can amend;")

While some discuss if near the other graves
　　Be room enough for this, and when a day
　　Suits best for carrying the corpse away,
With care about the banners, scarves and staves:
And still the man hears all, and only craves
　　He may not shame such tender love and stay.

Thus, I had so long suffered in this quest,
　　Heard failure prophesied so oft, been writ
　　So many times among "The Band"—to wit,
The knights who to the Dark Tower's search addressed
Their steps—that just to fail as they, seemed best,
　　And all the doubt was now—should I be fit?

So, quiet as despair, I turned from him,
　　That hateful cripple, out of his highway
　　Into the path he pointed. All the day

Had been a dreary one at best, and dim
Was settling to its close, yet shot one grim
  Red leer to see the plain catch its estray.

For mark! no sooner was I fairly found
  Pledged to the plain, after a pace or two,
  Than, pausing to throw backward a last view
O'er the safe road, 'twas gone; gray plain all round:
Nothing but plain to the horizon's bound.
  I might go on; naught else remained to do.

So, on I went. I think I never saw
  Such starved ignoble nature; nothing throve:
  For flowers—as well expect a cedar grove!
But cockle, spurge, according to their law
Might propagate their kind, with none to awe,
  You'd think: a burr had been a treasure trove.

No! penury, inertness and grimace,
  In some strange sort, were the land's portion. "See
  Or shut your eyes," said Nature peevishly,
"It nothing skills: I cannot help my case:
'Tis the Last Judgment's fire must cure this place,
  Calcine its clods and set my prisoners free."

If there pushed any ragged thistle-stalk
  Above its mates, the head was chopped; the bents
  Were jealous else. What made those holes and rents
In the dock's harsh swarth leaves, bruised as to balk
All hope of greenness? 'tis a brute must walk
  Pashing their life out, with a brute's intents.

As for the grass, it grew as scant as hair
  In leprosy; thin dry blades pricked the mud
  Which underneath looked kneaded up with blood.

One stiff blind horse, his every bone a-stare,
Stood stupefied, however he came there:
   Thrust out past service from the devil's stud!

Alive? he might be dead for aught I know,
   With that red gaunt and colloped neck a-strain,
   And shut eyes underneath the rusty mane;
Seldom went such grotesqueness with such woe;
I never saw a brute I hated so;
   He must be wicked to deserve such pain.

I shut my eyes and turned them on my heart.
   As a man calls for wine before he fights,
   I asked one draught of earlier, happier sights,
Ere fitly I could hope to play my part.
Think first, fight afterwards—the soldier's art:
   One taste of the old time sets all to rights.

Not it! I fancied Cuthbert's reddening face
   Beneath its garniture of curly gold,
   Dear fellow, till I almost felt him fold
An arm in mine to fix me to the place,
That way he used. Alas, one night's disgrace!
   Out went my heart's new fire and left it cold.

Giles then, the soul of honour—there he stands
   Frank as ten years ago when knighted first.
   What honest man should dare (he said) he durst.
Good—but the scene shifts—faugh! what hangman hands
Pin to his breast a parchment? His own bands
   Read it. Poor traitor, spit upon and curst!

Better this present than a past like that;
   Back therefore to my darkening path again!
   No sound, no sight as far as eye could strain.

Will the night send a howlet or a bat?
I asked: when something on the dismal flat
  Came to arrest my thoughts and change their train.

A sudden little river crossed my path
  As unexpected as a serpent comes.
  No sluggish tide congenial to the glooms;
This, as it frothed by, might have been a bath
For the fiend's glowing hoof—to see the wrath
  Of its black eddy bespate with flakes and spumes.

So petty yet so spiteful! All along,
  Low scrubby alders kneeled down over it;
  Drenched willows flung them headlong in a fit
Of mute despair, a suicidal throng:
The river which had done them all the wrong,
  Whate'er that was, rolled by, deterred no whit.

Which, while I forded,—good saints, how I feared
  To set my foot upon a dead man's cheek,
  Each step, or feel the spear I thrust to seek
For hollows, tangled in his hair or beard!
—It may have been a water-rat I speared,
  But, ugh! it sounded like a baby's shriek.

Glad was I when I reached the other bank.
  Now for a better country. Vain presage!
  Who were the strugglers, what war did they wage,
Whose savage trample thus could pad the dank
Soil to a plash? Toads in a poisoned tank,
  Or wild cats in a red-hot iron cage—

The fight must so have seemed in that fell cirque.
  What penned them there, with all the plain to choose?
  No footprint leading to that horrid mews,

None out of it. Mad brewage set to work
Their brains, no doubt, like galley-slaves the Turk
   Pits for his pastime, Christians against Jews.

And more than that—a furlong on—why, there!
   What bad use was that engine for, that wheel,
   Or brake, not wheel—that harrow fit to reel
Men's bodies out like silk? with all the air
Of Tophet's tool, on earth left unaware,
   Or brought to sharpen its rusty teeth of steel.

Then came a bit of stubbed ground, once a wood,
   Next a marsh, it would seem, and now mere earth
   Desperate and done with: (so a fool finds mirth,
Makes a thing and then mars it, till his mood
Changes and off he goes!) within a rood—
   Bog, clay and rubble, sand and stark black dearth.

Now blotches rankling, coloured gay and grim,
   Now patches where some leanness of the soil's
   Broke into moss or substances like boils;
Then came some palsied oak, a cleft in him
Like a distorted mouth that splits its rim
   Gaping at death, and dies while it recoils.

And just as far as ever from the end!
   Naught in the distance but the evening, naught
   To point my footstep further! At the thought,
A great black bird, Apollyon's bosom-friend,
Sailed past, nor beat his wide wing dragon-penned
   That brushed my cap—perchance the guide I sought.

For, looking up, aware I somehow grew,
   'Spite of the dusk, the plain had given place
   All round to mountains—with such name to grace

Mere ugly heights and heaps now stolen in view.
How thus they had surprised me,—solve it, you!
  How to get from them was no clearer case.

Yet half I seemed to recognize some trick
  Of mischief happened to me, God knows when—
  In a bad dream perhaps. Here ended, then,
Progress this way. When, in the very nick
Of giving up, one time more, came a click
  As when a trap shuts—you're inside the den!

Burningly it came on me all at once,
  This was the place! those two hills on the right,
  Crouched like two bulls locked horn in horn in fight;
While to the left, a tall scalped mountain . . . Dunce,
Dotard, a-dozing at the very nonce,
  After a life spent training for the sight!

What in the midst lay but the Tower itself?
  The round squat turret, blind as the fool's heart,
  Built of brown stone, without a counterpart
In the whole world. The tempest's mocking elf
Points to the shipman thus the unseen shelf
  He strikes on, only when the timbers start.

Not see? because of night perhaps?—why, day
  Came back again for that! before it left,
  The dying sunset kindled through a cleft:
The hills, like giants at a hunting, lay,
Chin upon hand, to see the game at bay,—
  "Now stab and end the creature—to the heft!"

Not hear? when noise was everywhere! it tolled
  Increasing like a bell. Names in my ears,
  Of all the lost adventurers my peers,—

How such a one was strong, and such was bold,
And such was fortunate, yet each of old
   Lost, lost! one moment knelled the woe of years.

There they stood, ranged along the hillsides, met
   To view the last of me, a living frame
   For one more picture! in a sheet of flame
I saw them and I knew them all. And yet
Dauntless the slug-horn to my lips I set,
   And blew. *"Childe Roland to the Dark Tower came."*

VI

THE word paradox comes from two Greek words, meaning simply, "beyond belief." As every one ought to know, a paradox is something that read literally is absurd, but if taken in the spirit in which it is uttered, may contain profound truth. Paradox is simply over-emphasis: and is therefore a favorite method of teaching. By the employment of paradox the teacher wishes to stress forcibly some aspect of the truth which otherwise may not be seen at all. Fine print needs a magnifying-glass; and the deep truth hidden in a paradox can not perhaps become clear unless enlarged by powerful emphasis. All teachers know the value of *italics*.

Socrates was very fond of paradox: the works of Ibsen, Nietzsche, Shaw and Chesterton are full of paradoxes: Our Lord's utterances in the New Testament are simply one paradox after another. No wonder His disciples were often in a maze. It requires centuries for the truth in some paradoxes to become manifest.

"This was some time a paradox, but now the time gives it proof."

Browning loved a paradox with all his heart. The original nature of his mind, his fondness for taking the other side, his over-subtlety, all drove him toward the paradox. He would have made a wonderful criminal lawyer. He loves to put some imaginary or historical character on the stand, and permit him to speak freely in his own defence; and he particularly loves to do this, when the person has received universal condemnation. Browning seems to say, "I wonder if the world is entirely right in this judgment: what would this individual say if given an opportunity for apologetic oratory?" Browning is the greatest master of special pleading in all literature. Although he detested Count Guido, he makes him present his case in the best possible light, so that for the moment he arouses our intellectual sympathy.

The Glove story is one of the best-known anecdotes in history; besides its French source, it has been told in German by Schiller, in English by Leigh Hunt, and has received thousands of allusory comments—but always from one point of view. The hooting and laughter that followed the Lady as she left the court, have been echoed in all lands. Browning pondered over this story, and took the woman's part. This may be accounted for by two causes. He is the most chivalrous poet that ever lived, and would naturally defend the Lady. What De Lorge ought to have done when he brought the glove back was to remind the Lady that she had another, and permit him the honor of retrieving that. But Browning saw also in this incident a true paradox— the Lady was right after all! Right in throwing the glove, right in her forecast of the event.

Like a good lawyer, he first proves that the Knight's achievement was slight. In the pit the Lion was not at that moment dangerous, because he was desperately homesick. He was lost in thoughts of his wild home, in imagination driving the flocks up the mountain, and took not the slightest notice of the glove. Then a page had leaped into the pit simply to recover his hat; and he had done that because he could not afford to buy a new one. No one applauded him. Think of the man who had originally caught the lion! He went out alone and trapped a lion, simply that his rude boys might be amused at the spectacle. In our degenerate days, we give our children a Teddy Bear. But in those strenuous times, the father said to his boys, "Come out into the back yard, and see the present I've got for you!" They came eagerly, and found a live lion. That man and his children were a hardy family. How they would have laughed at De Lorge's so-called heroism!

But the real truth of the matter is that De Lorge was a liar. The Lady suspected it all the time, and was saddened to have her judgment confirmed by the result. De Lorge had been boasting of his love, and of his eagerness to prove it. He had begged the Lady to test him—he would gladly die for her. Now it is important that a woman should know before marriage rather than after whether a lover's protestations are genuine or not—in short whether he is sincere and reliable, or whether he is a liar. The reason why men lie to women and not to men is because they know that a lie to a woman can not be avenged, they can not be made to pay any penalty; but when they lie to other men—in business affairs, for example—the penalty is severe.

How could the Lady satisfy her mind? How could she know whether De Lorge was sincere or not? There was no war, there was no tournament, there was no quest. Suddenly one method presented itself. She tossed her glove into the pit. He had to

go—he could never have held up his head otherwise.
But when he returned, he dashed the glove in the
Lady's face, ostensibly to teach her that a brave
man's life should not be risked by a woman's vanity.
This was even a better gallery-play than the recovery
of the glove, and succeeded splendidly. But the
Lady turned sadly away.

> The blow a glove gives is but weak:
> Does the mark yet discolour my cheek?
> But when the heart suffers a blow,
> Will the pain pass so soon, do you know?

What was the pain in her heart? Her wounded
vanity, her anguish at the Court's ostracism? Not
in the least. It was her pain at finding her opinion
of De Lorge justified. He was then, just as she
thought, a liar; he never meant to be taken at his
word. All his protestations of love and service were
mere phrases. His anger at the first test of his
boasting proves this. The pain in her heart is the
pain we all feel at reading of some cowardly or dis-
loyal act; one more man unfaithful, one more man
selfish, one more who lowers the level of human
nature.

The paradox teaches us the very simple lesson that
if we boast of our prowess, we must not be angry
when some one insists that we prove it.

THE GLOVE

1845

(PETER RONSARD *loquitur*)

"Heigho!" yawned one day King Francis,
"Distance all value enhances!
"When a man's busy, why, leisure
"Strikes him as wonderful pleasure:
"'Faith, and at leisure once is he?
"Straightway he wants to be busy.
"Here we've got peace; and aghast I'm
"Caught thinking war the true pastime.
"Is there a reason in metre?
"Give us your speech, master Peter!"
I who, if mortal dare say so,
Ne'er am at loss with my Naso,
"Sire," I replied, "joys prove cloudlets:
"Men are the merest Ixions"—
Here the King whistled aloud, "Let's
"—Heigho—go look at our lions!"
Such are the sorrowful chances
If you talk fine to King Francis.

And so, to the courtyard proceeding,
Our company, Francis was leading,
Increased by new followers tenfold
Before he arrived at the penfold;
Lords, ladies, like clouds which bedizen
At sunset the western horizon.
And Sir De Lorge pressed 'mid the foremost
With the dame he professed to adore most.
Oh, what a face! One by fits eyed
Her, and the horrible pitside;
For the penfold surrounded a hollow
Which led where the eye scarce dared follow,

And shelved to the chamber secluded
Where Bluebeard, the great lion, brooded.
The King hailed his keeper, an Arab
As glossy and black as a scarab,
And bade him make sport and at once stir
Up and out of his den the old monster.
They opened a hole in the wire-work
Across it, and dropped there a firework,
And fled: one's heart's beating redoubled;
A pause, while the pit's mouth was troubled,
The blackness and silence so utter,
By the firework's slow sparkling and sputter;
Then earth in a sudden contortion
Gave out to our gaze her abortion.
Such a brute! Were I friend Clement Marot
(Whose experience of nature's but narrow,
And whose faculties move in no small mist
When he versifies David the Psalmist)
I should study that brute to describe you
Illum Juda Leonem de Tribu.
One's whole blood grew curdling and creepy
To see the black mane, vast and heapy,
The tail in the air stiff and straining,
The wide eyes, nor waxing nor waning,
As over the barrier which bounded
His platform, and us who surrounded
The barrier, they reached and they rested
On space that might stand him in best stead:
For who knew, he thought, what the amazement,
The eruption of clatter and blaze meant,
And if, in this minute of wonder,
No outlet, 'mid lightning and thunder,
Lay broad, and, his shackles all shivered,
The lion at last was delivered?
Ay, that was the open sky o'erhead!

And you saw by the flash on his forehead,
By the hope in those eyes wide and steady,
He was leagues in the desert already,
Driving the flocks up the mountain,
Or catlike couched hard by the fountain
To waylay the date-gathering negress:
So guarded he entrance or egress.
"How he stands!" quoth the King: "we may well
     swear,
("No novice, we've won our spurs elsewhere
"And so can afford the confession,)
"We exercise wholesome discretion
"In keeping aloof from his threshold;
"Once hold you, those jaws want no fresh hold,
"Their first would too pleasantly purloin
"The visitor's brisket or surloin:
"But who's he would prove so fool-hardy?
"Not the best man of Marignan, pardie!"

The sentence no sooner was uttered,
Than over the rails a glove fluttered,
Fell close to the lion, and rested:
The dame 'twas, who flung it and jested
With life so, De Lorge had been wooing
For months past; he sat there pursuing
His suit, weighing out with nonchalance
Fine speeches like gold from a balance.

Sound the trumpet, no true knight's a tarrier!
De Lorge made one leap at the barrier,
Walked straight to the glove,—while the lion
Ne'er moved, kept his far-reaching eye on
The palm-tree-edged desert-spring's sapphire,
And the musky oiled skin of the Kaffir,—
Picked it up, and as calmly retreated,

Leaped back where the lady was seated,
And full in the face of its owner
Flung the glove.

        "Your heart's queen, you dethrone her?
"So should I!"—cried the King—" 'twas mere vanity,
"Not love, set that task to humanity!"
Lords and ladies alike turned with loathing
From such a proved wolf in sheep's clothing.

Not so, I; for I caught an expression
In her brow's undisturbed self-possession
Amid the Court's scoffing and merriment,—
As if from no pleasing experiment
She rose, yet of pain not much heedful
So long as the process was needful,—
As if she had tried in a crucible,
To what "speeches like gold" were reducible,
And, finding the finest prove copper,
Felt the smoke in her face was but proper;
To know what she had *not* to trust to,
Was worth all the ashes and dust too.
She went out 'mid hooting and laughter;
Clement Marot stayed; I followed after,
And asked, as a grace, what it all meant?
If she wished not the rash deed's recalment?
"For I"—so I spoke—"am a poet:
"Human nature,—behoves that I know it!"

She told me, "Too long had I heard
"Of the deed proved alone by the word:
"For my love—what De Lorge would not dare!
"With my scorn—what De Lorge could compare!
"And the endless descriptions of death
"He would brave when my lip formed a breath,

"I must reckon as braved, or, of course,
"Doubt his word—and moreover, perforce,
"For such gifts as no lady could spurn,
"Must offer my love in return.
"When I looked on your lion, it brought
"All the dangers at once to my thought,
"Encountered by all sorts of men,
"Before he was lodged in his den,—
"From the poor slave whose club or bare hands
"Dug the trap, set the snare on the sands,
"With no King and no Court to applaud,
"By no shame, should he shrink, overawed,
"Yet to capture the creature made shift,
"That his rude boys might laugh at the gift,
"—To the page who last leaped o'er the fence
"Of the pit, on no greater pretence
"Than to get back the bonnet he dropped,
"Lest his pay for a week should be stopped.
"So, wiser I judged it to make
"One trial what 'death for my sake'
"Really meant, while the power was yet mine,
"Than to wait until time should define
"Such a phrase not so simply as I,
"Who took it to mean just 'to die.'
"The blow a glove gives is but weak:
"Does the mark yet discolour my cheek?
"But when the heart suffers a blow,
"Will the pain pass so soon, do you know?"

I looked, as away she was sweeping,
And saw a youth eagerly keeping
As close as he dared to the doorway.
No doubt that a noble should more weigh
His life than befits a plebeian;
And yet, had our brute been Nemean—

(I judge by a certain calm fervour
The youth stepped with, forward to serve her)
—He'd have scarce thought you did him the worst turn
If you whispered "Friend, what you'd get, first earn!"
And when, shortly after, she carried
Her shame from the Court, and they married,
To that marriage some happiness, maugre
The voice of the Court, I dared augur.

For De Lorge, he made women with men vie,
Those in wonder and praise, these in envy;
And in short stood so plain a head taller
That he wooed and won . . . how do you call her?
The beauty, that rose in the sequel
To the King's love, who loved her a week well.
And 'twas noticed he never would honour
De Lorge (who looked daggers upon her)
With the easy commission of stretching
His legs in the service, and fetching
His wife, from her chamber, those straying
Sad gloves she was always mislaying,
While the King took the closet to chat in,—
But of course this adventure came pat in.
And never the King told the story,
How bringing a glove brought such glory,
But the wife smiled—"His nerves are grown firmer:
"Mine he brings now and utters no murmur."

Venienti occurrite morbo!
With which moral I drop my theorbo.

Browning wrote two poems on pedantry; the
former, in *Garden Fancies,* takes the conventional
view. How can a man with any blood in him pore
over miserable books, when life is so sweet? The

other, *A Grammarian's Funeral,* is the apotheosis of the scholar. The paradox here is that Browning has made a hero out of what seems at first blush impossible material. It is easy to make a hero out of a noble character; it is equally easy to make a hero out of a thorough scoundrel, a train-robber, or a murderer. Milton made a splendid hero out of the Devil. But a hero out of a nincompoop? A hero out of a dull, sexless pedant?

But this is exactly what Browning has done, nay, he has made this grammarian exactly the same kind of hero as a dashing cavalry officer leading a forlorn hope.

Observe that Browning has purposely made his task as difficult as possible. Had the scholar been a great discoverer in science, a great master in philosophical thought, a great interpreter in literature— then we might all take off our hats: but this hero was a grammarian. He spent his life not on Greek drama or Greek philosophy, but on Greek Grammar. He is dead: his pupils carry his body up the mountain, as the native disciples of Stevenson carried their beloved Tusitala to the summit of the island peak. These students are not weeping; they sing and shout as they march, for they are carrying their idol on their shoulders. His life and his death were

magnificent, an inspiration to all humanity. Hurrah!
Hurrah!

The swinging movement of the young men is in
exact accord with the splendid advance of the
thought. They tell us the history of their Teacher
from his youth to his last breath:

> This is our master, famous calm and dead,
> Borne on our shoulders.

It is a common error to suppose that missionaries,
nuns, and scholars follow their chosen callings because they are unfit for anything else. The judgment of the wise world is not always correct. It assumes that these strange folk never hear the call of
the blood. When John C. Calhoun was a student at
Yale, his comrades, returning at midnight from a
wild time, found him at his books. "Why don't you
come out, John, and be a man? You'll never be
young again." "I regard my work as more important," said John quietly. Milton's bitter cry

> Were it not better done, as others use,
> To sport with Amaryllis in the shade,
> Or with the tangles of Neæra's hair?

shows that it was not the absence of temptation, but
a tremendously powerful will, that kept him at his
desk. When a spineless milksop becomes a mission-

ary, when a gawk sticks to his books, when an ugly woman becomes a nun, the world makes no objection; but when a socially prominent man goes in for missions or scholarship, when a lovely girl takes the veil, the wise world says, "Ah, what a pity!"

Browning's Grammarian did not take up scholarship as a last resort. He could have done anything he liked.

> He was a man born with thy face and throat,
> Lyric Apollo!

He might have been an athlete, a social leader, a man of pleasure. He chose Greek Grammar. In the pursuit of this prize, he squandered his time and youth and health as recklessly as men squander these treasures on wine and women. When a young man throws away his youth and health in gambling, drink, and debauchery, the world expresses no surprise; he is known as a "splendid fellow," and is often much admired. But when a man spends all his gifts in scholarship, scientific discovery, or altruistic aims, he is regarded as an eccentric, lacking both blood and judgment.

I say that Browning has given his Grammarian not only courage and heroism, but the reckless, dashing, magnificent bravery of a cavalry leader. In the march for learning, this man lost his youth and health, and acquired painful diseases. Finally he comes to the end. When an officer in battle falls, and his friends bend over him to catch his last breath, he does not say, "I commend my soul to God," or "Give my love to my wife,"—he says, *"Did we win?"* and we applaud this passion in the last agony. So our Grammarian, full of diseases, paralysed from the waist down, the death rattle in his throat—what does he say to the faithful watchers? What are his last words? *He dictates Greek Grammar.*

The solitary student may be a paragon of courage, headstrong, reckless, tenacious as a bulldog, with a resolution entirely beyond the range of the children of this world.

SIBRANDUS SCHAFNABURGENSIS

1844

Plague take all your pedants, say I!
    He who wrote what I hold in my hand,
Centuries back was so good as to die,
    Leaving this rubbish to cumber the land;
This, that was a book in its time,
    Printed on paper and bound in leather,
Last month in the white of a matin-prime,
    Just when the birds sang all together.

Into the garden I brought it to read,
    And under the arbute and laurustine

Read it, so help me grace in my need,
   From title-page to closing line.
Chapter on chapter did I count,
   As a curious traveller counts Stonehenge;
Added up the mortal amount;
   And then proceeded to my revenge.

Yonder's a plum-tree with a crevice
   An owl would build in, were he but sage;
For a lap of moss, like a fine pont-levis
   In a castle of the Middle Age,
Joins to a lip of gum, pure amber;
   When he'd be private, there might he spend
Hours alone in his lady's chamber:
   Into this crevice I dropped our friend.

Splash, went he, as under he ducked,
   —At the bottom, I knew, rain-drippings stagnate;
Next, a handful of blossoms I plucked
   To bury him with, my bookshelf's magnate;
Then I went in-doors, brought out a loaf,
   Half a cheese, and a bottle of Chablis;
Lay on the grass and forgot the oaf
   Over a jolly chapter of Rabelais.

Now, this morning, betwixt the moss
   And gum that locked our friend in limbo,
A spider had spun his web across,
   And sat in the midst with arms akimbo:
So, I took pity, for learning's sake,
   And, *de profundis, accentibus lætis,*
Cantate! quoth I, as I got a rake;
   And up I fished his delectable treatise.

Here you have it, dry in the sun,
   With all the binding all of a blister,

And great blue spots where the ink has run,
   And reddish streaks that wink and glister
O'er the page so beautifully yellow:
   Oh, well have the droppings played their tricks!
Did he guess how toadstools grow, this fellow?
   Here's one stuck in his chapter six!

How did he like it when the live creatures
   Tickled and toused and browsed him all over,
And worm, slug, eft, with serious features,
   Came in, each one, for his right of trover?
—When the water-beetle with great blind deaf face
   Made of her eggs the stately deposit,
And the newt borrowed just so much of the preface
   As tiled in the top of his black wife's closet?

All that life and fun and romping,
   All that frisking and twisting and coupling,
While slowly our poor friend's leaves were swamping
   And clasps were cracking and covers suppling!
As if you had carried sour John Knox
   To the play-house at Paris, Vienna or Munich,
Fastened him into a front-row box,
   And danced off the ballet with trousers and tunic.

Come, old martyr! What, torment enough is it?
   Back to my room shall you take your sweet self.
Good-bye, mother-beetle; husband-eft, *sufficit!*
   See the snug niche I have made on my shelf!
A's book shall prop you up, B's shall cover you,
   Here's C to be grave with, or D to be gay,
And with E on each side, and F right over you,
   Dry-rot at ease till the Judgment-day!

A GRAMMARIAN'S FUNERAL

SHORTLY AFTER THE REVIVAL OF LEARNING IN EUROPE

1855

Let us begin and carry up this corpse,
    Singing together.
Leave we the common crofts, the vulgar thorpes
    Each in its tether
Sleeping safe on the bosom of the plain,
    Cared-for till cock-crow:
Look out if yonder be not day again
    Rimming the rock-row!
That's the appropriate country; there, man's thought,
    Rarer, intenser,
Self-gathered for an outbreak, as it ought,
    Chafes in the censer.
Leave we the unlettered plain its herd and crop;
    Seek we sepulture
On a tall mountain, citied to the top,
    Crowded with culture!
All the peaks soar, but one the rest excels;
    Clouds overcome it;
No! yonder sparkle is the citadel's
    Circling its summit.
Thither our path lies; wind we up the heights:
    Wait ye the warning?
Our low life was the level's and the night's;
    He's for the morning.
Step to a tune, square chests, erect each head,
    'Ware the beholders!
This is our master, famous calm and dead,
    Borne on our shoulders.

Sleep, crop and herd! sleep, darkling thorpe and croft,
    Safe from the weather!

He, whom we convoy to his grave aloft,
       Singing together,
He was a man born with thy face and throat,
       Lyric Apollo!
Long he lived nameless: how should spring take note
       Winter would follow?
Till lo, the little touch, and youth was gone!
       Cramped and diminished,
Moaned he, "New measures, other feet anon!
       "My dance is finished?"
No, that's the world's way: (keep the mountain-side,
       Make for the city!)
He knew the signal, and stepped on with pride
       Over men's pity;
Left play for work, and grappled with the world
       Bent on escaping:
"What's in the scroll," quoth he, "thou keepest furled?
       "Show me their shaping,
"Theirs who most studied man, the bard and sage,—
       "Give!"—So, he gowned him,
Straight got by heart that book to its last page:
       Learned, we found him.
Yea, but we found him bald too, eyes like lead,
       Accents uncertain:
"Time to taste life," another would have said,
       "Up with the curtain!"

This man said rather, "Actual life comes next?
       "Patience a moment!
"Grant I have mastered learning's crabbed text,
       "Still there's the comment.
"Let me know all! Prate not of most or least,
       "Painful or easy!
"Even to the crumbs I'd fain eat up the feast,
       "Ay, nor feel queasy."

Oh, such a life as he resolved to live,
      When he had learned it,
When he had gathered all books had to give!
      Sooner, he spurned it.
Image the whole, then execute the parts—
      Fancy the fabric
Quite, ere you build, ere steel strike fire from quartz,
      Ere mortar dab brick!

(Here's the town-gate reached: there's the market-place
      Gaping before us.)
Yea, this in him was the peculiar grace
      (Hearten our chorus!)
That before living he'd learn how to live—
      No end to learning:
Earn the means first—God surely will contrive
      Use for our earning.
Others mistrust and say, "But time escapes:
      "Live now or never!"
He said, "What's time? Leave Now for dogs and apes!
      "Man has Forever."
Back to his book then: deeper drooped his head:
      Calculus racked him:
Leaden before, his eyes grew dross of lead:
      Tussis attacked him.
"Now, master, take a little rest!"—not he!
      (Caution redoubled,
Step two abreast, the way winds narrowly!)
      Not a whit troubled
Back to his studies, fresher than at first,
      Fierce as a dragon
He (soul-hydroptic with a sacred thirst)
      Sucked at the flagon.
Oh, if we draw a circle premature,
      Heedless of far gain,

Greedy for quick returns of profit, sure
        Bad is our bargain!
Was it not great? did not he throw on God,
        (He loves the burthen)—
God's task to make the heavenly period
        Perfect the earthen?
Did not he magnify the mind, show clear
        Just what it all meant?
He would not discount life, as fools do here,
        Paid by instalment.
He ventured neck or nothing—heaven's success
        Found, or earth's failure:
"Wilt thou trust death or not?" He answered "Yes:
        "Hence with life's pale lure!"
That low man seeks a little thing to do,
        Sees it and does it:
This high man, with a great thing to pursue,
        Dies ere he knows it.
That low man goes on adding one to one,
        His hundred's soon hit:
This high man, aiming at a million,
        Misses an unit.
That, has the world here—should he need the next,
        Let the world mind him!
This, throws himself on God, and unperplexed
        Seeking shall find him.
So, with the throttling hands of death at strife,
        Ground he at grammar;
Still, thro' the rattle, parts of speech were rife:
        While he could stammer
He settled *Hoti's* business—let it be!—
        Properly based *Oun*—
Gave us the doctrine of the enclitic *De*,
        Dead from the waist down.

Well, here's the platform, here's the proper place:
    Hail to your purlieus,
All ye highfliers of the feathered race,
    Swallows and curlews!
Here's the top-peak; the multitude below
    Live, for they can, there:
This man decided not to Live but Know—
    Bury this man there?
Here—here's his place, where meteors shoot, clouds
    form,
    Lightnings are loosened,
Stars come and go! Let joy break with the storm,
    Peace let the dew send!
Lofty designs must close in like effects:
    Loftily lying,
Leave him—still loftier than the world suspects,
    Living and dying.

In the amusing poem, *Up at a Villa—Down in the City*, Browning compares the beauty of city and country life from an unusual point of view. It is generally assumed that the country is more poetical than the city; but it would be difficult to prove this, if we were put to the test. Natural scenery is now much admired, and mountains are in the height of fashion; every one is forced to express raptures, whether one feels them or not. But this has not always been the case. When Addison travelled to Italy, he regarded the Alps as disgusting; they were a disagreeable and dangerous barrier, that must be crossed before he could reach the object of his jour-

ney. He wrote home from Italy that he was delighted at the sight of a plain—a remark that would
damn a modern pilgrim. The first man in English
literature to bring out the real beauty of mountains
was Thomas Gray.

Very few people have a sincere and genuine love
of the country—as is proved by the way they flock
to the cities. We love the country for a change, for
a rest, for its novelty: how many of us would be
willing to live there the year around? We know
that Wordsworth loved the country, for he chose to
live among the lonely lakes when he could have lived
in London. But most intelligent persons live in
towns, and take to the country for change and recreation.

The speaker in Browning's poem is an absolutely
honest Philistine, who does not know that every
word he says spells artistic damnation. He is disgusted with the situation of his house:

> . . . . stuck like the horn of a bull
> Just on a mountain-edge as bare as the creature's skull.

In other words the site is so magnificent that to-day
expensive hotels are built there, and people come
from all over the world to enjoy the view. In fact
it is just this situation which Browning admires in
the poem *De Gustibus*.

What I love best in all the world
Is a castle, precipice-encurled,
In a gash of the wind-grieved Apennine.

But our man does not know what he *ought* to say;
he says simply what he really thinks.   The views of
a sincere Philistine on natural scenery, works of art,
pieces of music, are interesting because they are sincere.   The conventional admiration may or may not
be genuine.

This man says the city is much cooler in summer
than the country : that spring visits the city earlier :
that what we call the monotonous row of houses in
a city street is far more beautiful than the irregu-
larity of the country.   It appeals to his sense of
beauty.

Houses in four straight lines, not a single front awry.

But his real rapture over the city is because city
life is interesting.   There is something going on
every moment of the blessed day.   It is a perpetual theatre, admission free.   This is undoubtedly
the real reason why the poor prefer crowded, squalid
city tenements to the space, fresh air and hygienic
advantages of the country.   Many well-meaning folk
wonder why men with their families remain in city
slums, when they could easily secure work on farms,
where there would be abundance of fresh air, whole-

some food, and cool nights for sleep. Our Italian
gives the correct answer. People can not stand dullness and loneliness: they crave excitement, and this
is supplied day and night by the city street. Indeed
in some cases, where by the Fresh Air Fund, children are taken for a vacation to the country, they become homesick for the slums.

UP AT A VILLA—DOWN IN THE CITY

(AS DISTINGUISHED BY AN ITALIAN PERSON OF QUALITY)

1855

I

Had I but plenty of money, money enough and to spare,
The house for me, no doubt, were a house in the city-square;
Ah, such a life, such a life, as one leads at the window there!

II

Something to see, by Bacchus, something to hear, at least!
There, the whole day long, one's life is a perfect feast;
While up at a villa one lives, I maintain it, no more than a
      beast.

III

Well now, look at our villa! stuck like the horn of a bull
Just on a mountain-edge as bare as the creature's skull,
Save a mere shag of a bush with hardly a leaf to pull!
—I scratch my own, sometimes, to see if the hair's turned
      wool.

IV

But the city, oh the city—the square with the houses! Why?
They are stone-faced, white as a curd, there's something to
      take the eye!

Houses in four straight lines, not a single front awry;
You watch who crosses and gossips, who saunters, who hur-
    ries by;
Green blinds, as a matter of course, to draw when the sun
    gets high;
And the shops with fanciful signs which are painted properly.

V

What of a villa? Though winter be over in March by rights,
'Tis May perhaps ere the snow shall have withered well off
    the heights:
You've the brown ploughed land before, where the oxen steam
    and wheeze,
And the hills over-smoked behind by the faint grey olive-trees.

VI

Is it better in May, I ask you? You've summer all at once;
In a day he leaps complete with a few strong April suns.
'Mid the sharp short emerald wheat, scarce risen three fingers
    well,
The wild tulip, at end of its tube, blows out its great red bell
Like a thin clear bubble of blood, for the children to pick and
    sell.

VII

Is it ever hot in the square? There's a fountain to spout and
    splash!
In the shade it sings and springs; in the shine such foam-
    bows flash
On the horses with curling fish-tails, that prance and paddle
    and pash
Round the lady atop in her conch—fifty gazers do not abash,
Though all that she wears is some weeds round her waist in
    a sort of sash.

VIII

All the year long at the villa, nothing to see though you linger,
Except yon cypress that points like death's lean lifted fore-
       finger.
Some think fireflies pretty, when they mix i' the corn and
       mingle,
Or thrid the stinking hemp till the stalks of it seem a-tingle.
Late August or early September, the stunning cicala is shrill,
And the bees keep their tiresome whine round the resinous
       firs on the hill.
Enough of the seasons,—I spare you the months of the fever
       and chill.

IX

Ere you open your eyes in the city, the blessed church-bells
       begin:
No sooner the bells leave off than the diligence rattles in:
You get the pick of the news, and it costs you never a pin.
By-and-by there's the travelling doctor gives pills, lets blood,
       draws teeth;
Or the Pulcinello-trumpet breaks up the market beneath.
At the post-office such a scene-picture—the new play, piping
       hot!
And a notice how, only this morning, three liberal thieves
       were shot.
Above it, behold the Archbishop's most fatherly of rebukes,
And beneath, with his crown and his lion, some little new law
       of the Duke's!
Or a sonnet with flowery marge, to the Reverend Don So-and-
       so
Who is Dante, Boccaccio, Petrarca, Saint Jerome and Cicero,
"And moreover," (the sonnet goes rhyming,) "the skirts of
       Saint Paul has reached,
"Having preached us those six Lent-lectures more unctuous
       than ever he preached."

Noon strikes,—here sweeps the procession! our Lady borne
    smiling and smart
With a pink gauze gown all spangles, and seven swords stuck
    in her heart!
Bang-whang-whang goes the drum, *tootle-te-tootle* the fife;
No keeping one's haunches still: it's the greatest pleasure in
    life.

X

But bless you, it's dear—it's dear! fowls, wine, at double the
    rate.
They have clapped a new tax upon salt, and what oil pays
    passing the gate
It's a horror to think of. And so, the villa for me, not the
    city!
Beggars can scarcely be choosers: but still—ah, the pity, the
    pity!
Look, two and two go the priests, then the monks with cowls
    and sandals,
And the penitents dressed in white shirts, a-holding the yellow
    candles;
One, he carries a flag up straight, and another a cross with
    handles,
And the Duke's guard brings up the rear, for the better pre-
    vention of scandals:
Bang-whang-whang goes the drum, *tootle-te-tootle* the fife.
Oh, a day in the city-square, there is no such pleasure in life!

No poem of Browning's has given more trouble to
his whole-souled admirers than *The Statue and the
Bust:* and yet, if this is taken as a paradox, its meaning is abundantly clear.

The square spoken of in the poem is the Piazza
Annunziata in Florence: in the midst of the square

stands the equestrian statue of the Duke: and if one
follows the direction of the bronze eyes of the man,
it will appear that they rest steadfastly on the right
hand window in the upper storey of the palace. This
is the farthest window facing the East. There is no
bust there; but it is in this window that the lady sat
and regarded the daily passage of the Duke.

The reason why this poem has troubled the minds
of many good people is because it seems (on a very
superficial view) to sympathise with unlawful love;
even in certain circumstances to recommend the pursuit of it to fruition. Let us see what the facts are.
Before the Duke saw the bride, he was, as Browning
says, empty and fine like a swordless sheath. This is
a good description of many young men. They are
like an empty sheath. The sheath may be beautiful,
it may be exquisitely and appropriately enchased;
but a sheath is no good without a sword. So, many
young men are attractive and accomplished, their
minds are cultivated by books and travel, but they
have no driving purpose in life, no energy directed
to one aim, no end; and therefore all their attractive-
ness is without positive value. They are empty like
a handsome sheath minus the sword.

The moment the Duke saw the lady a great purpose filled his life: he became temporarily a resolute,

ambitious man, with capacity for usefulness. No
moral scruple kept the lovers apart; and they de-
termined to fly. This purpose was frustrated by pro-
crastination, trivial hindrances, irresolution, till it
was forever too late. Now the statue and the bust
gaze at each other in eternal ironical mockery, for
these lovers in life might as well have been made of
bronze and stone; they never really lived.

Contrary to his usual custom—it is only very seldom as in this poem and in *Bishop Blougram's
Apology,* and in both cases because he knew he
would otherwise be misunderstood—Browning
added a personal postscript. Where are these lovers
now? How do they spend their time in the spiritual
world? I do not know where they are, says Browning, but I know very well where they are *not:* they are
not with God. No, replies the reader, because they
wanted to commit adultery. Ah, says Browning,
they are not exiled from God because they wanted to
commit adultery: they are exiled because they did
not actually do it. This is the paradox.

Browning takes a crime to test character; for a
crime can test character as well as a virtue. We
must draw a clear distinction here between society
and the individual. It is a good thing for society
that people are restrained from crime by what are

you say? Is virtue the greatest thing in *your* life?
Do you strive to the uttermost toward that goal? Do
you really prefer virtue to your own ease, comfort
and happiness?

I find Browning's poem both clear and morally
stimulating. My one objection would be that he puts
rather too much value on mere energy. I do not believe that the greatest thing in life is striving, struggle, and force: there are deep, quiet souls who ac-
complish much in this world without being especially
strenuous. But in the sphere of virtue Browning
was essentially a fighting man.

THE STATUE AND THE BUST

1855

There's a palace in Florence, the world knows well,
And a statue watches it from the square,
And this story of both do our townsmen tell.

Ages ago, a lady there,
At the farthest window facing the East
Asked, "Who rides by with the royal air?"

The bridesmaids' prattle around her ceased;
She leaned forth, one on either hand;
They saw how the blush of the bride increased—

They felt by its beats her heart expand—
As one at each ear and both in a breath
Whispered, "The Great-Duke Ferdinand."

The selfsame instant, underneath,
The Duke rode past in his idle way,
Empty and fine like a swordless sheath.

Gay he rode, with a friend as gay,
Till he threw his head back—"Who is she?"
—"A bride the Riccardi brings home to-day."

Hair in heaps lay heavily
Over a pale brow spirit-pure—
Carved like the heart of the coal-black tree,

Crisped like a war-steed's encolure—
And vainly sought to dissemble her eyes
Of the blackest black our eyes endure,

And lo, a blade for a knight's emprise
Filled the fine empty sheath of a man,—
The Duke grew straightway brave and wise.

He looked at her, as a lover can;
She looked at him, as one who awakes:
The past was a sleep, and her life began.

Now, love so ordered for both their sakes,
A feast was held that selfsame night
In the pile which the mighty shadow makes.

(For Via Larga is three-parts light,
But the palace overshadows one,
Because of a crime, which may God requite!

To Florence and God the wrong was done,
Through the first republic's murder there
By Cosimo and his cursed son.)

The Duke (with the statue's face in the square)
Turned in the midst of his multitude
At the bright approach of the bridal pair.

Face to face the lovers stood
A single minute and no more,
While the bridegroom bent as a man subdued—

Bowed till his bonnet brushed the floor—
For the Duke on the lady a kiss conferred,
As the courtly custom was of yore.

In a minute can lovers exchange a word?
If a word did pass, which I do not think,
Only one out of a thousand heard.

That was the bridegroom. At day's brink
He and his bride were alone at last
In a bed chamber by a taper's blink.

Calmly he said that her lot was cast,
That the door she had passed was shut on her
Till the final catafalk repassed.

The world meanwhile, its noise and stir,
Through a certain window facing the East
She could watch like a convent's chronicler.

Since passing the door might lead to a feast,
And a feast might lead to so much beside,
He, of many evils, chose the least.

"Freely I choose too," said the bride—
"Your window and its world suffice,"
Replied the tongue, while the heart replied—

"If I spend the night with that devil twice,
May his window serve as my loop of hell
Whence a damned soul looks on paradise!

"I fly to the Duke who loves me well,
Sit by his side and laugh at sorrow
Ere I count another ave-bell.

" 'Tis only the coat of a page to borrow,
And tie my hair in a horse-boy's trim.
And I save my soul—but not to-morrow"—

(She checked herself and her eye grew dim)
"My father tarries to bless my state:
I must keep it one day more for him.

"Is one day more so long to wait?
Moreover the Duke rides past, I know;
We shall see each other, sure as fate."

She turned on her side and slept. Just so!
So we resolve on a thing and sleep:
So did the lady, ages ago.

That night the Duke said, "Dear or cheap
As the cost of this cup of bliss may prove
To body or soul, I will drain it deep."

And on the morrow, bold with love,
He beckoned the bridegroom (close on call,
As his duty bade, by the Duke's alcove)

And smiled " 'Twas a very funeral,
Your lady will think, this feast of ours,—
A shame to efface, whate'er befall!

"What if we break from the Arno bowers,
And try if Petraja, cool and green,
Cure last night's fault with this morning's flowers?"

The bridegroom, not a thought to be seen
On his steady brow and quiet mouth,
Said, "Too much favor for me so mean!

"But, alas! my lady leaves the South;
Each wind that comes from the Apennine
Is a menace to her tender youth:

"Nor a way exists, the wise opine,
If she quits her palace twice this year,
To avert the flower of life's decline."

Quoth the Duke, "A sage and a kindly fear.
Moreover Petraja is cold this spring:
Be our feast to-night as usual here!"

And then to himself—"Which night shall bring
Thy bride to her lover's embraces, fool—
Or I am the fool, and thou art the king!

"Yet my passion must wait a night, nor cool—
For to-night the Envoy arrives from France
Whose heart I unlock with thyself, my tool.

"I need thee still and might miss perchance
To-day is not wholly lost, beside,
With its hope of my lady's countenance:

"For I ride—what should I do but ride?
And passing her palace, if I list,
May glance at its window—well betide!"

So said, so done: nor the lady missed
One ray that broke from the ardent brow,
Nor a curl of the lips where the spirit kissed.

Be sure that each renewed the vow,
No morrow's sun should arise and set
And leave them then as it left them now.

But next day passed, and next day yet,
With still fresh cause to wait one day more
Ere each leaped over the parapet.

And still, as love's brief morning wore,
With a gentle start, half smile, half sigh,
They found love not as it seemed before.

They thought it would work infallibly,
But not in despite of heaven and earth:
The rose would blow when the storm passed by.

Meantime they could profit in winter's dearth
By store of fruits that supplant the rose:
The world and its ways have a certain worth:

And to press a point while these oppose
Were simple policy; better wait:
We lose no friends and we gain no foes.

Meantime, worse fates than a lover's fate,
Who daily may ride and pass and look
Where his lady watches behind the grate!

And she—she watched the square like a book
Holding one picture and only one,
Which daily to find she undertook:

When the picture was reached the book was done,
And she turned from the picture at night to scheme
Of tearing it out for herself next sun.

So weeks grew months, years; gleam by gleam
The glory dropped from their youth and love,
And both perceived they had dreamed a dream;

Which hovered as dreams do, still above:
But who can take a dream for a truth?
Oh, hide our eyes from the next remove!

One day as the lady saw her youth
Depart, and the silver thread that streaked
Her hair, and, worn by the serpent's tooth,

The brow so puckered, the chin so peaked,
And wondered who the woman was,
Hollow-eyed and haggard-cheeked,

Fronting her silent in the glass—
"Summon here," she suddenly said,
"Before the rest of my old self pass,

"Him, the Carver, a hand to aid,
Who fashions the clay no love will change,
And fixes a beauty never to fade.

"Let Robbia's craft so apt and strange
Arrest the remains of young and fair,
And rivet them while the seasons range.

"Make me a face on the window there,
Waiting as ever, mute the while,
My love to pass below in the square!

"And let me think that it may beguile
Dreary days which the dead must spend
Down in their darkness under the aisle,

"To say, 'What matters it at the end?
I did no more while my heart was warm
Than does that image, my pale-faced friend.'

"Where is the use of the lip's red charm,
The heaven of hair, the pride of the brow,
And the blood that blues the inside arm—

"Unless we turn, as the soul knows how,
The earthly gift to an end divine?
A lady of clay is as good, I trow."

But long ere Robbia's cornice, fine,
With flowers and fruits which leaves enlace,
Was set where now is the empty shrine—

(And, leaning out of a bright blue space,
As a ghost might lean from a chink of sky,
The passionate pale lady's face—

Eying ever, with earnest eye
And quick-turned neck at its breathless stretch,
Some one who ever is passing by—)

The Duke had sighed like the simplest wretch
In Florence, "Youth—my dream escapes!
Will its record stay?" And he bade them fetch

Some subtle moulder of brazen shapes—
"Can the soul, the will, die out of a man
Ere his body find the grave that gapes?

"John of Douay shall effect my plan,
Set me on horseback here aloft,
Alive, as the crafty sculptor can,

"In the very square I have crossed so oft:
That men may admire, when future suns
Shall touch the eyes to a purpose soft,

"While the mouth and the brow stay brave in bronze—
Admire and say, 'When he was alive
How he would take his pleasure once!'

"And it shall go hard but I contrive
To listen the while, and laugh in my tomb
At idleness which aspires to strive."

———————

So! While these wait the trump of doom,
How do their spirits pass, I wonder,
Nights and days in the narrow room?

Still, I suppose, they sit and ponder
What a gift life was, ages ago,
Six steps out of the chapel yonder.

Only they see not God, I know,
Nor all that chivalry of his,
The soldier-saints who, row on row,

Burn upward each to his point of bliss—
Since, the end of life being manifest,
He had burned his way through the world to this.

I hear you reproach, "But delay was best,
For their end was a crime."—Oh, a crime will do
As well, I reply, to serve for a test,

As a virtue golden through and through,
Sufficient to vindicate itself
And prove its worth at a moment's view!

Must a game be played for the sake of pelf?
Where a button goes, 'twere an epigram
To offer the stamp of the very Guelph.

The true has no value beyond the sham:
As well the counter as coin, I submit,
When your table's a hat, and your prize, a dram.

Stake your counter as boldly every whit,
Venture as warily, use the same skill,
Do your best, whether winning or losing it,

If you choose to play!—is my principle.
Let a man contend to the uttermost
For his life's set prize, be it what it will!

The counter our lovers staked was lost
As surely as if it were lawful coin:
And the sin I impute to each frustrate ghost

Is—the unlit lamp and the ungirt loin,
Though the end in sight was a vice, I say.
You of the virtue (we issue join)
How strive you? *De te, fabula!*

The two volumes of *Dramatic Idyls* are full of paradoxes, for Browning became fonder and fonder of the paradox as he descended into the vale of years. The Russian poem *Ivan Ivanovitch* justly condemns mothers who prefer their own safety to that of their children. When a stranger gives up his life for another, as happens frequently in crises of fire and shipwreck, we applaud: but when a mother sacrifices her life for that of her child, she does the natural and expected thing. The woman in this poem was a monster of wickedness and did not deserve to live. She started with three children and arrived with none. Now there are some things in life for which no apology and no explanation suffice. What do we care about her story? Who cares to hear her defence? What difference does it make whether she actively threw out the children or allowed the wolves to take them? She arrives safe and sound without them and there is no mistaking the fact that she rejoices in her own salvation. She does not rejoice long, however, for Ivan, who is Browning's ideal of resolution, neatly removes her head. Practically and literally Ivan is a murderer: but paradoxically he is God's servant, for the woman is not fit to live, and he eliminates her.

From the practical point of view there is a diffi-

culty ahead. The husband is due; when he hears
that the children are lost, he will suffer horribly, and
will enquire anxiously as to the fate of his wife.
When he learns that she arrived in good condition
and that then Ivan knocked her head off, he may not
fully appreciate the ethical beauty of Ivan's deed.
But this detail does not affect the moral significance
of the story. Yet I can not help thinking that a man
with such strong convictions as Ivan ought not to
carry an axe.

Ivan, however, is still needed in Russia. Two or
three years ago, immediately after a wedding cere-
mony, the bride and groom, with the whole wedding
party, set out in sledges for the next town. The
wolves attacked them and ate every member of the
party except the four in the first sledge—husband,
wife, and two men. As the wolves drew near, these
two heroes advised the husband to throw out the
bride, for if he did so, the three left might be saved,
as their haven was almost in sight. Naturally the
bridegroom declined. Then the two men threw out
both bride and groom, and just managed to reach
the town in safety, the sole survivors of the whole
party. I wish that Ivan had been there to give them
the proper welcome.

The poem *Clive* is a psychological analysis of

courage and fear, two of the most interesting of human sensations. Clive seems to have been an instrument in the hands of Destiny. When an obscure young man, he twice tried to commit suicide, and both times the pistol missed fire. A born gambler, he judged that he was reserved for something great. He was: he conquered India. Then, after his life-work was fully accomplished, his third attempt at suicide was successful.

After describing the dramatic incident at card-play, which he gave to the old buck as the only time in his life when he felt afraid, his companion remarked that it was enough to scare anybody to face a loaded pistol. But here comes the paradox. Clive was intensely angry because his friend failed to see the point. "Why, I wasn't afraid he would shoot, I was afraid he wouldn't." Suppose the general had said contemptuously that young Clive was not worth the powder and ball it would take to kill him—suppose he had sent him away wholly safe and wholly disgraced. Then Clive would have instantly killed himself. Either the general was not clever enough to play this trump, or the clear unwinking eyes of his victim convicted him of sin.

Clive was one of those exceedingly rare individuals who have never known the sensation of physical fear. But I do not think he was really so brave as those men, who, cursed with an imagination that fills their minds with terror, nevertheless advance toward danger. For your real hero is one who does not allow the desires of his body to control his mind. The body, always eager for safety, comfort, and pleasure, cries out against peril: but the mind, up in the conning-tower of the brain, drives the protesting and shivering body forward. Napoleon, who was a good judge of courage, called Ney the bravest of the brave: and I admired Ney more intensely when I learned that in battle he was in his heart always afraid.

The courage of soldiers in the mass seems sublime, but it is the commonest thing on earth: all nations show it: it is probably an inexplicable compound of discipline, pride, shame, and rage: but individuals differ from one another as sharply in courage as they do in mental ability. In sheer physical courage Clive has never been surpassed, and Browning, who loved the manly virtues, saw in this corrupt and cruel man a great hero.

The poem *Muléykeh,* which is one of the oldest of Oriental stories, is really an analysis of love. The mare was dearer to her owner than life itself: yet he intentionally surrendered her to his rival rather than have her disgraced. His friends called him an idiot and a fool: but he replied, "You never have loved my Pearl." And indeed, from his point of view, they did not know the meaning of love. What is love? Simply the desire for possession, or the desire that the beloved object should be imcomparably pure and unsullied by defeat and disgrace? The man who owned Muléykeh really loved her, since her honor was more precious to him than his own happiness.

The short poem *Which?* published on the last day of Browning's life, is a splendid paradox. In the Middle Ages, when house-parties assembled, an immense amount of time was taken up by the telling of stories and by the subsequent discussions thereupon. The stock subject was Love, and the ideal lover was a favorite point of debate. In this instance, the three court ladies argue, and to complete the paradox, a Priest is chosen for referee. Perhaps he was thought to be out of it altogether, and thus ready to judge with an unprejudiced mind.

The Duchess declares that her lover must be a man she can respect: a man of religion and patriotism. He must love his God, and his country; then comes his wife, who holds the third place in his affections.

> I could not love thee, dear, so much,
> Loved I not honour more.

The Marquise insists that her lover must be a man who has done something. He must not only be a man inspired by religious and patriotic motives, but must have actually suffered in her service. He has received wounds in combat, he is pointed out everywhere as the man who has accomplished great deeds. I can not love him unless I can be proud of his record.

The Comtesse says that her ideal lover must love her first: he must love her more than he loves God, more than he loves his country, more than he loves his life—yes, more than he loves his own honor. He must be willing, if necessary, not only to sacrifice his health and life in her behalf, indeed, any true knight would do that: he must be willing to sacrifice his good name, be false to his religion and a traitor to his country. What do I care whether he be a coward, a craven, a scoundrel, a hissing and a byword, so long as he loves me most of all?

This is a difficult position for the Abbé, the man of God: but he does not flinch. His decision is that the third lover is the one of whom Almighty God would approve.

One thing is certain: the third man really loved

his Lady. We do not know whether the other two
loved or not. When a man talks a great deal about
his honor, his self-respect, it is just possible that he
loves himself more than he loves any one else. But
the man who would go through hell to win a woman
really loves that woman. Browning abhors selfish-
ness. He detests a man who is kept from a certain
course of action by thoughts of its possible results to
his reputation. Ibsen has given us the standard example of what the first and second lover in this poem
might sink to in a real moral crisis. In *A Doll's
House,* the husband curses his wife because she has
committed forgery, and his good name will suffer.
She replied that she committed the crime to save his
life—her motive was Love: and she had hoped that
when the truth came out the miracle would happen:
her husband would step forward and take the blame
all on himself. "What fools you women are," said
he, angrily: "you know nothing of business. I
would work my fingers to the bone for you: I would
give up my life for you: but you can't expect a man
to sacrifice his *honor* for a woman." Her retort is
one of the greatest in literature. "Millions of
women have done it."

WHICH?

1889

So, the three Court-ladies began
   Their trial of who judged best
   In esteeming the love of a man:
Who preferred with most reason was thereby confessed
Boy-Cupid's exemplary catcher and cager;
An Abbé crossed legs to decide on the wager.

First the Duchesse: "Mine for me—
   Who were it but God's for Him,
   And the King's for—who but he?
Both faithful and loyal, one grace more shall brim
His cup with perfection: a lady's true lover,
He holds—save his God and his king—none above her."

"I require"—outspoke the Marquise—
   "Pure thoughts, ay, but also fine deeds:
   Play the paladin must he, to please
My whim, and—to prove my knight's service exceeds
Your saint's and your loyalist's praying and kneeling—
Show wounds, each wide mouth to my mercy appealing."

Then the Comtesse: "My choice be a wretch,
   Mere losel in body and soul,
   Thrice accurst! What care I, so he stretch
Arms to me his sole saviour, love's ultimate goal,
Out of earth and men's noise—names of 'infidel,' 'traitor,'
Cast up at him? Crown me, crown's adjudicator!"

And the Abbé uncrossed his legs,
   Took snuff, a reflective pinch,
   Broke silence: "The question begs
Much pondering ere I pronounce. Shall I flinch?
The love which to one and one only has reference
Seems terribly like what perhaps gains God's preference."

VII

AMONG all modern thinkers and writers,
Browning is the foremost optimist. He has
left not the slightest doubt on this point; his belief is
stated over and over again, running like a vein of
gold through all his poems from *Pauline* to *Asolando*. The shattered man in *Pauline* cries at the
very last,

> I believe in God and Truth and Love.

This staunch affirmation, "I believe!" is the common
chord in Browning's music. His optimism is in
striking contrast to the attitude of his contemporaries, for the general tone of nineteenth century
literature is pessimistic. Amidst the wails and
lamentations of the poets, the clear, triumphant voice
of Browning is refreshing even to those who are not
convinced.

Browning suffered for his optimism. It is generally thought that the optimist must be shallow and
superficial; whilst pessimism is associated with pro-

found and sincere thinking. Browning felt this criticism, and replied to it with a scriptural insult in his
poem *At the Mermaid*. I can not possibly be a great
poet, he said sneeringly, because I have never said I
longed for death; I have enjoyed life and loved it,
and have never assumed a peevish attitude. In another poem he declared that pessimists were liars,
because they really loved life while pretending it was
all suffering.

It is only fair to Browning to remember that his
optimism has a philosophical basis, and is the logical
result of a firmly-held view of the universe. Many
unthinking persons declare that Browning, with his
jaunty good spirits, gets on their nerves; he dodges
or leaps over the real obstacles in life, and thinks he
has solved difficulties when he has only forgotten
them. They miss in Browning the note of sorrow,
of internal struggle, of despair; and insist that he
has never accurately portrayed the real bitterness of
the heart's sufferings. These critics have never read
attentively Browning's first poem.

The poem *Pauline* shows that Browning had his
Sturm und Drang, in common with all thoughtful
young men. Keats' immortal preface to *Endymion*
would be equally applicable to this youthful work.
"The imagination of a boy is healthy, and the ma-

ture imagination of a man is healthy; but there is a
space of life between, in which the soul is in a fer-
ment, the character undecided, the way of life un-
certain, the ambition thick-sighted: thence proceeds
mawkishness, and all the thousand bitters which
those men I speak of must necessarily taste in going
over the following pages." The astonishing thing is,
that Browning emerged from the slough of despond
at just the time when most young men are entering
it. He not only climbed out, but set his face reso-
lutely toward the Celestial City.

The poem *Pauline* shows that young Browning
passed through skepticism, atheism, pessimism, cynicism, and that particularly dark state when the mind
reacts on itself; when enthusiasms, high hopes, and
true faith seem childish; when wit and mockery take
the place of zeal, this diabolical substitution seeming
for the moment to be an intellectual advance. But
although he suffered from all these diseases of the
soul, he quickly became convalescent and *Paracelsus*
proves that his cure was complete.

Browning's optimism is not based on any discount
of the sufferings of life, nor any attempt to overlook
such gross realities as sin and pain. No pessimist
has realised these facts more keenly than he. The
Pope, who is the poet's mouthpiece, calls the world

a dread machinery of sin and sorrow. The world is full of sin and sorrow, but it is machinery—and machinery is meant to make something; in this instance the product is human character, which can not be made without obstacles, struggles, and torment. In *Reverie,* Browning goes even farther than this in his description of terrestrial existence.

> Head praises, but heart refrains
> From loving's acknowledgment.
> Whole losses outweigh half-gains:
> Earth's good is with evil blent:
> Good struggles but evil reigns.

Such an appraisal of life can hardly be called a blind and jaunty optimism.

Browning declares repeatedly that the world shows clearly two attributes of God: immense force and immense intelligence. We can not worship God, however, merely because He is strong and wise; He must be better than we are to win our respect and homage. The third necessary attribute, Love, is not at all clear in the spectacle furnished by science and history. Where then shall we seek it? His answer is, in the revelation of God's love through Jesus Christ.

> What lacks then of perfection fit for God
> But just the instance which this tale supplies
> Of love without a limit?

Browning's philosophy therefore is purely Christian.
The love of God revealed in the Incarnation and
in our own ethical natures—our imperfect souls containing here and now the possibilities of infinite development—makes Browning believe that this is
God's world and we are God's children. He con-
ceives of our life as an eternal one, our existence
here being merely probation. No one has ever believed more rationally and more steadfastly in the
future life than our poet; and his optimism is based
solidly on this faith. The man who believes in the
future life, he seems to say, may enjoy whole-heart-
edly and enthusiastically the positive pleasures of
this world, and may endure with a firm mind its
evils and its terrible sufferings. Take Christianity
out of Browning, and his whole philosophy, with its
cheerful outlook, falls to the ground. Of all true
English poets, he is the most definitely Christian, the
most sure of his ground. He wrote out his own
evangelical creed in *Christmas-Eve* and *Easter Day;*
but even if we did not have these definite assurances,
poems like *A Death in the Desert* and *Gold Hair*
would be sufficient.

Sequels are usually failures: the sequel to *Saul* is
a notable exception to the rule. The first part of the
poem, including the first nine stanzas, was published

among the *Dramatic Romances* in 1845: in 1855, among the *Men and Women,* appeared the whole work, containing ten additional stanzas. This sequel is fully up to the standard of the original in artistic beauty, and contains a quite new climax, of even greater intensity. The ninth stanza closes with the cry "King Saul!"—he represents the last word of physical manhood, the finest specimen on earth of the athlete. The eighteenth stanza closes with the cry "See the Christ stand!"—He represents the climax of all human history, the appearance on earth of God in man. The first man is of the earth, earthy: the second man is the Lord from heaven. And as we have borne the image of the earthy, we shall also bear the image of the heavenly.

No modern Pagan has ever sung the joy of life with more gusto than Browning trots it out in the ninth stanza. The glorious play of the muscles, the rapture of the chase, the delight of the plunge into cold water, the delicious taste of food and wine, the unique sweetness of deep sleep. No shame attaches to earthly delights: let us rejoice in our health and strength, in exercise, recreation, eating and sleeping. Saul was a cowboy before he was a King; and young David in his music takes the great monarch back to the happy carefree days on the pasture, before the

responsibilities of the crown had given him melan-
cholia.   The effect of music on patients suffering
from nervous depression is as well known now as it
was in Saul's day; Shakespeare knew something
about it.   His physicians are sometimes admirable;
the great nervous specialist called in on Lady Macbeth's case is a model of wisdom and discretion: the
specialist that Queen Cordelia summoned to pre-
scribe for her father, after giving him trional, or
something of that nature, was careful to have his
return to consciousness accompanied by suitable
music.   Such terrible fits of melancholy as afflicted
Saul were called in the Old Testament the visitations
of an evil spirit; and there is no better diagnosis to-
day.   The Russian novelist Turgenev suffered exactly in the manner in which Browning describes
Saul's sickness of heart: for several days he would
remain in an absolute lethargy, like the king-serpent
in his winter sleep.   And, as in the case of Saul,
music helped him more than medicine.

When David had carried the music to its fullest
extent, the spirit of prophecy came upon him, as in
the Messianic Psalms, and in the eighteenth stanza,
he joyfully infers from the combination of man's
love and man's weakness, that God's love is equal to
God's power.   Man's will is powerless to change the

world of atoms: from God's will stream the stars.
Yet if man's will were equal in power to his benevo-
lence, how quickly would I, David, restore Saul to
happiness! The fact that I love my King with such
intensity, whilst I am powerless to change his condition, makes me believe in the coming of Him who
shall have my wish to help humanity with the accom-
panying power. Man is contemptible in his strength,
but divine in his ideals. 'Tis not what man Does
which exalts him, but what man Would do!

The last stanza of the poem has been thought by
some critics to be a mistake, worse than superfluous.
For my part, I am very glad that Browning added it.
Up to this point, we have had exhibited the effect of
the music on Saul: now we see the effect on the man
who produced it, David. While it is of course impossible even to imagine how a genius must feel
immediately after releasing some immortal work
that has swollen his heart, we can not help making
conjectures. If we are so affected by *hearing* the
Ninth Symphony, what must have been the sensations of Beethoven at its birth? When Händel
wrote the Hallelujah Chorus, he declared that he
saw the heavens opened, and the Son of God sitting
in glory, and I think he spoke the truth. After
Thackeray had written a certain passage in *Vanity*

Fair, he rushed wildly about the room, shouting "That's Genius!"

Now no man in the history of literature has been more reticent than Browning in describing his emotions after virtue had passed out of him. He never talked about his poetry if he could help it; and the hundreds of people who met him casually met a fluent and pleasant conversationalist, who gave not the slightest sign of ever having been on the heights. We know, for example, that on the third day of January, 1852, Browning wrote in his Paris lodgings to the accompaniment of street omnibuses the wonderful poem *Childe Roland:* what a marvellous day that must have been in his spiritual life! In what a frenzy of poetic passion must have passed the hours when he saw those astounding visions, and heard the blast of the horn in the horrible sunset! He must have been inspired by the very demon of poetry. And yet, so far as we know, he never told any one about that day, nor left any written record either of that or any other of the great moments in his life. In *The Ring and the Book,* he tells us of the passion, mystery and wonder that filled his soul on the night of the day when he had found the old yellow volume: but he has said nothing of his sensations when he wrote the speech of Pompilia.

This is why I am glad he added the last stanza to *Saul*. It purports to be a picture of David's drunken rapture, when, after the inspiration had flowed through his soul, he staggered home through the night. About him were angels, powers, unuttered, unseen, alive, aware. The whole earth was awakened, hell loosed with her crews; the stars of night beat with emotion. David is Browning himself; and the poet is trying to tell us, in the only way possible to a man like Browning, how the floods of his own genius affected him. He gives a somewhat similar picture in *Abt Vogler*. It is not in the least surprising that he could not write or talk to his friends about such marvellous experiences. Can a man who has looked on the face of God, and dwelt in the heavenly places, talk about it to others?

Furthermore this nineteenth stanza of *Saul* contains a picture of the dawn that has never been surpassed in poetry. Only those who have spent nights in the great woods can really understand it.

SAUL

1845–1855

I

Said Abner, "At last thou art come! Ere I tell, ere thou
    speak,
Kiss my cheek, wish me well!" Then I wished it, and did kiss
    his cheek.

And he: "Since the King, O my friend, for thy countenance
    sent,
Neither drunken nor eaten have we; nor until from his tent
Thou return with the joyful assurance the King liveth yet,
Shall our lip with the honey be bright, with the water be wet.
For out of the black mid-tent's silence, a space of three days,
Not a sound hath escaped to thy servants, of prayer nor of
    praise,
To betoken that Saul and the Spirit have ended their strife,
And that, faint in his triumph, the monarch sinks back upon
    life.

II

"Yet now my heart leaps, O beloved! God's child with his
    dew
On thy gracious gold hair, and those lilies still living and blue
Just broken to twine round thy harp-strings, as if no wild
    heat
Were now raging to torture the desert!"

III

                            Then I, as was meet,
Knelt down to the God of my fathers, and rose on my feet,
And ran o'er the sand burnt to powder. The tent was un-
    looped;
I pulled up the spear that obstructed, and under I stooped;
Hands and knees on the slippery grass-patch, all withered and
    gone,
That extends to the second enclosure, I groped my way on
Till I felt where the foldskirts fly open. Then once more I
    prayed,
And opened the foldskirts and entered, and was not afraid
But spoke, "Here is David, thy servant!" And no voice re-
    plied.
At the first I saw naught but the blackness: but soon I de-
    scried

A something more black than the blackness—the vast, the up-
    right
Main prop which sustains the pavilion: and slow into sight
Grew a figure against it, gigantic and blackest of all.
Then a sunbeam, that burst through the tent-roof, showed
    Saul.

IV

He stood as erect as that tent-prop, both arms stretched out
    wide
On the great cross-support in the centre, that goes to each
    side;
He relaxed not a muscle, but hung there as, caught in his
    pangs
And waiting his change, the king-serpent all heavily hangs,
Far away from his kind, in the pine, till deliverance come
With the spring-time,—so agonized Saul, drear and stark,
    blind and dumb.

V

Then I tuned my harp,—took off the lilies we twine round
    its chords
Lest they snap 'neath the stress of the noontide—those sun-
    beams like swords!
And I first played the tune all our sheep know, as, one after
    one,
So docile they come to the pen-door till folding be done.
They are white and untorn by the bushes, for lo, they have
    fed
Where the long grasses stifle the water within the stream's
    bed;
And now one after one seeks its lodging, as star follows star
Into eve and the blue far above us,—so blue and so far!

VI

—Then the tune for which quails on the corn-land will each
     leave his mate

To fly after the player; then, what makes the crickets elate

Till for boldness they fight one another; and then, what has
     weight

To set the quick jerboa a-musing outside his sand house—

There are none such as he for a wonder, half bird and half
     mouse!

God made all the creatures and gave them our love and our
     fear,

To give sign, we and they are his children, one family here.

VII

Then I played the help-tune of our reapers, their wine-song,
     when hand

Grasps at hand, eye lights eye in good friendship, and great
     hearts expand

And grow one in the sense of this world's life.—And then, the
     last song

When the dead man is praised on his journey—"Bear, bear
     him along,

With his few faults shut up like dead flowerets! Are balm
     seeds not here

To console us? The land has none left such as he on the bier.

Oh, would we might keep thee, my brother!"—And then, the
     glad chaunt

Of the marriage,—first go the young maidens, next, she whom
     we vaunt

As the beauty, the pride of our dwelling.—And then, the great
     march

Wherein man runs to man to assist him and buttress an arch

Naught can break; who shall harm them, our friends? Then,
     the chorus intoned

As the Levites go up to the altar in glory enthroned.
But I stopped here: for here in the darkness Saul groaned.

VIII

And I paused, held my breath in such silence, and listened
      apart;
And the tent shook, for mighty Saul shuddered: and sparkles
      'gan dart
From the jewels that woke in his turban, at once with a start,
All its lordly male-sapphires, and rubies courageous at heart.
So the head: but the body still moved not, still hung there
      erect.
And I bent once again to my playing, pursued it unchecked,
As I sang:—

IX

  "Oh, our manhood's prime vigour! No spirit feels waste,
Not a muscle is stopped in its playing nor sinew unbraced.
Oh, the wild joys of living! the leaping from rock up to rock,
The strong rending of boughs from the fir-tree, the cool silver
      shock
Of the plunge in a pool's living water, the hunt of the bear,
And the sultriness showing the lion is couched in his lair.
And the meal, the rich dates yellowed over with gold dust
      divine,
And the locust-flesh steeped in the pitcher, the full draught of
      wine,
And the sleep in the dried river-channel where bulrushes tell
That the water was wont to go warbling so softly and well.
How good is man's life, the mere living! how fit to employ
All the heart and the soul and the senses forever in joy!
Hast thou loved the white locks of thy father, whose sword
      thou didst guard
When he trusted thee forth with the armies, for glorious re-
      ward?

Didst thou see the thin hands of thy mother, held up as men
  sung
The low song of the nearly-departed, and hear her faint
  tongue
Joining in while it could to the witness, 'Let one more attest,
I have lived, seen God's hand through a lifetime, and all was
  for best'?
Then they sung through their tears in strong triumph, not
  much, but the rest.
And thy brothers, the help and the contest, the working
  whence grew
Such result as, from seething grape-bundles, the spirit
  strained true:
And the friends of thy boyhood—that boyhood of wonder
  and hope,
Present promise and wealth of the future beyond the eye's
  scope,—
Till lo, thou art grown to a monarch; a people is thine;
And all gifts, which the world offers singly, on one head com-
  bine!
On one head, all the beauty and strength, love and rage (like
  the throe
That, a-work in the rock, helps its labour and lets the gold go)
High ambition and deeds which surpass it, fame crowning
  them,—all
Brought to blaze on the head of one creature—King Saul!"

X

And lo, with that leap of my spirit,—heart, hand, harp and
  voice,
Each lifting Saul's name out of sorrow, each bidding rejoice
Saul's fame in the light it was made for—as when, dare I say,
The Lord's army, in rapture of service, strains through its
  array,

And upsoareth the cherubim-chariot—"Saul!" cried I, and
    stopped, .

And waited the thing that should follow. Then Saul, who
    hung propped

By the tent's cross-support in the centre, was struck by his
    name.

Have ye seen when Spring's arrowy summons goes right to
    the aim,

And some mountain, the last to withstand her, that held (he
    alone,

While the vale laughed in freedom and flowers) on a broad
    bust of stone

A year's snow bound about for a breastplate,—leaves grasp of
    the sheet?

Fold on fold all at once it crowds thunderously down to his
    feet,

And there fronts you, stark, black, but alive yet, your moun-
    tain of old,

With his rents, the successive bequeathings of ages untold—

Yea, each harm got in fighting your battles, each furrow and
    scar

Of his head thrust 'twixt you and the tempest—all hail, there
    they are!

—Now again to be softened with verdure, again hold the nest

Of the dove, tempt the goat and its young to the green on his
    crest

For their food in the ardours of summer. One long shudder
    thrilled

All the tent till the very air tingled, then sank and was stilled

At the King's self left standing before me, released and
    aware.

What was gone, what remained? All to traverse 'twixt hope
    and despair,

Death was past, life not come: so he waited. Awhile his **right**
 hand
Held the brow, helped the eyes left too vacant forthwith **to**
 remand
To their place what new objects should enter: 'twas Saul as
 before.
I looked up and dared gaze at those eyes, nor was hurt any
 more
Than by slow pallid sunsets in autumn, we watch from the
 shore,
At their sad level gaze o'er the ocean—a sun's slow decline
Over hills which, resolved in stern silence, o'erlap and entwine
Base with base to knit strength more intensely; so, arm folded
 arm
O'er the chest whose slow heavings subsided.

XI

      What spell or what charm,
(For awhile there was trouble within me,) what next should
 I urge
To sustain him where song had restored him?—Song filled to
 the verge
His cup with the wine of this life, pressing all that it yields
Of mere fruitage, the strength and the beauty: beyond, on
 what fields,
Glean a vintage more potent and perfect to brighten the eye
And bring blood to the lip, and commend them the cup they
 put by?
He saith, "It is good;" still he drinks not: he lets me praise
 life,
Gives assent, yet would die for his own part.

XII

Then fancies grew rife

Which had come long ago on the pasture, when round me the
   sheep

Fed in silence—above, the one eagle wheeled slow as in sleep;

And I lay in my hollow and mused on the world that might
   lie

'Neath his ken, though I saw but the strip 'twixt the hill and
   the sky:

And I laughed—"Since my days are ordained to be passed
   with my flocks,

Let me people at least, with my fancies, the plains and the
   rocks,

Dream the life I am never to mix with, and image the show

Of mankind as they live in those fashions I hardly shall know!

Schemes of life, its best rules and right uses, the courage
   that gains,

And the prudence that keeps what men strive for." And now
   these old trains

Of vague thought came again; I grew surer; so, once more
   the string

Of my harp made response to my spirit, as thus—

XIII

"Yea, my King,"

I began—"thou dost well in rejecting mere comforts that
   spring

From the mere mortal life held in common by man and by
   brute:

In our flesh grows the branch of this life, in our soul it bears
   fruit.

Thou hast marked the slow rise of the tree,—how its stem
   trembled first

Till it passed the kid's lip, the stag's antler; then safely outburst

The fan-branches all round; and thou mindest when these
    too, in turn,
Broke a-bloom and the palm-tree seemed perfect: yet more
    was to learn,
E'en the good that comes in with the palm-fruit. Our dates
    shall we slight,
When their juice brings a cure for all sorrow? or care for the
    plight
Of the palm's self whose slow growth produced them? Not
    so! stem and branch
Shall decay, nor be known in their place, while the palm-wine
    shall stanch
Every wound of man's spirit in winter. I pour thee such wine.
Leave the flesh to the fate it was fit for! the spirit be thine!
By the spirit, when age shall o'ercome thee, thou still shalt
    enjoy
More indeed, than at first when inconscious, the life of a boy.
Crush that life, and behold its wine running! Each deed thou
    hast done
Dies, revives, goes to work in the world; until e'en as the sun
Looking down on the earth, though clouds spoil him, though
    tempests efface,
Can find nothing his own deed produced not, must everywhere
    trace
The results of his past summer-prime,—so, each ray of thy
    will,
Every flash of thy passion and prowess, long over, shall thrill
Thy whole people, the countless, with ardor, till they too give
    forth
A like cheer to their sons, who in turn, fill the South and the
    North
With the radiance thy deed was the germ of. Carouse in the
    past!
But the license of age has its limit; thou diest at last:

As the lion when age dims his eyeball, the rose at her height,
So with man—so his power and his beauty forever take flight.
No! Again a long draught of my soul-wine! Look forth o'er
    the years!
Thou hast done now with eyes for the actual; begin with the
    seer's!
Is Saul dead? In the depth of the vale make his tomb—bid
    arise
A gray mountain of marble heaped four-square, till, built to
    the skies,
Let it mark where the great First King slumbers: whose fame
    would ye know?
Up above see the rock's naked face, where the record shall go
In great characters cut by the scribe,—Such was Saul, so he
    did;
With the sages directing the work, by the populace chid,—
For not half, they'll affirm, is comprised there! Which fault
    to amend,
In the grove with his kind grows the cedar, whereon they
    shall spend
(See, in tablets 'tis level before them) their praise, and record
With the gold of the graver, Saul's story,—the statesman's
    great word
Side by side with the poet's sweet comment. The river's
    a-wave
With smooth paper-reeds grazing each other when prophet-
    winds rave:
So the pen gives unborn generations their due and their part
In thy being! Then, first of the mighty, thank God that thou
    art!"

XIV

And behold while I sang . . . but O Thou who didst grant me
    that day,
And before it not seldom hast granted thy help to essay,

Carry on and complete an adventure,—my shield and my
 sword
In that act where my soul was thy servant, thy word was my
 word,—
Still be with me, who then at the summit of human endeavour
And scaling the highest, man's thought could, gazed hopeless
 as ever
On the new stretch of heaven above me—till, mighty to save,
Just one lift of thy hand cleared that distance—God's throne
 from man's grave!
Let me tell out my tale to its ending—my voice to my heart
Which can scarce dare believe in what marvels last night I
 took part,
As this morning I gather the fragments, alone with my sheep,
And still fear lest the terrible glory evanish like sleep!
For I wake in the gray dewy covert, while Hebron upheaves
The dawn struggling with night on his shoulder, and Kidron
 retrieves
Slow the damage of yesterday's sunshine.

XV

                                    I say then,—my song
While I sang thus, assuring the monarch, and ever more
 strong
Made a proffer of good to console him—he slowly resumed
His old motions and habitudes kingly. The right hand re-
 plumed
His black locks to their wonted composure, adjusted the
 swathes
Of his turban, and see—the huge sweat that his countenance
 bathes,
He wipes off with the robe; and he girds now his loins as of
 yore,
And feels slow for the armlets of price, with the clasp set
 before.

He is Saul, ye remember in glory,—ere error had bent
The broad brow from the daily communion; and still, though
    much spent
Be the life and the bearing that front you, the same, God did
    choose,
To receive what a man may waste, desecrate, never quite lose.
So sank he along by the tent-prop till, stayed by the pile
Of his armour and war-cloak and garments, he leaned there
    awhile,
And sat out my singing,—one arm round the tent-prop, to
    raise
His bent head, and the other hung slack—till I touched on the
    praise
I foresaw from all men in all time, to the man patient there;
And thus ended, the harp falling forward. Then first I was
    'ware
That he sat, as I say, with my head just above his vast knees
Which were thrust out on each side around me, like oak roots
    which please
To encircle a lamb when it slumbers. I looked up to know
If the best I could do had brought solace: he spoke not, but
    slow
Lifted up the hand slack at his side, till he laid it with care
Soft and grave, but in mild settled will, on my brow: through
    my hair
The large fingers were pushed, and he bent back my head, with
    kind power—
All my face back, intent to peruse it, as men do a flower.
Thus held he me there with his great eyes that scrutinized
    mine—
And oh, all my heart how it loved him! but where was the
    sign?
I yearned—"Could I help thee, my father, inventing a bliss,
I would add, to that life of the past, both the future and this;

I would give thee new life altogether, as good, ages hence,
As this moment,—had love but the warrant, love's heart to
    dispense!"

XVI

Then the truth came upon me.   No harp more—no song more!
    outbroke—

XVII

"I have gone the whole round of creation: I saw and I spoke:
I, a work of God's hand for that purpose, received in my brain
And pronounced on the rest of his handwork—returned him
    again
His creation's approval or censure: I spoke as I saw:
I report, as a man may of God's work—all's love, yet all's law.
Now I lay down the judgeship he lent me.   Each faculty
    tasked
To perceive him, has gained an abyss, where a dewdrop was
    asked.
Have I knowledge? confounded it shrivels at Wisdom laid
    bare.
Have I forethought? how purblind, how blank, to the Infinite
    Care!
Do I task any faculty highest, to image success?
I but open my eyes,—and perfection, no more and no less,
In the kind I imagined, full-fronts me, and God is seen God
In the star, in the stone, in the flesh, in the soul and the clod.
And thus looking within and around me, I ever renew
(With that stoop of the soul which in bending upraises it too)
The submission of man's nothing-perfect to God's all-complete,
As by each new obeisance in spirit, I climb to his feet.
Yet with all this abounding experience, this deity known,
I shall dare to discover some province, some gift of my own.
There's a faculty pleasant to exercise, hard to hoodwink,
I am fain to keep still in abeyance, (I laugh as I think)

Lest, insisting to claim and parade in it, wot ye, I worst
E'en the Giver in one gift.—Behold, I could love if I durst!
But I sink the pretension as fearing a man may o'ertake
God's own speed in the one way of love: I abstain for love's
    sake.
—What, my soul? see thus far and no farther? when doors
    great and small,
Nine-and-ninety flew ope at our touch, should the hundredth
    appall?
In the least things have faith, yet distrust in the greatest of
    all?
Do I find love so full in my nature, God's ultimate gift,
That I doubt his own love can compete with it? Here, the
    parts shift?
Here, the creature surpass the Creator,—the end, what Began?
Would I fain in my impotent yearning do all for this man,
And dare doubt he alone shall not help him, who yet alone
    can?
Would it ever have entered my mind, the bare will, much less
    power,
To bestow on this Saul what I sang of, the marvellous dower
Of the life he was gifted and filled with? to make such a soul,
Such a body, and then such an earth for insphering the whole?
And doth it not enter my mind (as my warm tears attest)
These good things being given, to go on, and give one more,
    the best?
Ay, to save and redeem and restore him, maintain at the height
This perfection,—succeed with life's day-spring, death's minute
    of night?
Interpose at the difficult minute, snatch Saul the mistake,
Saul the failure, the ruin he seems now,—and bid him awake
From the dream, the probation, the prelude, to find himself set
Clear and safe in new light and new life,—a new harmony yet

To be run, and continued, and ended—who knows?—or endure!
The man taught enough by life's dream, of the rest to make
sure;
By the pain-throb, triumphantly winning intensified bliss,
And the next world's reward and repose, by the struggles in
this.

XVIII

"I believe it! 'Tis thou, God, that givest, 'tis I who receive:
In the first is the last, in thy will is my power to believe.
All's one gift: thou canst grant it moreover, as prompt to my
prayer
As I breathe out this breath, as I open these arms to the air.
From thy will stream the worlds, life and nature, thy dread
Sabaoth:
I will?—the mere atoms despise me! Why am I not loth
To look that, even that in the face too? Why is it I dare
Think but lightly of such impuissance? What stops my de-
spair?
This;—'tis not what man Does which exalts him, but what
man Would do!
See the King—I would help him but cannot, the wishes fall
through.
Could I wrestle to raise him from sorrow, grow poor to en-
rich,
To fill up his life, starve my own out, I would—knowing
which,
I know that my service is perfect. Oh, speak through me
now!
Would I suffer for him that I love? So wouldst thou—so wilt
thou!
So shall crown thee the topmost, ineffablest, uttermost crown—
And thy love fill infinitude wholly, nor leave up nor down

One spot for the creature to stand in! It is by no breath,
Turn of eye, wave of hand, that salvation joins issue with
    death!
As thy Love is discovered almighty, almighty be proved
Thy power, that exists with and for it, of being Beloved!
He who did most, shall bear most; the strongest shall stand
    the most weak.
'Tis the weakness in strength, that I cry for! my flesh, that I
    seek
In the Godhead! I seek and I find it. O Saul, it shall be
A Face like my face that receives thee; a Man like to me,
Thou shalt love and be loved by, forever: a Hand like this
    hand
Shall throw open the gates of new life to thee! See the
    Christ stand!"

XIX

I know not too well how I found my way home in the night.
There were witnesses, cohorts about me, to left and to right,
Angels, powers, the unuttered, unseen, the alive, the aware:
I repressed, I got through them as hardly, as strugglingly
    there,
As a runner beset by the populace famished for news—
Life or death. The whole earth was awakened, hell loosed
    with her crews;
And the stars of night beat with emotion, and tingled and shot
Out in fire the strong pain of pent knowledge: but I fainted
    not,
For the Hand still impelled me at once and supported, sup-
    pressed
All the tumult, and quenched it with quiet, and holy behest,
Till the rapture was shut in itself, and the earth sank to rest.
Anon at the dawn, all that trouble had withered from earth—
Not so much, but I saw it die out in the day's tender birth;

In the gathered intensity brought to the grey of the hills;
In the shuddering forests' held breath; in the sudden wind-
        thrills;
In the startled wild beasts that bore off, each with eye sidling
        still
Though averted with wonder and dread; in the birds stiff and
        chill
That rose heavily, as I approached them, made stupid with
        awe:
E'en the serpent that slid away silent,—he felt the new law.
The same stared in the white humid faces upturned by the
        flowers;
The same worked in the heart of the cedar and moved the
        vine-bowers:
And the little brooks witnessing murmured, persistent and low,
With their obstinate, all but hushed voices—"E'en so, it is so!"

On a clear, warm day in March, 1912, I stood on
the Piazza Michel Angelo in Florence, with a copy
of Browning in my hand, and gazed with delight on
the panorama of the fair city below. Then I read
aloud the first two stanzas of *Old Pictures in Florence,* and realised for the thousandth time the defi-
niteness of Browning's poetry. This particular
poem is a mixture of art and doggerel; but even the
latter is interesting to lovers of Florence.

Not a churlish saint, Lorenzo Monaco?

Did you ever stand in front of the picture by Lorenzo that Browning had in mind, and observe the
churlish saints? Most saints in Italian pictures look

either happy or complacent; because they have just been elected to the society of heaven and are in for life. But for some strange reason, Lorenzo's saints, although in the Presence, and worshipping with music, look as if they were suffering from acute indigestion. If one will wander about the galleries of Florence, and take along Browning, one will find the poet more specifically informing than Baedeker.

The philosophy of this poem is Browning's favorite philosophy of development. He compares the perfection of Greek art with the imperfection of the real human body. We know what a man ought to look like; and if we have forgotten, we may behold a representation by a Greek sculptor. Stand at the corner of a city street, and watch the men pass; they are caricatures of the manly form. Yet ludicrously ugly as they are, the intention is clear; we see even in these degradations, what the figure of a man ought to be. In Greek art

> The Truth of Man, as by God first spoken,
> Which the actual generations garble,
> Was reuttered.

Which the actual generations garble—men as we see them are clumsy and garbled versions of the original. But there is no value in lamenting this; it is idle for men to gaze with regret and longing at the

Apollo Belvedere. It is much better to remember
that Perfection and Completion spell Death: only
Imperfection has a future. What if the souls in our
ridiculously ugly bodies become greater and grander
than the marble men of Pheidias? Giotto's unfinished
Campanile is nobler than the perfect zero he drew
for the Pope. In our imperfect minds, housed in
our over-fat, over-lean, and always commonplace
bodies, exists the principle of development, for
whose steady advance eternity is not too long.
Statues belong to time: man has Forever.

For some strange reason, no tourist ever goes to
Fano. One reason why I went there was simply because I had never met a person of any nationality
who had ever seen the town. Yet it is easily accessi-
ble, very near Ancona, the scene of the *Grammarian's Funeral,* and the place where Browning wrote
The Guardian Angel. One day Mr. and Mrs. Browning, walking about Fano, came to the church of San
Agostino, in no way a remarkable edifice, and there
in the tiny chapel, over the altar, they found Guercino's masterpiece. Its calm and serene beauty
struck an immortal poem out of Browning's heart;
and thanks to the poet, the picture is now one of the
most familiar in the world. But no copy comes near

the ineffable charm of the original, as one sees it in
the dim light of the chapel.

The child on the tomb is looking past the angel's
face into the glory of heaven; but the poet, who
wishes that he might take the place of the little child,
declares that he would gaze, not toward heaven, but
into the gracious face of the bird of God. If we
could only see life as the angel sees it, if we could
only see the whole course of history, we should then
realise that

> All is beauty:
> And knowing this, is love, and love is duty.

We can not see the forest for the trees: the last place
to obtain an idea of the range, grandeur, and beauty
of a forest, is in it: one should climb a high mountain and look over its vast extent. So we, in life,
"where men sit and hear each other groan," believe
that the world is some dreadful mistake, full of
meaningless anguish. This is because we are in the
midst of it all: we can not see far: the nearest objects, though infinitesimal in size, loom enormous, as
with the palm of your hand you can cut off the sun.
But if we could only see the end from the beginning,
if we could get the angel's view-point, the final re-

sult would be beauty.   Browning is not satisfied with
Keats's doctrine

> "Beauty is truth, truth beauty,"—that is all
> Ye know on earth, and all ye need to know.

He shows us what happened to Aprile with this philosophy.   Browning adds the doctrine of love.   The
moment we realise that the universe is conceived in
terms of beauty, love fills our hearts: love for our
fellow-beings, who are making the journey through
life with us; and love for God, the author of it all,
just as a child loves one who gives it the gift of its
heart's desire.   That the supreme duty of life is love
is simply one more illustration of Browning's stead-
fast adherence to the Gospel of Christ.

THE GUARDIAN-ANGEL

A PICTURE AT FANO

1855

I

> Dear and great Angel, wouldst thou only leave
>   That child, when thou hast done with him, for me!
> Let me sit all the day here, that when eve
>   Shall find performed thy special ministry,
> And time come for departure, thou, suspending
> Thy flight, mayst see another child for tending,
>   Another still, to quiet and retrieve.

II

Then I shall feel thee step one step, no more,
  From where thou standest now, to where I gaze,
—And suddenly my head is covered o'er
  With those wings, white above the child who prays
Now on that tomb—and I shall feel thee guarding
Me, out of all the world; for me, discarding
  Yon heaven thy home, that waits and opes its door.

III

I would not look up thither past thy head
  Because the door opes, like that child, I know,
For I should have thy gracious face instead,
  Thou bird of God! And wilt thou bend me low
Like him, and lay, like his, my hands together,
And lift them up to pray, and gently tether
  Me, as thy lamb there, with thy garment's spread?

IV

If this was ever granted, I would rest
  My head beneath thine, while thy healing hands
Close-covered both my eyes beside thy breast,
  Pressing the brain, which too much thought expands,
Back to its proper size again, and smoothing
Distortion down till every nerve had soothing,
  And all lay quiet, happy and suppressed.

V

How soon all worldly wrong would be repaired!
  I think how I should view the earth and skies
And sea, when once again my brow was bared
  After thy healing, with such different eyes.
O world, as God has made it! All is beauty:
And knowing this, is love, and love is duty.
  What further may be sought for or declared?

VI

Guercino drew this angel I saw teach
    (Alfred, dear friend!)—that little child to pray,
Holding the little hands up, each to each
    Pressed gently,—with his own head turned away
Over the earth where so much lay before him
Of work to do, though heaven was opening o'er him,
    And he was left at Fano by the beach.

VII

We were at Fano, and three times we went
    To sit and see him in his chapel there,
And drink his beauty to our soul's content
    —My angel with me too: and since I care
For dear Guercino's fame (to which in power
And glory comes this picture for a dower,
    Fraught with a pathos so magnificent)—

VIII

And since he did not work thus earnestly
    At all times, and has else endured some wrong—
I took one thought his picture struck from me,
    And spread it out, translating it to song.
My love is here. Where are you, dear old friend?
How rolls the Wairoa at your world's far end?
    This is Ancona, yonder is the sea.

The three poems, *Caliban on Setebos, Rabbi Ben Ezra,* and *A Death in the Desert,* should be read in that order; for there is a logical order in the thought. The first is God as an amphibious brute would imagine him: the second is noble Hebrew theism: the third is the Christian God of Love. Whilst the second is the finest poem of the three, the first is the most original. The word "upon" is ironical: it is Caliban's treatise on theology. We read Caliban on God, as we read Mill on Political Economy: for Caliban, like many a human theologian, does not scruple to speak the last word on the nature of the Supreme Being. The citation from the Psalms is a rebuke to gross anthropomorphism: Caliban, like the Puritans, has simply made God in his own image.

The difference between Shakespeare's and Browning's Caliban is simply the difference between Shakespeare and Browning. Shakespeare made the monster for decorative purposes, to satisfy his love of the grotesque, as an architect placed gargoyles on a cathedral: the grotesque is an organic part of romantic art. Browning is interested not in Caliban's appearance, but in his processes of thought. Suppose a monster, half fish, half beast, living with supreme comfort in the slime, could think: what kind of God would he imagine had created this world?

Caliban speaks in the third person (does Brown-

ing make a slip when he changes occasionally to the
first?) in order to have indicated the low order of
his intelligence; just as a little child says, "Don't
hurt her: she hasn't done anything wrong." He is
lying in liquid refuse, with little lizards deliciously
tickling his spine (such things are entirely a matter
of taste, what would be odious to us would be heaven
to a sow) and having nothing to do for the moment,
like a man in absolute leisure, turns his thoughts to
God. He believes that God is neither good nor bad,
but simply capricious. What's the use of being God,
if you can't do what you like? He treats earth's
creatures as a wanton boy treats his toys; they belong to me; why shouldn't I break them if I choose?
No one ought to complain of misfortunes: you can
not expect God is going to reward the virtuous and
punish the guilty. He has no standards whatever.
Just as I, Caliban, sit here and watch a procession of
crabs: I might lazily make up my mind, in a kind of
sporting interest, to count them as they pass; to let
twenty go in safety, and smash the twenty-first, loving not, hating not, just choosing so. When I feel
like it, I help some creatures; if in another mood, I
torment others; that's the way God treats us, that's
the way I would act if I were God.

As Caliban's theology has much of the human in it, so his practical reasoning is decidedly human in its superstition. Granted that we are in the hands of a childish and capricious God, who amuses himself with torturing us, who laughs at our faces distorted with pain, what is the thing we ought to do? How shall we best manage? Caliban's advice is clear: don't let Him notice you: don't get prominent: above all, never boast of your good fortune, for that will surely draw God's attention, and He will put you where you belong. This superstition, that God is against us, is deep-seated in human nature, as the universal practice of "touching wood" sufficiently demonstrates. If a man says, "I haven't had a cold this winter," his friends will advise him to touch wood; and if he wakes up the next morning snuffling, he will probably soliloquise, "What a fool I was! Why couldn't I keep still? Why did I have to mention it? Now see what I've got!"

Caliban disagreed with his mother Sycorax on one important point. She believed in the future life. Caliban says such a belief is absurd. There can be nothing worse than this life. Its good moments are simply devices of God to strengthen us so that He can torture us again, just as in the good old times the executioners gave the sufferers they were tormenting some powerful stimulant, so that they might return to consciousness and suffer; for nothing cheated the spectators worse than to have the victim die during the early stages of the torture. The object was to keep the wretch alive as long as possible. Thus in this life we have moments of comparative ease and rest, wherein we recuperate a little, just as the cat lets the mouse recover strength enough to imagine he is going to get away.

Caliban is of course an absolute and convinced pessimist. A malevolent giant is not so bad a God as an insane child. And Browning means that pessimism is what we should naturally expect from so rudimentary an intellect as Caliban's, which judges the whole order of the universe from proximate and superficial evidences.

The close of the poem is a good commentary on some human ideas of what kind of service is pleasing to God. Poor Caliban! he had saved up some quails, meaning to have a delicious meal. But in his fear he cries to God, I will let them fly, if you will only spare me this time! I will not eat whelks for a month, I will eat no chocolates during Lent, anything to please God!

CALIBAN UPON SETEBOS; OR, NATURAL THEOLOGY IN THE ISLAND

1864

"Thou thoughtest that I was altogether such a one as thyself."

['Will sprawl, now that the heat of day is best,
Flat on his belly in the pit's much mire,
With elbows wide, fists clenched to prop his chin.
And, while he kicks both feet in the cool slush,
And feels about his spine small eft-things course,
Run in and out each arm, and make him laugh:
And while above his head a pompion-plant,
Coating the cave-top as a brow its eye,
Creeps down to touch and tickle hair and beard,
And now a flower drops with a bee inside,
And now a fruit to snap at, catch and crunch,—
He looks out o'er yon sea which sunbeams cross
And recross till they weave a spider-web
(Meshes of fire, some great fish breaks at times)
And talks to his own self, howe'er he please,
Touching that other, whom his dam called God.
Because to talk about Him, vexes—ha,
Could He but know! and time to vex is now,
When talk is safer than in winter-time.
Moreover Prosper and Miranda sleep
In confidence he drudges at their task,
And it is good to cheat the pair, and gibe,
Letting the rank tongue blossom into speech.]

Setebos, Setebos, and Setebos!
'Thinketh, He dwelleth i' the cold o' the moon.

'Thinketh He made it, with the sun to match,
But not the stars; the stars came otherwise;
Only made clouds, winds, meteors, such as that:

Also this isle, what lives and grows thereon,
And snaky sea which rounds and ends the same.
'Thinketh, it came of being ill at ease:
He hated that He cannot change His cold,
Nor cure its ache. 'Hath spied an icy fish
That longed to 'scape the rock-stream where she lived,
And thaw herself within the lukewarm brine
O' the lazy sea her stream thrusts far amid,
A crystal spike 'twixt two warm walls of wave;
Only, she ever sickened, found repulse
At the other kind of water, not her life,
(Green-dense and dim-delicious, bred o' the sun)
Flounced back from bliss she was not born to breathe,
And in her old bounds buried her despair,
Hating and loving warmth alike: so He.

'Thinketh, He made thereat the sun, this isle,
Trees and the fowls here, beast and creeping thing.
Yon otter, sleek-wet, black, lithe as a leech;
Yon auk, one fire-eye in a ball of foam,
That floats and feeds; a certain badger brown
He hath watched hunt with that slant white-wedge eye
By moonlight; and the pie with the long tongue
That pricks deep into oakwarts for a worm,
And says a plain word when she finds her prize,
But will not eat the ants; the ants themselves
That build a wall of seeds and settled stalks
About their hole—He made all these and more,
Made all we see, and us, in spite: how else?
He could not, Himself, make a second self
To be His mate; as well have made Himself:
He would not make what he mislikes or slights,
An eyesore to Him, or not worth His pains:
But did, in envy, listlessness or sport,
Make what Himself would fain, in a manner, be—

Weaker in most points, stronger in a few,
Worthy, and yet mere playthings all the while,
Things He admires and mocks too,—that is it.
Because, so brave, so better though they be,
It nothing skills if He begin to plague.
Look now, I melt a gourd-fruit into mash,
Add honeycomb and pods, I have perceived,
Which bite like finches when they bill and kiss,—
Then, when froth rises bladdery, drink up all,
Quick, quick, till maggots scamper through my brain;
Last, throw me on my back i' the seeded thyme,
And wanton, wishing I were born a bird.
Put case, unable to be what I wish,
I yet could make a live bird out of clay:
Would not I take clay, pinch my Caliban
Able to fly?—for, there, see, he hath wings,
And great comb like the hoopoe's to admire,
And there, a sting to do his foes offence,
There, and I will that he begin to live,
Fly to yon rock-top, nip me off the horns
Of grigs high up that make the merry din,
Saucy through their veined wings, and mind me not.
In which feat, if his leg snapped, brittle clay,
And he lay stupid-like,—why, I should laugh;
And if he, spying me, should fall to weep,
Beseech me to be good, repair his wrong,
Bid his poor leg smart less or grow again,—
Well, as the chance were, this might take or else
Not take my fancy: I might hear his cry,
And give the mankin three sound legs for one,
Or pluck the other off, leave him like an egg,
And lessoned he was mine and merely clay.
Were this no pleasure, lying in the thyme,
Drinking the mash, with brain become alive,
Making and marring clay at will? So He.

'Thinketh, such shows nor right nor wrong in Him,
Nor kind, nor cruel: He is strong and Lord.
'Am strong myself compared to yonder crabs
That march now from the mountain to the sea;
'Let twenty pass, and stone the twenty-first,
Loving not, hating not, just choosing so.
'Say, the first straggler that boasts purple spots
Shall join the file, one pincer twisted off;
'Say, this bruised fellow shall receive a worm,
And two worms he whose nippers end in red;
As it likes me each time, I do: so He.

Well then, 'supposeth He is good i' the main,
Placable if His mind and ways were guessed,
But rougher than His handiwork, be sure!
Oh, He hath made things worthier than Himself,
And envieth that, so helped, such things do more
Than He who made them! What consoles but this?
That they, unless through Him, do nought at all,
And must submit: what other use in things?
'Hath cut a pipe of pithless elder-joint
That, blown through, gives exact the scream o' the jay
When from her wing you twitch the feathers blue:
Sound this, and little birds that hate the jay
Flock within stone's throw, glad their foe is hurt:
Put case such pipe could prattle and boast forsooth
"I catch the birds, I am the crafty thing,
"I make the cry my maker cannot make
"With his great round mouth; he must blow through mine!"
Would not I smash it with my foot? So He.

But wherefore rough, why cold and ill at ease?
Aha, that is a question! Ask, for that,
What knows,—the something over Setebos
That made Him, or He, may be, found and fought,

Worsted, drove off and did to nothing, perchance.
There may be something quiet o'er His head,
Out of His reach, that feels nor joy nor grief,
Since both derive from weakness in some way.
I joy because the quails come; would not joy
Could I bring quails here when I have a mind:
This Quiet, all it hath a mind to, doth.
'Esteemeth stars the outposts of its couch,
But never spends much thought nor care that way.
It may look up, work up,—the worse for those
It works on! 'Careth but for Setebos
The many-handed as a cuttle-fish,
Who, making Himself feared through what He does,
Looks up, first, and perceives he cannot soar
To what is quiet and hath happy life;
Next looks down here, and out of very spite
Makes this a bauble-world to ape yon real,
These good things to match those as hips do grapes.
'Tis solace making baubles, ay, and sport.
Himself peeped late, eyed Prosper at his books
Careless and lofty, lord now of the isle:
Vexed, 'stitched a book of broad leaves, arrow-shaped,
Wrote thereon, he knows what, prodigious words;
Has peeled a wand and called it by a name;
Weareth at whiles for an enchanter's robe
The eyed skin of a supple oncelot;
And hath an ounce sleeker than youngling mole,
A four-legged serpent he makes cower and couch,
Now snarl, now hold its breath and mind his eye,
And saith she is Miranda and my wife:
'Keeps for his Ariel a tall pouch-bill crane
He bids go wade for fish and straight disgorge;
Also a sea-beast, lumpish, which he snared,
Blinded the eyes of, and brought somewhat tame,
And split its toe-webs, and now pens the drudge

In a hole o' the rock and calls him Caliban;
A bitter heart that bides its time and bites.
'Plays thus at being Prosper in a way,
Taketh his mirth with make-believes: so He.

His dam held that the Quiet made all things
Which Setebos vexed only: 'holds not so.
Who made them weak, meant weakness He might vex.
Had He meant other, while His hand was in,
Why not make horny eyes no thorn could prick,
Or plate my scalp with bone against the snow,
Or overscale my flesh 'neath joint and joint,
Like an orc's armour? Ay,—so spoil His sport!
He is the One now: only He doth all.
'Saith, He may like, perchance, what profits Him.
Ay, himself loves what does him good; but why?
'Gets good no otherwise. This blinded beast
Loves whoso places flesh-meat on his nose,
But, had he eyes, would want no help, but hate
Or love, just as it liked him: He hath eyes.
Also it pleaseth Setebos to work,
Use all His hands, and exercise much craft,
By no means for the love of what is worked.
'Tasteth, himself, no finer good i' the world
When all goes right, in this safe summer-time,
And he wants little, hungers, aches not much,
Than trying what to do with wit and strength.
'Falls to make something: 'piled yon pile of turfs,
And squared and stuck there squares of soft white chalk,
And, with a fish-tooth, scratched a moon on each,
And set up endwise certain spikes of tree,
And crowned the whole with a sloth's skull a-top,
Found dead i' the woods, too hard for one to kill.
No use at all i' the work, for work's sole sake;
'Shall some day knock it down again: so He.

'Saith He is terrible: watch His feats in proof!
One hurricane will spoil six good months' hope.
He hath a spite against me, that I know,
Just as He favours Prosper, who knows why?
So it is, all the same, as well I find.
'Wove wattles half the winter, fenced them firm
With stone and stake to stop she-tortoises
Crawling to lay their eggs here: well, one wave,
Feeling the foot of Him upon its neck,
Gaped as a snake does, lolled out its large tongue,
And licked the whole labour flat: so much for spite.
'Saw a ball flame down late (yonder it lies)
Where, half an hour before, I slept i' the shade:
Often they scatter sparkles: there is force!
'Dug up a newt He may have envied once
And turned to stone, shut up inside a stone.
Please Him and hinder this?—What Prosper does?
Aha, if He would tell me how! Not He!
There is the sport: discover how or die!
All need not die, for of the things o' the isle
Some flee afar, some dive, some run up trees;
Those at His mercy,—why, they please Him most
When . . . when . . . well, never try the same way twice!
Repeat what act has pleased, He may grow wroth.
You must not know His ways, and play Him off,
Sure of the issue. 'Doth the like himself:
'Spareth a squirrel that it nothing fears
But steals the nut from underneath my thumb,
And when I threat, bites stoutly in defence:
'Spareth an urchin that contrariwise,
Curls up into a ball, pretending death
For fright at my approach: the two ways please.
But what would move my choler more than this,
That either creature counted on its life
To-morrow and next day and all days to come,

Saying, forsooth, in the inmost of its heart,
"Because he did so yesterday with me,
"And otherwise with such another brute,
"So must he do henceforth and always."—Ay?
Would teach the reasoning couple what "must" means!
'Doth as he likes, or wherefore Lord? So He.

'Conceiveth all things will continue thus,
And we shall have to live in fear of Him
So long as He lives, keeps His strength: no change,
If He have done His best, make no new world
To please Him more, so leave off watching this,—
If He surprise not even the Quiet's self
Some strange day,—or, suppose, grow into it
As grubs grow butterflies: else, here are we,
And there is He, and nowhere help at all.

Believeth with the life, the pain shall stop.
His dam held different, that after death
He both plagued enemies and feasted friends:
Idly! He doth His worst in this our life,
Giving just respite lest we die through pain,
Saving last pain for worst,—with which, an end.
Meanwhile, the best way to escape His ire
Is, not to seem too happy. 'Sees, himself,
Yonder two flies, with purple films and pink,
Bask on the pompion-bell above: kills both.
'Sees two black painful beetles roll their ball
On head and tail as if to save their lives:
Moves them the stick away they strive to clear.

Even so, 'would have Him misconceive, suppose
This Caliban strives hard and ails no less,
And always, above all else, envies Him;
Wherefore he mainly dances on dark nights,
Moans in the sun, gets under holes to laugh,

And never speaks his mind save housed as now:
Outside, 'groans, curses. If He caught me here,
O'erheard this speech, and asked "What chucklest at?"
'Would, to appease Him, cut a finger off,
Or of my three kid yearlings burn the best,
Or let the toothsome apples rot on tree,
Or push my tame beast for the orc to taste:
While myself lit a fire, and made a song
And sung it, *"What I hate, be consecrate*
"To celebrate Thee and Thy state, no mate
"For Thee; what see for envy in poor me?"
Hoping the while, since evils sometimes mend,
Warts rub away and sores are cured with slime,
That some strange day, will either the Quiet catch
And conquer Setebos, or likelier He
Decrepit may doze, doze, as good as die.

————————

[What, what? A curtain o'er the world at once!
Crickets stop hissing; not a bird—or, yes,
There scuds His raven that has told Him all!
It was fool's play, this prattling! Ha! The wind
Shoulders the pillared dust, death's house o' the move,
And fast invading fires begin! White blaze—
A tree's head snaps—and there, there, there, there, there,
His thunder follows! Fool to gibe at Him!
Lo! 'Lieth flat and loveth Setebos!
'Maketh his teeth meet through his upper lip,
Will let those quails fly, will not eat this month
One little mess of whelks, so he may 'scape!]

In the great poem *Rabbi Ben Ezra,* a quite different reason from that of Caliban's is suggested for
the drawbacks and sufferings of life. They are a

part of the divine machinery employed by infinite wisdom to further human development, to make us ultimately fit to see His face. There can be no true progress without obstacles: no enjoyment without its opposite: no vacation without duties: no virtue without sin.

The second line of the poem is startling in its direct contradiction of the language and lamentation of conventional poetry. Regret for lost youth and terror before old age are stock ideas in poetry, and in human meditation; but here we are invited to look forward to old age as the best time of life. Not to grow old gracefully, in resignation, but to grow old eagerly, in triumph—this is the Rabbi's suggestion. There is not the slightest doubt that he is right, provided one lives a mental, rather than an animal existence. A short time ago, Mr. Joseph H. Choate was addressing a large company in New York: he said, "Unquestionably the best period of life is the time between seventy and eighty years of age: and I advise you all to hurry up and get there as soon as you can."

God loveth whom He chasteneth. Our doubts and fears, our sorrows and pains, are spurs, stimulants to advance; rejoice that we have them, for they are proofs that we are alive and moving!

In the seventh stanza comes an audacious but cheering thought. Many thinkers regard the deepest sorrow of life as rising from the disparity between our ideals and our achievement; Schiller, in his poem, *Das Ideal und das Leben,* has expressed this cause of woe in beautiful language. Browning says boldly,

> What I aspired to be,
> And was not, *comforts* me:

This paradox, which comforts while it mocks, means, "My achievements are ridiculously small in comparison with my hopes, my ambitions, my dreams: thank God for all this! Thank God I was not content with low aims, thank God I had my aspirations and have them still: they point to future development."

In the twenty-third, twenty-fourth and twenty-fifth stanzas, Browning suddenly returns to this idea: in the appraisement of the human soul, efforts, which if unsuccessful, count for nothing in worldly estimation, pay an enormous ultimate dividend, and must therefore be rated high. The reason why the world counts only things done and not things attempted, is because the world's standards are too coarse: they are adapted only for gross and obvious results. You can not weigh diamonds on hay scales:

the indicator would show precisely nothing. And yet one diamond, too fine for these huge scales, might be of more value than thousands of tons of hay.

From the twenty-sixth stanza to the end, Browning takes up the figure of the Potter, the Wheel, and the Clay. I think that he was drawn to use this metaphor, not from Scripture, but as a protest against the use of it in Fitzgerald's *Omar Khayyám.* Fitzgerald published his translation in 1859; and although it attracted no public attention, it is certainly possible that Browning saw it. He would have enjoyed its melodious beauty, but the philosophy of the poem would have been to him detestable and abhorrent. Much is made there of the Potter, meaning blind destiny: and the moral is, "Drink! the Past gone, seize To-day!" Browning explicitly rejects and scorns this teaching: it is propounded by fools for the benefit of other fools.

> Fool! all that is, at all,
> Lasts ever, past recall;
> Earth changes, but thy soul and God stand sure:
> What entered into thee,
> *That* was, is, and shall be:
> Time's wheel runs back or stops: Potter and clay endure.

In Browning's metaphor, the Potter is God: the

Wheel is the whirling course of life's experiences: the Clay is man. God holds us on the wheel to turn us into the proper shape. Owing to our flaws, the strain is sometimes too great, and some of us are warped and twisted by this stern discipline: other characters, made of better material, constantly grow more beautiful and more serviceable under the treatment. Browning had suffered the greatest sorrow of his life when he wrote this poem, and yet he had faith enough to say in the thirty-first stanza, that *not even while the whirl was worst,* did he, bound dizzily to the terrible wheel of life, once lose his belief that he was in God's hands and that the deep cuttings were for his ultimate benefit.

In the making of a cup, the Potter engraved around the base lovely images of youth and pleasure, and near the rim skulls and signs of death: but what is a cup for? It is meant for the Master's lips. The nearer therefore we approach to death, the nearer we are to God's presence, who is making us fit to slake His thirst. Finished at last, we are done forever with life's wheel: we come to the banquet, the festal board, lamp's flash and trumpet's peal, the glorious appearance of the Master.

RABBI BEN EZRA

1864

I

Grow old along with me!
The best is yet to be,
The last of life, for which the first was made:
Our times are in His hand
Who saith "A whole I planned,
"Youth shows but half; trust God: see all nor be afraid!"

II

Not that, amassing flowers,
Youth sighed "Which rose make ours,
"Which lily leave and then as best recall?"
Not that, admiring stars,
It yearned "Nor Jove, nor Mars;
"Mine be some figured flame which blends, transcends them
　　all!"

III

Not for such hopes and fears
Annulling youth's brief years,
Do I remonstrate: folly wide the mark!
Rather I prize the doubt
Low kinds exist without,
Finished and finite clods, untroubled by a spark.

IV

Poor vaunt of life indeed,
Were man but formed to feed
On joy, to solely seek and find and feast:
Such feasting ended, then
As sure an end to men;
Irks care the crop-full bird? Frets doubt the maw-crammed
　　beast?

V

Rejoice we are allied
To That which doth provide
And not partake, effect and not receive!
A spark disturbs our clod;
Nearer we hold of God
Who gives, than of His tribes that take, I must believe.

VI

Then, welcome each rebuff
That turns earth's smoothness rough,
Each sting that bids nor sit nor stand but go!
Be our joys three-parts pain!
Strive, and hold cheap the strain;
Learn, nor account the pang; dare, never grudge the throe!

VII

For thence,—a paradox
Which comforts while it mocks,—
Shall life succeed in that it seems to fail:
What I aspired to be,
And was not, comforts me:
A brute I might have been, but would not sink i' the scale.

VIII

What is he but a brute
Whose flesh has soul to suit,
Whose spirit works lest arms and legs want play?
To man, propose this test—
Thy body at its best,
How far can that project thy soul on its lone way?

IX

Yet gifts should prove their use:
I own the Past profuse
Of power each side, perfection every turn:

Eyes, ears took in their dole,
Brain treasured up the whole;
Should not the heart beat once "How good to live and learn?"

X

Not once beat "Praise be Thine!
"I see the whole design,
"I, who saw power, see now love perfect too:
"Perfect I call Thy plan:
"Thanks that I was a man!
"Maker, remake, complete,—I trust what Thou shalt do!"

XI

For pleasant is this flesh;
Our soul, in its rose-mesh
Pulled ever to the earth, still yearns for rest;
Would we some prize might hold
To match those manifold
Possessions of the brute,—gain most, as we did best!

XII

Let us not always say
"Spite of this flesh to-day
"I strove, made head, gained ground upon the whole!"
As the bird wings and sings,
Let us cry "All good things
"Are ours, nor soul helps flesh more, now, than flesh helps
    soul!"

XIII

Therefore I summon age
To grant youth's heritage,
Life's struggle having so far reached its term:
Thence shall I pass, approved
A man, for aye removed
From the developed brute; a god though in the germ.

XIV

And I shall thereupon
Take rest, ere I be gone
Once more on my adventure brave and new:
Fearless and unperplexed,
When I wage battle next,
What weapons to select, what armour to indue.

XV

Youth ended, I shall try
My gain or loss thereby;
Leave the fire ashes, what survives is gold:
And I shall weigh the same,
Give life its praise or blame:
Young, all lay in dispute; I shall know, being old.

XVI

For note, when evening shuts,
A certain moment cuts
The deed off, calls the glory from the grey:
A whisper from the west
Shoots—"Add this to the rest,
"Take it and try its worth: here dies another day."

XVII

So, still within this life,
Though lifted o'er its strife,
Let me discern, compare, pronounce at last,
"This rage was right i' the main,
"That acquiescence vain:
"The Future I may face now I have proved the Past."

XVIII

For more is not reserved
To man, with soul just nerved
To act to-morrow what he learns to-day:

Here, work enough to watch
The Master work, and catch
Hints of the proper craft, tricks of the tool's true play.

XIX

As it was better, youth
Should strive, through acts uncouth,
Toward making, than repose on aught found made:
So, better, age, exempt
From strife, should know, than tempt
Further.　Thou waitedest age: wait death nor be afraid!

XX

Enough now, if the Right
And Good and Infinite
Be named here, as thou callest thy hand thine own,
With knowledge absolute,
Subject to no dispute
From fools that crowded youth, nor let thee feel alone.

XXI

Be there, for once and all,
Severed great minds from small,
Announced to each his station in the Past!
Was I, the world arraigned,
Were they, my soul disdained,
Right?　Let age speak the truth and give us peace at last!

XXII

Now, who shall arbitrate?
Ten men love what I hate,
Shun what I follow, slight what I receive;
Ten, who in ears and eyes
Match me: we all surmise,
They this thing, and I that: whom shall my soul believe?

XXIII

Not on the vulgar mass
Called "work," must sentence pass,
Things done, that took the eye and had the price;
O'er which, from level stand,
The low world laid its hand,
Found straightway to its mind, could value in a trice:

XXIV

But all, the world's coarse thumb
And finger failed to plumb,
So passed in making up the main account;
All instincts immature,
All purposes unsure,
That weighed not as his work, yet swelled the man's amount:

XXV

Thoughts hardly to be packed
Into a narrow act,
Fancies that broke through language and escaped;
All I could ever be,
All, men ignored in me,
This, I was worth to God, whose wheel the pitcher shaped.

XXVI

Ay, note that Potter's wheel,
That metaphor! and feel
Why time spins fast, why passive lies our clay,—
Thou, to whom fools propound,
When the wine makes its round,
"Since life fleets, all is change; the Past gone, seize to-day!"

XXVII

Fool! All that is, at all,
Lasts ever, past recall;
Earth changes, but thy soul and God stand sure:

What entered into thee,
That was, is, and shall be:
Time's wheel runs back or stops: Potter and clay endure

XXVIII

He fixed thee mid this dance
Of plastic circumstance,
This Present, thou, forsooth, wouldst fain arrest:
Machinery just meant
To give thy soul its bent,
Try thee and turn thee forth, sufficiently impressed.

XXIX

What though the earlier grooves
Which ran the laughing loves
Around thy base, no longer pause and press?
What though, about thy rim,
Scull-things in order grim
Grow out, in graver mood, obey the sterner stress?

XXX

Look not thou down but up!
To uses of a cup,
The festal board, lamp's flash and trumpet's peal,
The new wine's foaming flow,
The Master's lips a-glow!
Thou, heaven's consummate cup, what need'st thou with earth's
    wheel?

XXXI

But I need, now as then,
Thee, God, who mouldest men;
And since, not even while the whirl was worst,
Did I,—to the wheel of life
With shapes and colours rife,
Bound dizzily,—mistake my end, to slake Thy thirst:

XXXII

So, take and use Thy work:
Amend what flaws may lurk,
What strain o' the stuff, what warpings past the aim!
My times be in Thy hand!
Perfect the cup as planned!
Let age approve of youth, and death complete the same!

Browning wrote four remarkable poems dealing with music: *A Toccata of Galuppi's, Master Hugues of Saxe-Gotha, Abt Vogler,* and *Charles Avison.* In *Abt Vogler* the miracle of extemporisation has just been accomplished. The musician sits at the keys, tears running down his face: tears of weakness, because of the storm of divine inspiration that has passed through him: tears of sorrow, because he never can recapture the fine, careless rapture of his unpremeditated music: tears of joy, because he knows that on this particular day he has been the channel chosen by the Infinite God.

If he had only been an architect, his dream would have remained in a permanent form. The armies of workmen would have done his will, and the world would have admired it for ages. If he had only been a poet or a painter, his inspiration would have taken the form of fixed type or enduring shape and color: but in the instance of music, the armies of thoughts that have worked together in absolute har-

mony to elevate the noble building of sound, which
has risen like an exhalation, have vanished together
with the structure they animated. It has gone like
the wonderful beauty of some fantastic cloud.

His sorrow at this particular irreparable loss gives
way to rapture as he reflects on the source whence
came the inspiration. He could not possibly have
constructed such wonderful music: it was the God
welling up within him: for this past hour divine inspiration has spoken through him. He has had one
glimpse at the Celestial Radiance. How can he now
think that the same God who expanded his heart
lacks the power to fill it? The Source from whence
this river came must be inexhaustible, and it was
vouchsafed to him to feel for a short time its infinite
richness. The broken arcs on earth are the earnest
of the perfect round in heaven.

Abt Vogler says that the philosophers may each
make his guess at the meaning of this earthly scheme
of weal and woe: but the musicians, the musicians
who have felt in their own bosoms the presence of
the Divine Power and heard its marvellous voice,—
why, the philosophers may reason and welcome: 'tis
we musicians know!

ABT VOGLER

<small>(AFTER HE HAS BEEN EXTEMPORISING UPON THE MUSICAL
INSTRUMENT OF HIS INVENTION)</small>

1864

I

Would that the structure brave, the manifold music I build,
 Bidding my organ obey, calling its keys to their work,
Claiming each slave of the sound, at a touch, as when Solomon
  willed
 Armies of angels that soar, legions of demons that lurk,
Man, brute, reptile, fly,—alien of end and of aim,
 Adverse, each from the other heaven-high, hell-deep re-
  moved,—
Should rush into sight at once as he named the ineffable Name,
 And pile him a palace straight, to pleasure the princess he
  loved!

II

Would it might tarry like his, the beautiful building of mine,
 This which my keys in a crowd pressed and importuned to
  raise!
Ah, one and all, how they helped, would dispart now and now
  combine,
 Zealous to hasten the work, heighten their master his praise!
And one would bury his brow with a blind plunge down to
  hell,
 Burrow awhile and build, broad on the roots of things,
Then up again swim into sight, having based me my palace
  well,
 Founded it, fearless of flame, flat on the nether springs.

III

And another would mount and march, like the excellent
   minion he was,
   Ay, another and yet another, one crowd but with many a
      crest,
Raising my rampired walls of gold as transparent as glass,
   Eager to do and die, yield each his place to the rest:
For higher still and higher (as a runner tips with fire,
   When a great illumination surprises a festal night—
Outlined round and round Rome's dome from space to spire)
   Up, the pinnacled glory reached, and the pride of my soul
      was in sight.

IV

In sight? Not half! for it seemed, it was certain, to match
   man's birth,
   Nature in turn conceived, obeying an impulse as I;
And the emulous heaven yearned down, made effort to reach
   the earth,
   As the earth had done her best, in my passion, to scale the
      sky:
Novel splendors burst forth, grew familiar and dwelt with
   mine,
   Not a point nor peak but found and fixed its wandering
      star;
Meteor-moons, balls of blaze: and they did not pale nor pine,
   For earth had attained to heaven, there was no more near
      nor far.

V

Nay more; for there wanted not who walked in the glare and
   glow,
   Presences plain in the place; or, fresh from the Protoplast,
Furnished for ages to come, when a kindlier wind should blow,
   Lured now to begin and live, in a house to their liking at
      last;

Or else the wonderful Dead who have passed through the body
   and gone,
   But were back once more to breathe in an old world worth
      their new:
What never had been, was now; what was, as it shall be anon;
   And what is,—shall I say, matched both? for I was made
      perfect too.

VI

All through my keys that gave their sounds to a wish of my
      soul,
   All through my soul that praised as its wish flowed visibly
      forth,
All through music and me! For think, had I painted the whole,
   Why, there it had stood, to see, nor the process so wonder-
      worth:
Had I written the same, made verse—still, effect proceeds
      from cause,
   Ye know why the forms are fair, ye hear how the tale is
      told;
It is all triumphant art, but art in obedience to laws,
   Painter and poet are proud in the artist-list enrolled:—

VII

But here is the finger of God, a flash of the will that can,
   Existent behind all laws, that made them and, lo, they are!
And I know not if, save in this, such gift be allowed to man,
   That out of three sounds he frame, not a fourth sound, but
      a star.
Consider it well: each tone of our scale in itself is naught:
   It is everywhere in the world—loud, soft, and all is said:
Give it to me to use! I mix it with two in my thought:
   And there! Ye have heard and seen: consider and bow the
      head!

VIII

Well, it is gone at last, the palace of music I reared;
  Gone! and the good tears start, the praises that come too
    slow;
For one is assured at first, one scarce can say that he feared,
  That he even gave it a thought, the gone thing was to go.
Never to be again! But many more of the kind
  As good, nay, better perchance: is this your comfort to me?
To me, who must be saved because I cling with my mind
  To the same, same self, same love, same God: ay, what was,
    shall be.

IX

Therefore to whom turn I but to thee, the ineffable Name.
  Builder and maker, thou, of houses not made with hands!
What, have fear of change from thee who art ever the same?
  Doubt that thy power can fill the heart that thy power ex-
    pands?
There shall never be one lost good! What was, shall live as
    before;
  The evil is null, is naught, is silence implying sound;
What was good shall be good, with, for evil, so much good
    more;
  On the earth the broken arcs; in the heaven a perfect round.

X

All we have willed or hoped or dreamed of good shall exist;
  Not its semblance, but itself; no beauty, nor good, nor power
Whose voice has gone forth, but each survives for the melodist
  When eternity affirms the conception of an hour.
The high that proved too high, the heroic for earth too hard,
  The passion that left the ground to lose itself in the sky,
Are music sent up to God by the lover and the bard;
  Enough that he heard it once: we shall hear it by and by.

XI

And what is our failure here but a triumph's evidence
  For the fulness of the days? Have we withered or agonized?
Why else was the pause prolonged but that singing might issue
      thence?
  Why rushed the discords in, but that harmony should be
      prized?
Sorrow is hard to bear, and doubt is slow to clear,
  Each sufferer says his say, his scheme of the weal and woe:
But God has a few of us whom he whispers in the ear;
  The rest may reason and welcome: 'tis we musicians know.

XII

Well, it is earth with me; silence resumes her reign:
  I will be patient and proud, and soberly acquiesce.
Give me the keys. I feel for the common chord again,
  Sliding by semitones till I sink to the minor,—yes,
And I blunt it into a ninth, and I stand on alien ground,
  Surveying awhile the heights I rolled from into the deep;
Which, hark, I have dared and done, for my resting-place is
      found,
  The C Major of this life: so, now I will try to sleep.

In the autumn following his wife's death Browning wrote the poem *Prospice*, which title means *Look Forward!* This is the most original poem on death in English Literature. It shows that Browning strictly and consistently followed the moral appended to *The Glove*—*Venienti occurrite morbo,* run to meet approaching disaster!

Although the prayer-book expresses the wish that

the Good Lord will deliver us from battle, murder, and sudden death, that hope was founded on the old superstition that it was more important how a man died than how he lived. If a man who had lived a righteous, sober and godly life died while playing cards or in innocent laughter, with no opportunity for the ministrations of a priest, his chances for the next world were thought to be slim. On the other hand, a damnable scoundrel on the scaffold, with the clergyman's assurances assented to, was supposed to be jerked into heaven. This view of life and death was firmly held even by so sincere and profound a thinker as Hamlet: which explains his anguish at the fate of his father killed in his sleep, and his own refusal to slay the villain Claudius at prayer.

It is probable that thousands of worshippers who now devoutly pray to be delivered from sudden death, would really prefer that exit to any other. The reason is clear enough: it is to avoid the pain of slow dissolution, the sufferings of the death-bed, and the horrible fear of the dark. Now Browning boldly asks that he may be spared nothing of all these grim terrors. True to his conception of a poet, as a man who should understand all human experiences, he hopes that he may pass conscious and aware through the wonderful experience of dying. Most sick folk

become unconscious hours before death and slip
over the line in total coma: Browning wants to stay
awake.

> I would hate that death bandaged my eyes, and forbore,
> And bade me creep past.

I want to taste it all, the physical suffering, the fear
of the abyss: I want to hear the raving of the fiend-
voices, to be in the very thick of the fight. He adds
the splendid line,

> For sudden the worst turns the best to the brave.

Brave hearts turn defeat into victory.

Browning died twenty-eight years after he wrote
this poem, and his prayer was granted. He was
conscious almost up to the last second, and fully
aware of the nearness of death. Even the manner
of death, as described in the first line of the poem,
came to be his own experience: for he died of bronchitis.

PROSPICE

1864

> Fear death?—to feel the fog in my throat,
> The mist in my face,
> When the snows begin, and the blasts denote
> I am nearing the place,
> The power of the night, the press of the storm,
> The post of the foe;
> Where he stands, the Arch Fear in a visible form,

> Yet the strong man must go:
> For the journey is done and the summit attained,
>   And the barriers fall,
> Though a battle's to fight ere the guerdon be gained,
>   The reward of it all.
> I was ever a fighter, so—one fight more,
>   The best and the last!
> I would hate that death bandaged my eyes, and forbore,
>   And bade me creep past.
> No! let me taste the whole of it, fare like my peers
>   The heroes of old,
> Bear the brunt, in a minute pay glad life's arrears
>   Of pain, darkness and cold.
> For sudden the worst turns the best to the brave,
>   The black minute's at end,
> And the elements' rage, the fiend-voices that rave,
>   Shall dwindle, shall blend,
> Shall change, shall become first a peace out of pain,
>   Then a light, then thy breast,
> O thou soul of my soul! I shall clasp thee again,
>   And with God be the rest!

One can hardly repress a smile at Browning's thorough-going optimism, when he reads the poem, *Apparent Failure,* and then glances back at the title. *Apparent* failure! Of all the defeated sons of earth, the nameless suicides whose wretched bodies are taken to the public morgue, ought surely, we should imagine, to be classed as absolute failures. But Browning does not think so. It is possible, he says, that the reason why these poor outcasts abandoned life, was because their aspirations were so tremen-

dously high that dull reality overpowered their
spirits. Goodness is better than badness: meekness
better than ferocity: calm sense than mad ravings.
But, after all, these poor fellows were God's creatures. His sun will eventually pierce the darkest
cloud earth can stretch. Somewhere, after many
ages in the next life, these men will develop into
something better under the sunshine of the smile of
God.

APPARENT FAILURE

1864

"We shall soon lose a celebrated building."
Paris Newspaper.

I

No, for I'll save it! Seven years since,
  I passed through Paris, stopped a day
To see the baptism of your Prince;
  Saw, made my bow, and went my way:
Walking the heat and headache off,
  I took the Seine-side, you surmise,
Thought of the Congress, Gortschakoff,
  Cavour's appeal and Buol's replies,
So sauntered till—what met my eyes?

II

Only the Doric little Morgue!
  The dead-house where you show your drowned:
Petrarch's Vaucluse makes proud the Sorgue,
  Your Morgue has made the Seine renowned.
One pays one's debt in such a case;

I plucked up heart and entered,—stalked,
Keeping a tolerable face
    Compared with some whose cheeks were chalked:
Let them ! No Briton's to be baulked !

III

First came the silent gazers; next,
    A screen of glass, we're thankful for;
Last, the sight's self, the sermon's text,
    The three men who did most abhor
Their life in Paris yesterday,
    So killed themselves: and now, enthroned
Each on his copper couch, they lay
    Fronting me, waiting to be owned.
I thought, and think, their sin's atoned.

IV

Poor men, God made, and all for that !
    The reverence struck me; o'er each head
Religiously was hung its hat,
    Each coat dripped by the owner's bed,
Sacred from touch: each had his berth,
    His bounds, his proper place of rest,
Who last night tenanted on earth
    Some arch, where twelve such slept abreast,—
Unless the plain asphalte seemed best.

V

How did it happen, my poor boy?
    You wanted to be Buonaparte
And have the Tuileries for toy,
    And could not, so it broke your heart?
You, old one by his side, I judge,

Were, red as blood, a socialist,
A leveller! Does the Empire grudge
  You've gained what no Republic missed?
Be quiet, and unclench your fist!

VI

And this—why, he was red in vain,
  Or black,—poor fellow that is blue!
What fancy was it turned your brain?
  Oh, women were the prize for you!
Money gets women, cards and dice
  Get money, and ill-luck gets just
The copper couch and one clear nice
  Cool squirt of water o'er your bust,
The right thing to extinguish lust!

VII

It's wiser being good than bad;
  It's safer being meek than fierce:
It's fitter being sane than mad.
  My own hope is, a sun will pierce
The thickest cloud earth ever stretched;
  That, after Last, returns the First,
Though a wide compass round be fetched;
  That what began best, can't end worst,
Nor what God blessed once, prove accurst.

The poem *Rephan*, the title of which was taken from the Book of Acts, has the same pleasant teaching we find in the play by Ludwig Fulda, called *Schlaraffenland*, published in 1899. In this drama, a boy, ragged, cold, and chronically hungry, falls asleep in a miserable room, and dreams that he is in a country of unalloyed delight. Broiled chickens fly slowly by, easy to clutch and devour : expensive wardrobes await his immediate pleasure, and every conceivable wish is instantly and completely fulfilled. For a short time the boy is in ecstasies of joy : then the absence of effort, of counterbalancing privation, begins to make his heart dull : finally the paradise becomes so intolerable that he wakes with a scream— wakes in a dark, cold room, wakes in rags with his belly empty : and wakes in rapture at finding the good old earth of struggle and toil around him.

Contentment is stagnation : development is happiness. The mystery of life, its uncertainty, its joys paid for by effort, these make human existence worth while.

Browning delights to prove that the popular longing for static happiness would result in misery : that the sharp sides of life sting us into the real joy of living. He loves to take popular proverbs, which sum up the unconscious pessimism of humanity, and then show how false they are to fact. For example, we hear every day the expression, "No rose without a thorn," and we know very well what is meant. In *The Ring and the Book,* Browning says

So a thorn comes to the aid of and completes the rose.

REPHAN

1889

How I lived, ere my human life began
In this world of yours,—like you, made man,—
When my home was the Star of my God Rephan?

Come then around me, close about,
World-weary earth-born ones! Darkest doubt
Or deepest despondency keeps you out?

Nowise! Before a word I speak,
Let my circle embrace your worn, your weak,
Brow-furrowed old age, youth's hollow cheek—

Diseased in the body, sick in soul,
Pinched poverty, satiate wealth,—your whole
Array of despairs! Have I read the roll?

All here? Attend, perpend! O Star
Of my God Rephan, what wonders are
In thy brilliance fugitive, faint and far!

Far from me, native to thy realm,
Who shared its perfections which o'erwhelm
Mind to conceive. Let drift the helm,

Let drive the sail, dare unconfined
Embark for the vastitude, O Mind,
Of an absolute bliss! Leave earth behind!

Here, by extremes, at a mean you guess:
There, all's at most—not more, not less:
Nowhere deficiency nor excess.

No want—whatever should be, is now:
No growth—that's change, and change comes—how
To royalty born with crown on brow?

Nothing begins—so needs to end:
Where fell it short at first? Extend
Only the same, no change can mend!

I use your language: mine—no word
Of its wealth would help who spoke, who heard,
To a gleam of intelligence. None preferred,

None felt distaste when better and worse
Were uncontrastable: bless or curse
What—in that uniform universe?

Can your world's phrase, your sense of things
Forth-figure the Star of my God? No springs,
No winters throughout its space. Time brings

No hope, no fear: as to-day, shall be
To-morrow: advance or retreat need we
At our stand-still through eternity?

All happy: needs must we so have been,
Since who could be otherwise? All serene:
What dark was to banish, what light to screen?

Earth's rose is a bud that's checked or grows
As beams may encourage or blasts oppose:
Our lives leapt forth, each a full-orbed rose—

Each rose sole rose in a sphere that spread
Above and below and around—rose-red:
No fellowship, each for itself instead.

One better than I—would prove I lacked
Somewhat: one worse were a jarring fact
Disturbing my faultlessly exact.

How did it come to pass there lurked
Somehow a seed of change that worked
Obscure in my heart till perfection irked?—

Till out of its peace at length grew strife—
Hopes, fears, loves, hates,—obscurely rife,—
My life grown a-tremble to turn your life?

Was it Thou, above all lights that are,
Prime Potency, did Thy hand unbar
The prison-gate of Rephan my Star?

In me did such potency wake a pulse
Could trouble tranquillity that lulls
Not lashes inertion till throes convulse

Soul's quietude into discontent?
As when the completed rose bursts, rent
By ardors till forth from its orb are sent

New petals that mar—unmake the disc—
Spoil rondure: what in it ran brave risk,
Changed apathy's calm to strife, bright, brisk,

Pushed simple to compound, sprang and spread
Till, fresh-formed, facetted, floretted,
The flower that slept woke a star instead?

No mimic of Star Rephan! How long
I stagnated there where weak and strong,
The wise and the foolish, right and wrong,

Are merged alike in a neutral Best,
Can I tell? No more than at whose behest
The passion arose in my passive breast,

And I yearned for no sameness but difference
In thing and thing, that should shock my sense
With a want of worth in them all, and thence

Startle me up, by an Infinite
Discovered above and below me—height
And depth alike to attract my flight,

Repel my descent: by hate taught **love.**
Oh, gain were indeed to see above
Supremacy ever—to move, remove,

Not reach—aspire yet never attain
To the object aimed at! Scarce in vain,—
As each stage I left nor touched again.

To suffer, did pangs bring the loved one bliss,
Wring knowledge from ignorance,—just for this—
To add one drop to a love-abyss!

Enough: for you doubt, you hope, O men,
You fear, you agonize, die: what then?
Is an end to your life's work out of ken?

Have you no assurance that, earth at end,
Wrong will prove right? Who made shall mend
In the higher sphere to which yearnings tend?

Why should I speak? You divine the test.
When the trouble grew in my pregnant breast
A voice said "So wouldst thou strive, not rest?

"Burn and not smoulder, win by worth,
Not rest content with a wealth that's dearth?
Thou art past Rephan, thy place be Earth!"

Browning was an optimist with his last breath.
In the *Prologue* to *Asolando,* a conventional person
is supposed to be addressing the poet: he says, "Of
course your old age must be sad, because you have
now lost all your youthful illusions. Once you
looked on the earth with rose-colored spectacles,

but now you see the naked and commonplace reality of the things you used to think so radiant."

Browning's answer is significant, and the figure he uses wonderfully apt. Suppose you are going to travel in Europe: you go to the optician, and you ask for a first-rate magnifying-glass, that you may scan the ocean, and view the remote corners of cathedrals. Now imagine him saying that he has for you something far better than that: he has a lovely kaleidoscope: apply your eye to the orifice, turn a little wheel, and you will behold all sorts of pretty colored rosettes. You would be naturally indignant. "Do you take me for a child to be amused with a rattle? I don't want pretty colors: I want something that will bring the object, *exactly as it is,* as near to my eyes as it can possibly be brought."

Indeed, when one buys a glass for a telescope, if one has sufficient cash, one buys a glass made of crown and flint glass placed together, which destroys color, which produces what is called an *achromatic* lens. Now just as we judge of the value of a glass by its ability to bring things as they are within the range of our vision, so, says Browning, old age is much better than youth. In age our old eyes become achromatic. The rosy illusions of youth vanish, thank God for it! The colors which we imagined belonged to the object were in reality in our imperfect eyes—as we grow older these pretty colors disappear and we see what? We see life itself. Life is a greater and grander thing than any fool's illusion about it. The world of nature and man is infinitely more interesting and wonderful as it is than in any mistaken view of it. Therefore old age is better than youth.

PROLOGUE

1889

"The Poet's age is sad: for why?
　In youth, the natural world could show
No common object but his eye
　At once involved with alien glow—
His own soul's iris-bow.

"And now a flower is just a flower:
　Man, bird, beast are but beast, bird, man—
Simply themselves, uncinct by dower
　Of dyes which, when life's day began,
Round each in glory ran."

Friend, did you need an optic glass,
　Which were your choice? A lens to drape
In ruby, emerald, chrysopras,
　Each object—or reveal its shape
Clear outlined, past escape,

The naked very thing?—so clear
　That, when you had the chance to gaze,
You found its inmost self appear
　Through outer seeming—truth ablaze,
Not falsehood's fancy-haze?

How many a year, my Asolo,
    Since—one step just from sea to land—
I found you, loved yet feared you so—
    For natural objects seemed to stand
Palpably fire-clothed! No—

No mastery of mine o'er these!
    Terror with beauty, like the Bush
Burning but unconsumed. Bend knees,
    Drop eyes to earthward! Language? Tush!
Silence 'tis awe decrees.

And now? The lambent flame is—where?
    Lost from the naked world: earth, sky,
Hill, vale, tree, flower,—Italia's rare
    O'er-running beauty crowds the eye—
But flame? The Bush is bare.

Hill, vale, tree, flower—they stand distinct,
    Nature to know and name. What then?
A Voice spoke thence which straight unlinked
    Fancy from fact: see, all's in ken:
Has once my eyelid winked?

No, for the purged ear apprehends
    Earth's import, not the eye late dazed:
The Voice said "Call my works thy friends!
    At Nature dost thou shrink amazed?
God is it who transcends."

It is an interesting and dramatic parallel in literary history that Tennyson and Browning should each have published the last poem that appeared in his life-time in the same month of the same year, and that each farewell to the world should be so exactly characteristic of the poetic genius and spiritual temperament of the writer. In December, 1889, came from the press *Demeter and Other Poems,* closing with *Crossing the Bar*—came also *Asolando,* closing with the *Epilogue.* Tennyson's lyric is exquisite in its tints of sunset, a serene close to a long and calmly beautiful day. It is the perfect tone of dignified departure, with the admonition to refrain from weeping, with the quiet assurance that all is well. Browning's *Epilogue* is full of excitement and strenuous rage: there is no hint of acquiescence; it is a wild charge with drum and trumpet on the hidden foe. Firm in the faith, full of plans for the future, he looks not on the darkening night, but on to-morrow's sunrise.

He tells us not to pity him. He is angry at the thought that people on the streets of London, when they hear of his death will say, "Poor Browning! He's gone! How he loved life!" Rather he wishes that just as in this life when a friend met him in the city with a face lighted up by the pleasure of the sudden encounter, with a shout of hearty welcome— so now, when your thoughts perhaps turn to me, let it not be with sorrow or pity, but with eager recognition. I shall be striving there as I strove here: greet me with a cheer!

EPILOGUE

1889

At the midnight in the silence of the sleep-time,
    When you set your fancies free,
Will they pass to where—by death, fools think, imprisoned—
Low he lies who once so loved you, whom you loved so,
                —Pity me?

Oh to love so, be so loved, yet so mistaken!
    What had I on earth to do
With the slothful, with the mawkish, the unmanly?
Like the aimless, helpless, hopeless, did I drivel
                —Being—who?

One who never turned his back but marched breast forward,
    Never doubted clouds would break,
Never dreamed, though right were worsted, wrong would
        triumph,
Held we fall to rise, are baffled to fight better,
                Sleep to wake.

No, at noonday in the bustle of man's work-time
    Greet the unseen with a cheer!
Bid him forward, breast and back as either should be,
"Strive and thrive!" cry "Speed,—fight on, fare ever
                There as here!"

THE END

INDEX

INDEX

Abt Vogler, 125, 303, 351-357.

Addison, J., disgust for the Alps, 266.

Andrea del Sarto, 206-216.

Another Way of Love, 99.

Apparent Failure, 360-363.

Artemis Prologizes, 101.

Asolando, Prologue and *Epilogue,* 368-373.

Asolo: Browning's visits to, its place in his work, 8; last summer passed there, 26.

Austin, Alfred, compared with F. Thompson, 69.

Bad Dreams, 166, 168.

Bells and Pomegranates, meaning of title, 101.

Bishop Blougram's Apology, 46, 274.

Bishop Orders His Tomb, The, 193-199.

Blot in the 'Scutcheon, A, 7, 25, 83 169.

Boy and the Angel, The, 99.

Browning, Elizabeth Barrett: engagement, 8-10; her sonnets, 12; described by her son, 23; her ill health, 24; invented name "Dramatic Lyric," 58; her assistance in R. Browning's poems, 97.

Browning, Robert: parentage and early life, 1-4; education, 4-6; visit to Russia, 6; play-writing, 7; first visit to Italy, 7; marriage, 8-12; travels in Italy and lives at Paris, 22; domestic life in Florence described by Hawthorne, 23; death, 27; personal habits, 28; peculiarities, 29; piano-playing, 29, 30; enthusiasm, 30; friendship with Tennyson, 31; normality in appearance, 32; excellence in character, 32, 33; his theory of poetry, 34, ff; his sonnets, 74, 75; his favorite feature the brow, 141, 142; fondness for yellow hair, 142; his "rejected lovers," 143, ff.

Browning, Robert Barrett: death at Asolo, 8; my conversation with, 23.

Bryant, W. C., visits Browning, 23.

Byron, Lord, lyrical power, 71.

By the Fireside, 141.

Caliban on Setebos, 326-339.

Campion, T., his lyrical power compared with Donne's, 72.

Carlyle, T.: travels to Paris with the Brownings, 22; his smoking, 28.
Cavalier Tunes, 110-114.
Charles Avison, 351.
"*Childe Roland,*" 22, 231-244, 302.
Choate, J. H., his remark on old age, 340.
Christmas-Eve, 25, 44, 52, 97, 98, 298.
Cleon, 148, 216, 220-222.
Clive, 287-289.
Confessions, 163-165.
Count Gismond, 100, 120, 142, 177-183.
Cristina, 115-127.

Death in the Desert, A, 125, 163, 298, 326.
De Gustibus, 267, 268.
Dis Aliter Visum, 120.
Donne, J.: compared with Browning, 69; compared with Campion, 72.
Dramatic Lyric, origin of name, 58.
Dramatic Lyrics, 37, 98, 99, 100, 101.
Dramatic Romances, 97, 98, 100, 101.
Dramatis Personæ, 23, 25, 97.

Eliot, George, *Daniel Deronda* and *My Last Duchess,* 172.
Emerson, R. W.: pie and optimism, 28; his opinion of Tennyson's *Ulysses,* 99, 100.
Epistle, An, Containing Strange Medical Experience of Karshish, 216-219, 222-231.
Eurydice, 142.
Evelyn Hope, 47, 120, 124, 130-132, 141, 142.
"*Eyes Calm Beside Thee,*" 75.

Face, A, 87.
Fano: seldom visited, 322; scene of picture of *Guardian Angel,* 322.
Fifine at the Fair: 29; *Epilogue* to, 88-90.
Forster, J., his praise of *Paracelsus,* 7.
Fra Lippo Lippi, 22, 203-206.
Fulda, L., his play *Schlaraffenland* compared with *Rephan,* 363.

Garden Fancies, Sibrandus Schafnaburgensis, 255, 259-261.
Glove, The, 47, 246-255, 357.
Goethe, doctrine of elective affinities, 116-118.
Gold Hair, 142, 298.
Grammarian's Funeral, A, 256-259, 262-266.
Gray, T., early appreciation of mountain scenery, 267.
Guardian Angel, The, 322-326.

Hallam, A. H., home in Wimpole Street, 10.
Hawthorne, N., visits Browning in Florence, 23.
Holy Cross Day, 46.
Home-Thoughts, from Abroad, 83-86, 100.
Home-Thoughts, from the Sea, 83-86.
How It Strikes a Contemporary, 50, 54.
"*How They Brought the Good News*," 101, 139, 189-193.

Ibsen, H.: an original genius, 36, 37; *When We Dead Awaken*, 148; *A Doll's House*, 292.
In a Balcony, 169.
In a Gondola, 100, 120, 142, 154-156.
Incident of the French Camp, 100, 139.
Ivàn Ivànovitch, 7, 286, 287.

James Lee's Wife, 67, 86.
Jocoseria, Prologue to, 94.
Johannes Agricola in Meditation, 103, 107-110.
Jonson, B., his remarks on Donne, 69.

Karshish (see *Epistle, An*).
Keats, J.: prosody in *Endymion*, 41, 171; *Bright Star*, 71; his conception of beauty, 167; preface to *Endymion*, 295; his doctrine of beauty, 324.
Kipling, R., allusions to Browning in *Stalky and Co.*, 195.

Laboratory, The, 199-203.
Landor, W. S., his poetic tribute to Browning, 68.
Lanier, S., his criticism of *The Ring and the Book*, 37.
La Saisiaz, Prologue to, 93.
Last Ride Together, The, 46, 141, 146-154.
LeMoyne, Sarah Cowell, her reading aloud *Meeting at Night*, 133, 134.
Lessing, G. E., his remark about truth, 148.
Longfellow, H. W.: a better sonneteer than either Tennyson or Browning, 74; *Paul Revere's Ride* compared with "*How They Brought*," etc., 189.
Lost Leader, The, 100, 110, 114, 144.
Lost Mistress, The, 144, 149.
Love Among the Ruins, 42, 46, 142, 156-161.
Lover's Quarrel, A, 99.
Luria, 70, 97.

Macbeth: German translation of, 47; pessimistic speech by, 102, 103.
Macready, W. C., relations with Browning, 7.
Maeterlinck, M.: scene in *Monna Vanna* taken from *Luria*, 70; his praise of Browning's poetry, 70.

Master Hugues of Saxe-Gotha, 351.
Meeting at Night, 59, 132-140.
Men and Women, 22, 25, 96, 97, 98, 99.
Mesmerism, 99.
Mill, J. S., his opinion of *Pauline,* 73.
Muléykeh, 289, 290.
My Last Duchess, 101, 170-177, 186.
My Star, 165, 167.

Nationality in Drinks, 98.

Old Pictures in Florence, 320-322.
Omar Khayyam, his figure of the Potter compared with
    Browning's, 342.
One Way of Love, 144, 145, 149.
One Word More, 13, 14, 15-21.

Pacchiarotto: 61; *Epilogue* to, 63, 70; *Prologue* to, 92.
Paracelsus, 7, 25, 76-79, 123, 128-130.
Parting at Morning (see *Meeting at Night*).
Pauline, 6, 24, 25, 37, 42, 47, 73, 84, 294, 296.
Pippa Passes, 8, 25, 61, 67, 80-83, 102, 135.
Pope: popularity of *Essay on Man,* 34; his prosody compared
    with that of Keats, 171.
Porphyria's Lover, 103-107.
Prince Hohenstiel-Schwangau, 96.
Prospice, 357-360.

Rabbi Ben Ezra, 62, 122, 326, 339-351.
Rephan, 363-368.
Respectability, 161-163.
Reverie, 297.
Ring and the Book, The, 25, 37, 45, 59, 60, 62, 97, 116, 364.
Rossetti, D. G.: draws picture of Tennyson, 22; his opinion of
    Pauline, 73, 74.
Rossetti, W. M., meets the Brownings and the Tennysons, 22.
Rudel to the Lady of Tripoli, 101.
Ruskin, J., his remark on *The Bishop Orders His Tomb,* 193,
    194.

Saul, 98, 298-320.
Schiller, F.: his poem *Der Handschuh,* 246; his poem *Das
    Ideal und das Leben,* 341.
Schopenhauer, A.: father's financial help similar to Brown-
    ing's, 3; his late-coming fame similar to Browning's, 24;
    his remark on Rafael's *St. Cecilia,* 208.
Schumann, R. and Mrs., presentation to the Scandinavian
    king, 26.

Shakespeare, W., Browning declares him to be the supreme poet, 44.
Sharp, W., characterization of *Sordello*, 66.
Shelley, P. B.: his vegetarianism imitated by Browning, 27; his lyrical power, 71.
Sibrandus Schafnaburgensis (see *Garden Fancies*).
Sludge (Mr.) the Medium, 46, 133.
Soliloquy of the Spanish Cloister, 183-189.
Soul's Tragedy, A, 97, 98.
Sordello, 8, 66, 67.
Statue and the Bust, The, 120, 141, 142, 272-285.
Stedman (mother of the poet, E. C.), her remarks on the health of Mrs. Browning in Florence, 24.
Summum Bonum, 166, 168.

Tennyson, A.: reading aloud from *Maud*, 22; Browning's letter to him, 31; a genius for adaptation, 36; wrote to please critics, 39; compared with Browning, 65; his lyrical power, 71; his lyrics compared with Browning's 72; wrote no good sonnets, 74; *Lotos-Eaters*, 76; *Ulysses*, 99; *Crossing the Bar*, 102; *St. Agnes' Eve* compared with *Johannes Agricola*, 110; *Locksley Hall*, 119; his "rejected lovers" compared with Browning's, 143; his criticism of *The Laboratory*, 200; *Crossing the Bar* compared with *Epilogue* to *Asolando*, 372.
Thackeray, *Vanity Fair*, 302.
Thompson, F., his poetry compared with Austin's, 69.
Time's Revenges, 143.
Toccata of Galuppi's, A, 142, 351.
Transcendentalism, 48, 52, 115.
Twins, The, 61, 62.
Two Poets of Croisic, the *Epilogue* to, 91.

Up at a Villa—Down in the City, 266-272.

Wagner, R.: his originality, 36, 37; his slow-coming fame, 40; his operas, 64.
Which, 290-293.
Wister, O., criticism of Browning's poetry in his novel *The Virginian*, 135, 138, 139, 191.
Wordsworth, W.: served as model for *The Lost Leader*, 110; his sincere love of the country, 267.

Youth and Art, 120.